YALE HISTORICAL PUBLICATIONS

LEWIS P. CURTIS, *Editor*

HISTORY OF ART: VI

THE THIRTY-FIRST VOLUME PUBLISHED UNDER

THE DIRECTION OF THE DEPARTMENT OF HISTORY ON THE

KINGSLEY TRUST ASSOCIATION PUBLICATION FUND

ESTABLISHED BY THE SCROLL AND KEY SOCIETY

OF YALE COLLEGE, AND WITH THE COOPERATION OF

THE DEPARTMENT OF THE HISTORY OF ART

AND THE AID OF THE HISTORY OF ART PUBLICATION FUND

Architecture and Town Planning in Colonial Connecticut

by Anthony N. B. Garvan

YALE UNIVERSITY PRESS

NEW HAVEN : 1951

LONDON : GEOFFREY CUMBERLEGE

OXFORD UNIVERSITY PRESS

TO F.P.G. AND J.M.S.A.

Preface

Late in the spring of 1941 I began an investigation of the relationship between domestic architecture and the demography and national origins of colonial Connecticut, under the guidance and with the approval of the late John M. S. Allison and Leonard W. Labaree of Yale University. It soon became apparent that the colony's racial homogeneity failed to explain its architectural variety. Moreover the thread of colonial house design wove through the whole tapestry of seventeenth-century life and could not be understood independently of town planning and land ownership. Wartime experience in research further emphasized the intelligence to be drawn from aerial photographs and manuscript land surveys. Alexander O. Vietor of the Yale University Library made many friendly suggestions of new sources of cartographical information.

In the preparation and organization, as throughout the research of my thesis, my Yale friends Leonard Labaree and George Kubler were understanding and patient critics. Sumner Crosby, George Hamilton, Franklin Baumer, John M. Phillips, Christopher Tunnard, William Jordy, and Henry Russell Hitchcock of Smith College all made specific suggestions which so far as they were carried out extended the validity of my conclusions.

In the final preparation of this book the discerning humor of Lewis P. Curtis sharpened the faulty images he found in my text. That many of my stylistic shortcomings have proved too much for his editorial pencil results from my impatience and not his oversight. To Miss Roberta Yerkes and

Miss Ella Holliday of the Yale University Press I extend my thanks for their most helpful editing and styling. Kathryn S. Leslie prepared several graphs; Frederick Ludwig gave invaluable guidance in problems of photographic research; and Wayne Andrews kindly let me print some of his photographic studies of Connecticut houses. Finally I thank Walter Creese, editor of the *Journal for the Society of Architectural Historians,* for permission to reprint part of Chapter VI.

ANTHONY N. B. GARVAN

Whitemarsh, Pennsylvania
March, 1951.

Contents

Illustrations

1. The People

The builders and planners of colonial towns tend to be anonymous. Provincialism, poverty, and a paucity of records have combined to obscure their humble personalities. Their work cannot be explained in terms of individuals and biography, since few architects are known by name and almost none has left an explanation of his aims. Under such conditions demographic evidence, even of the most general kind, becomes significant. The cultural origin of its people forms the highly imperfect framework upon which any description of seventeenth-century Connecticut architecture and town planning must hang.

Every Connecticut town plan and indeed every Connecticut house poses a question for the curious observer. Since he can rarely know who created the sure proportions of the ancient chimney stack or ample common which arouses his admiration, he must satisfy himself with a lesser query: what kind of man designed these things? Was he husbandman, surveyor, servant, squire, or lord? Was he English and, if so, did he hail from Yorkshire or Middlesex, Devon or Oxfordshire? With these questions answered the architectural tradition of the Connecticut colonist will be implied, and the task remains to discover the degree of rebellion against conventions with which these almost anonymous architects and planners built their simple but handsome towns.

Moreover, the movements of the colonial population modified architectural practice in Connecticut: the order in which towns were settled, the rapidity of their growth, urban class structure, the flow of commerce within the colony were expressed in architectural development. The founding date of a town indicates its place in the chronology of city planning; a chart of the growth of that town mirrors its need for new building; and along the main paths of commerce and settlement architectural details were carried as easily as grain, pork, or barrel staves.

Fortunately Connecticut demography is simple. Unlike the colorful variety of the middle colonies Connecticut had a homogeneous population. Few travelers or census takers before 1800 failed to remark the existence of an almost pure English stock or to contrast this condition with that of neighboring colonies.[1] Jedidiah Morse in 1797 described the inhabitants of Connecticut as "almost entirely of English descent. There are no Dutch, French or Germans and very few Scotch or Irish people in any part of the state."[2] Negroes formed less than one part in forty of the population in 1756 and exerted little social pressure on the colony's architecture. Connecticut was a colony of Englishmen whose increase in numbers the governor, Thomas Fitch, cautiously attributed "to an industrious, temperate life and early marriage."[3]

Thomas Fitch's opinion of the value of a businesslike philosophy toward marriage did not miss the mark. Estimates of colonial population indicate that the initial migration before 1660 supplied most of the colony's inhabitants. To an extraordinary degree the colony grew by natural increase and was little affected by later migration.

Connecticut had only some 5,000 square miles of land and, at the end of the colonial period, only 237,946 persons, including 2,648 slaves. Seven states had larger populations; outside New England only Delaware, New Jersey, and Georgia had fewer inhabitants in 1790; Virginia had three times as many settlers, but Connecticut's population density of 49.1 persons per square mile ranked second only to Rhode Island.[4] The narrow compass of her boundaries, only one eighth of the Virginia colony, had held little promise for the land-hungry immigrant of the eighteenth century.

What else restricted the colony's growth is not certain. Its population increased throughout the colonial period, but at varying rates. It had grown rapidly in the early seventeenth century, but until 1676 the incomplete tax lists fail to chart the change. In that year the threat of war and a need for soldiers forced the first accurate count of the militia, and from this list the total population of the colony may be placed at about 9,000 persons.[5] In 1700, almost

1. *New England Historical and Genealogical Register,* XXVI, 301–305. Spot comparisons of United States Bureau of the Census, *Heads of Families at the First Census of the United States Taken in the Year 1790,* "Connecticut" (Washington, Government Printing Office, 1907–8), and Charles W. E. Bardsley, *A Dictionary of English and Welsh Names* (New York, H. Frowde, 1901) bore out this conclusion. See also Emberson E. Proper, *Colonial Immigration Laws* (New York, Columbia University Press, 1900), pp. 33–34; *The Public Records of the Colony of Connecticut* (Hartford, 1877), X, 617–618; XIV, 483–492 (hereafter abbreviated to *P.R. Col. Conn.*).

2. Jedidiah Morse, *The American Gazetteer* (Boston, 1797), "Connecticut."

3. In answer to John Pownall's query on behalf of the Board of Trade, see *P. R. Col. Conn.,* X, 622.

4. Bureau of the Census, *Heads of Families,* "Connecticut," p. 8.

5. *Ibid.,* II, 207. Evarts B. Greene and Virginia D. Harrington, *American Population before the Federal Census of 1790* (New York, Columbia University Press, 1932), p. xxiii.

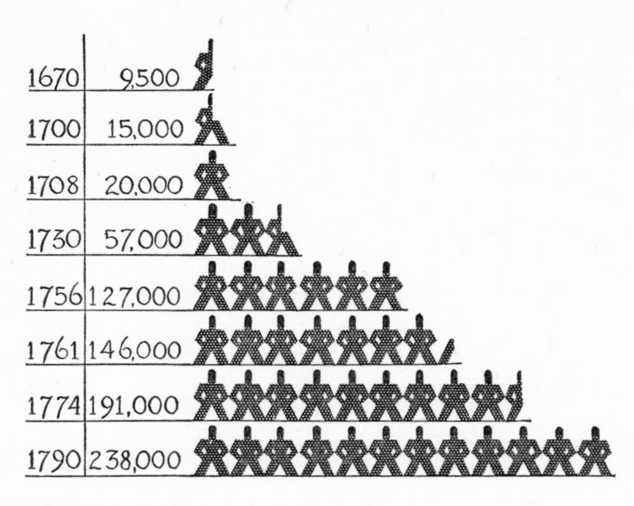

1. Growth of Connecticut population, 1670–1790

a quarter of a century later, some 3,800 persons paid taxes to the colony. The total population in that year may therefore be roughly estimated at 15,000 persons, showing an average annual increase between 1676 and 1700 of only 250 persons.[6] (Fig. 1.)

During the next decade the rate of population increase accelerated. The population in 1708 reached a total of 20,000 persons. This growth of 5,000 persons, or about 600 annually, in the main went to the new towns then being added to the tax lists and not to the older established communities. New Haven's population, based on such lists, would appear to have actually declined; Branford, a small town, had a relatively stable number of inhabitants, but Canterbury, Mansfield, and Durham, absent on earlier lists, registered respectable totals at the end of the period.[7]

For the years 1708 to 1756 no complete lists have survived, but it is clear that the colony grew rapidly. In 1756, 127,000 white colonists and some 2,000 slaves lived in Connecticut.[8] Only a guess can now be made as to the rate of growth in the near half-century between censuses. Dexter estimated the population in 1730 at 57,000, a figure that suggests a regularly increasing rate of population growth; but he felt that more than 20,000 persons had settled in the colony by 1708, which later writers deny.[9]

Even during the French and Indian War the population rose steadily to a total of 146,000 in 1761, and by 1774 it numbered 191,343. The Revolutionary

6. *P. R. Col. Conn.*, IV, 329.

7. *Ibid.*, IV, 71.

8. *Ibid.*, X, 617–618.

9. Franklin B. Dexter, "Estimates of Population in the American Colonies," American Antiquarian Society, *Proceedings* (1887), V, 32.

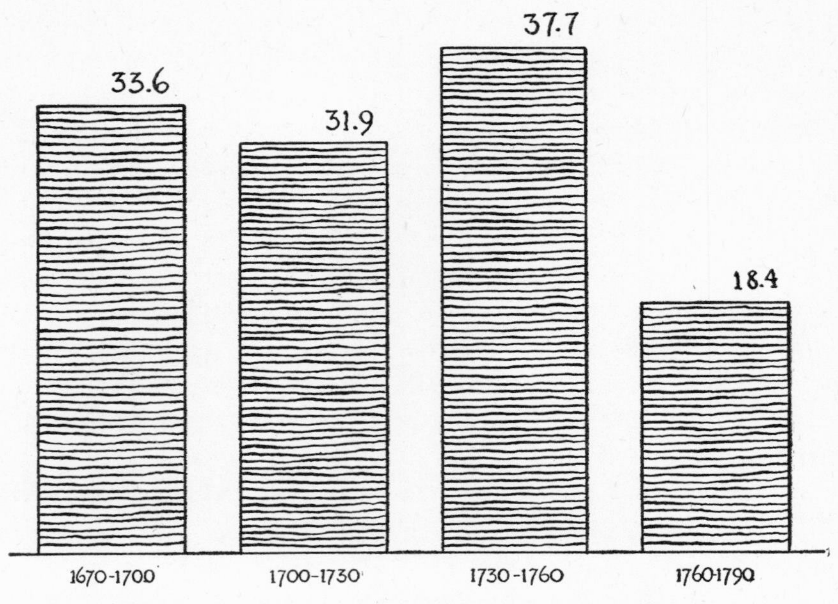

2. Rate of decennial increase of Connecticut population, 1670–1790

War only slowed the increase, and the census of 1782 showed a total of 209,177 persons of all races in the new state. The first federal census of 1790 credited Connecticut with 238,000 persons, an increase of about 15 per cent in eight years. Since the colony depended little on foreign migration to swell her population, wars had less effect upon her than upon her neighbors, New York and Massachusetts.[10] (Fig. 1.)

Actually migration at the end of the eighteenth century changed the nature of the colony's population far less than earlier and smaller increases. These numerical gains obscure a significant decline in the rate of increase in population. The plot of this rate either as a percentage or in terms of the number of persons needed to produce an annual unit increase in population indicates that the rate of growth fell steadily from 1676 until sometime shortly after 1730. Then it began to rise slowly until the census of 1756 and the beginning of the French and Indian War. At the end of the war the rate of increase continued to decline, although the population itself slowly increased up to the Revolutionary War. Thereafter the annual rate of increase rose to about 2 per cent, a small fraction of the soaring populations of New York and Pennsylvania.[11] (Fig. 2.)

Increases in population brought a steady demand for new buildings. The

10. *P.R. Col. Conn.*, XI, 630; XIV, 485–492. Jedidiah Morse, *The American Geography* (London, 1792), p. 218, corrected total for 1782. Bureau of the Census, *Heads of Families,* "Connecticut," p. 9.

11. Bureau of the Census, *Heads of Families,* "Connecticut," p. 8.

census of 1790 indicated that for every six persons recorded the assistant marshals named one family head. Since Congress enacted "that every person whose usual place of abode shall be in any family . . . shall be returned as of that family," families were distinguished from one another by the ownership of separate houses. It follows, therefore, that at the end of the colonial period an average of six persons occupied each house.[12]

Certainly no less than six persons inhabited the average house in the seventeenth century. (Greene estimates "at least seven persons.") In 1700, therefore, Connecticut colonists occupied at most only some 2,500 houses, perhaps only 2,100. For the last quarter of the seventeenth century population increase required only thirty-five to forty new houses annually, apart from any lost by fire or neglect. A decade later population growth throughout the colony still required less than one hundred new houses each year. Today only some twenty, less than 1 per cent of the houses built, have any serious claim to origin before 1700. The remainder, like their builders, have disappeared and left their mark only in the plans and details of eighteenth-century successors.

Free of sudden demands for new homes, Connecticut builders were slow to change their architecture, and this conservatism renders an analysis of the colony's early settlers valuable. The models which they developed before 1680 dominated the colony's domestic architecture for nearly two centuries; the background of these settlers, geographic, social, and economic, determined the shape of the local architectural idiom along the shore from Greenwich to Groton and up the Connecticut River from Saybrook to Windsor. Reasonable conformity became synonymous with beauty; the latest English fashion appeared chiefly in moldings and panels; floor plans and elevations remained almost static.

Connecticut settlers were English; they came from the counties of southeastern England, southwestern England, northern, and central England, in that order. This distribution is not surprising, since the settlers of New England as a whole came from the same parts of the British Isles. Despite the contrary opinions of many scholars geographical origin seems to have no clear economic or religious significance.[13] (Fig. 3.)

12. *Ibid.*, p. 7.

13. Although each decade genealogists add new names to the long lists of emigrants traced to their English homes, the proportions do not seem to vary. The most complete account is given in Charles E. Banks, *Topographical Dictionary of 2,885 English Emigrants to New England, 1620–1650* (Philadelphia, The Bertram Press, 1937), see p. xiii for map. Other partial lists are Henry R. Stiles, *The History and Genealogies of Ancient Windsor* (Hartford Case, Lockwood & Brainard Company, 1891); *The History of Ancient Wethersfield* (New York, Grafton Press, 1904); "List of Officers, Military and Civil, March 1636–December 1665, in the Colonies of Connecticut and New Haven," *New Haven Genealogical Magazine*, IV (Rome, New York, 1927), 966–1016; George F. T. Sherwood, *American Colonists in English Records* (London, G. Sherwood, 1932–33).

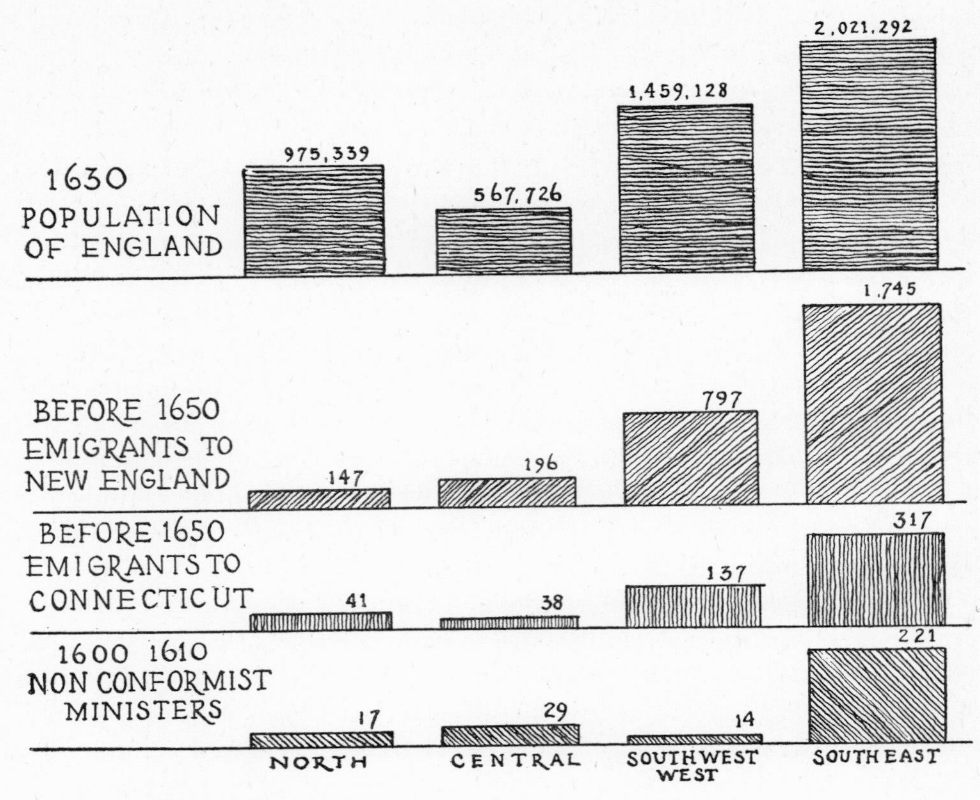

3. Emigrants and sources of migration

Some years ago James Truslow Adams chose the Great Migration to Connecticut, Rhode Island, and Massachusetts as a classic example of economic determinism. He presumed that migration proceeded from those areas in England which were economically maladjusted. He then linked the southeastern origin of Puritans and New England settlers to the progress of enclosures and the depression in the cloth industry in those same areas at the end of the sixteenth and the beginning of the seventeenth centuries. Since enclosures were concentrated in the southeast and the crisis in the cloth industry had its nucleus in the vicinity of the Wash, it was easy to connect both with those emigrants from the same counties who left for America.[14]

Other authorities contested Adams' theory and found in religious motivation a primary explanation of seventeenth-century migration to New England. The Puritans formed one of the first religious groups in whose history

14. James T. Adams, *The Founding of New England* (Boston, Little, Brown & Co., 1933), pp. 121–134; Richard J. Tawney, *The Agrarian Problem in the Sixteenth Century* (New York, Longmans, Green & Co., 1912), pp. 8–9. For some conclusions with a radically different method, see Gilbert Slater, "The Inclosure of Common Fields Considered Geographically," *Geographical Journal,* XXIX (1907), 40–44.

the influence of geographical and economic factors can be plotted from their beginning. Since Puritan distribution traditionally followed a pattern of concentration in the southeast and around the Wash, scholars linked the New England migration to Archbishop Laud's persecution.[15] Moreover, the religious historians pointed out that migration continued in full force after the economic depression had subsided but stopped at the end of the religious persecution of the Puritans.[16]

In further support of the latter conclusion the distribution of Puritan ministers, the class from which many of the leaders of the migration to New England were drawn, has been plotted. An analysis of ministers who were known to be Nonconformist between 1600 and 1610 indicated the highest concentration in Middlesex, Suffolk, Essex, and Northamptonshire. The southwestern and northern counties were relatively free of Puritan clerics with the exception of a considerable pocket of ministers in southern Lancashire, but oddly enough the counties south of the Thames had only a few scattered Puritan clergy centered in Sussex.[17] (Fig. 3.)

Important as the economic and religious interpretations may be, their sponsors have so far erroneously assumed that population was evenly distributed. On the contrary more Englishmen lived in southeastern England than in the northern counties; more Englishmen lived in western England than in Leicestershire and nearby counties. In general the number of Connecticut settlers from each part of England corresponded roughly to the size of that section's population in 1630. Populous counties sent many settlers; barren and sparse counties sent few.[18] (Fig. 3.)

Not every county sent precisely its proportion of New England settlers, but this occasionally happened. For example, Northumberland had a population of 97,771 in 1630. The same estimate credits Lancashire with 220,022 inhabitants and Yorkshire with 432,226 persons, and this ratio of 1:2:4 is exactly repeated in the emigrants to New England who have been traced to their places of origin; 19 came from Northumberland, 43 from Lancashire, and 81 from Yorkshire.[19]

In other counties religious or economic discontent increased migration to New England. From a population of only 174,229 at least 298 Suffolk men

15. Nellis M. Crouse, "Causes of the Great Migration, 1630–1640," *New England Quarterly*, V, 27–29.

16. *Ibid.*, pp. 14–15.

17. Roland G. Usher, *The Reconstruction of the English Church* (London, D. Appleton & Co., 1910), I, 250 map, 255. This compilation represents about 85 per cent of seventeenth-century estimates of Puritan clergy.

18. Parliamentary Papers, *Reports from the Commissioners* (1843), XXII, 36.

19. *Ibid.* Cf. C. E. Banks, *Topographical Dictionary*, p. xiii. Since all the persons listed by Banks are male his list represents about a quarter of the total migration.

settled in New England before 1650. Two hundred sixty-six Essex men came from a county with a population of only about 183,000.[20] Essentially these ratios must be viewed as minor modifications of the basic pattern of the distribution of English population. The marked prominence of the southwest and populous counties throughout England indicates that the migration was a general one touching every part of England. Neither enclosure nor Puritan sentiment alone suffices to explain the great attraction of New England's coastline in the early seventeenth century.[21] The Great Migration was a symptom of nationwide discontent and distress.

Every class of English society responded to the cry of Westward Ho. Often uncertain as to the colony in which they would settle, the departing emigrants would vaguely name their destination as Virginia or New England in the port records, swear a hurried oath of allegiance and supremacy and list their family and occupation before embarking upon some such ship as "the *Confidence* of London of C C tounes. John Jobson Mr." [22] Only when they had met these conditions correctly could the New England emigrants set sail. The anxiety which such formalities entailed is reflected in a warrant issued in February, 1633, in which "the severall ships following bound for New England and now lying in the River of Thames were made staye of untill further order: viz. the Clement & Job, the Reformation, the True Love, The Elizabeth Benadventure, the Sea Flower, The Mary & John, the Plantor, the Elizabeth & Dorcas, the Hercules, and the Neptune." Finally on the last day of February the ten ships, after crews and passengers had officially affirmed their allegiance to king and church, were allowed to weigh anchor.[23]

Despite the vigilance of port authorities, time and fire have destroyed most seventeenth-century passenger lists. What once was a complete description of the trades and families of departing emigrants has dwindled to a mere handful of documents. But from these a suggestive if fragmentary picture of the New England planter emerges.

On these lists the husbandman appears most frequently. The class or social station of husbandman was first of all rural and concerned with the land. No clear-cut line separated the husbandman from the yeoman, who also farmed and generally had a freehold, but the two classes might merge in one family—the head of the family and his eldest son be classed as yeomen, the younger sons as husbandmen. The husbandman was a kind of meaner yeoman who

20. *Ibid.*

21. It is interesting to note that John Winthrop mentioned that interest in New England was widespread throughout England. John Winthrop, *History of New England* (New York, C. Scribner's Sons, 1908), I, 164.

22. Samuel G. Drake, *Result of Some Researches among the British Archives* (Boston, 1860), p. 51.

23. *Ibid.*, p. 69.

might with the improvement of his estate become a yeoman himself. Certainly wide variations in husbandmen's property appeared in the port lists. Many husbandmen transported two or more servants across the seas, while others traveled alone with few goods of value, but in each instance the husbandman came to the dock from a rural district, proud of his occupation as a farmer.[24]

On most passenger lists of the early seventeenth-century servants, often attached to the large family of a husbandman or yeoman, comprised the second most numerous group. In this early period the indentured servant rarely traveled alone or in the household of a merchant. Apparently the class was generally made up of countrymen; rural distress shared with the husbandmen made both groups migrate, and the husbandman paid the poorer servant's fare in return for his promise of labor.[25]

Many other households came from the agricultural English village. Plowrights and carpenters, sawyers and joiners, practicing trades essential to the more specialized and diversified life of the seventeenth-century countryside, joined the migration to Connecticut. Fishermen and fishmongers from the west of England came in smaller numbers. An occasional miller or a cooper saw in the voyage a chance to better himself. Masons were rare, since most of the settlers came from the timber-growing parts of England. Common laborers were seldom classified and cannot be either included or excluded on the basis of surviving evidence; the large body of such unclassified emigrants who lacked servants and were not engaged in trade suggests that they were landless tenants. If that is so, almost every sort of seventeenth-century village artisan and laborer migrated to New England.[26]

Had the New England migration been purely religious its character would

24. Other possible definitions are: a man who tills or cultivates the soil, i.e., until *ca.* 1660 husbandry did not include the raising and care of livestock, which is its common modern meaning. A more precise but too restricted use of the term is "a holder of the orthodox husband-land consisting of two ox-gangs," *A New English Dictionary on Historical Principles* (Oxford, Clarendon Press, 1888–1928). For an exhaustive investigation of the term, see Mildred Campbell, *The English Yeoman* (New Haven, Yale University Press, 1942), pp. 21–33.

25. That indentured servants came over early and were largely drawn from the dispossessed class of agricultural laborers is known. Marcus W. Jernegan, *Laboring and Dependent Classes in Colonial America* (Chicago, University of Chicago Press, 1931), pp. 46–47. In New England, however, it is generally believed that the majority of persons listed as servants were free. Abbot E. Smith, *Colonists in Bondage* (Chapel Hill, University of North Carolina Press, 1947), pp. v–vi, 308–310, 316–317.

26. The bulk of the information about the occupation of settlers is drawn from published port lists, of which the following were the most helpful: John C. Hotten, *The Original Lists of Persons of Quality; . . . 1600–1700* (New York, 1874), pp. 43, 45–49, 53–56, 58, 59, 61–66, 76, 88, 91, 97, 100–101, 105, 107, 108, 283–286, 289–295; Drake, *Result of Some Researches*, pp. 15–18, 30–35, 40–43, 45–50, 55, 61, 82–85. Both sets of lists give parallel results.

have been very different, as is illustrated by the Marian exile of 1553–59 to the Continent, a clear-cut religious protest against the reforms of Mary Tudor. Almost 40 per cent of these sixteenth-century migrants were listed as gentry; clergy and theological students made up another 40 per cent. Only some forty merchants or roughly 10 per cent of the total went into that voluntary exile. The remaining 10 per cent included chiefly artisans and printers; the migration failed to attract the husbandman, rural craftsman, and indentured servant. While the clergy and those of independent means could almost alone support a purely religious protest like the Marian exile, a far wider economic and especially agricultural base was needed for the New England migration, which became thereby a rural land movement as well as a religious release.[27]

Even village and city artisans who went to New England relied almost wholly upon rural prosperity for their livelihood. Weavers and tailors sailed in considerable numbers along with clothiers, drapers, glovers, curriers, shoemakers, and tanners. Few of the many other urban occupations listed in the English port records were unconnected with the wool trade. Occasionally a merchant, mercer, lawyer, or chirurgeon embarked for New England. The smaller artisans of the town dependent upon the sheep and cattle of country districts made up the urban share of the Great Migration.

Leadership, however, rested outside the bulk of the emigrants. The men who gave the migration its ideals and its ships belonged to more restricted classes of English society. Gentlemen and an occasional esquire, ministers of considerable property like Henry Whitfield, radical Nonconformists, men of affairs like John Winthrop, a few military engineers among whom Lion Gardiner was prominent, led the seventeenth-century settlers to Connecticut. Behind the poorer emigrant stood the money of the mercantile class and a firm Puritan faith.[28]

Faith and wealth blended conspicuously in the government of New Haven and Connecticut. The personalities of Theophilus Eaton and John Davenport were shaped by the problems of the Puritan merchant and minister early in the seventeenth century. The two were boyhood friends, a difference of only seven years separating their ages: in 1637 Eaton was almost fifty years old, while Davenport was forty-three. Before 1625 neither had been interested in New England, and not until a decade later did the prospect of settling there seize hold of either man.[29] Each succeeded in his chosen pursuit. Eaton was apprenticed at the age of fourteen to one of the livery companies of London,

27. Christina H. Garrett, *The Marian Exiles* (Cambridge, University Press, 1938), pp. 67–349.

28. Charles M. Andrews, *The Colonial Period of American History* (New Haven, Yale University Press, 1934), I, 76–77.

29. New Haven Historical Society, *Papers,* VII, 19; Isabel MacB. Calder, *The New Haven Colony* (New Haven, Yale University Press, 1934), p. 29.

in all probability the Mercers. At any rate he entered the employ of the Eastland Company, which held a monopoly of the Baltic trade, and in behalf of this company he spent several years in the north of Europe; before 1617 he had been elected a deputy-governor of the company.[30] In 1622 he married in London and sailed for Copenhagen. He returned to London in 1624 with a commission to buy undyed wool for Christian IV, King of Denmark. In 1625 he settled in St. Nicholas Acorns parish. That same year his first wife, Grace Hiller, died.

Late in 1629 Eaton moved to the parish of St. Stephen, Coleman Street. This wealthy congregation had as their minister John Davenport, who had been called in 1624. Although only twenty-seven years old when he left the Church of St. Lawrence Jewry, Davenport was a well-known and popular preacher, more than a little suspect in his Puritan leanings. Only through the efforts on his behalf of Sir Edward Conway and Lady Vere was he inducted as Vicar of St. Stephen's.[31] His new office did not lessen his radical activities. As one of four clergymen, together with an equal number of lawyers and London citizens, he administered the London Society, the principal aim of which was the distribution of funds to "preaching, conformable ministers appointed by the group." These funds were raised by the purchase of ecclesiastical revenues in lay hands.[32]

After 1629 Davenport and Eaton both contributed to the Massachusetts Bay Company. Eaton served in the first Court of Assistants; Davenport as a member of the commonalty. In January, 1633, Davenport nearly had to stand trial for his part in the purchase and control of lay livings, and when in August Laud was appointed archbishop Davenport fled to Holland.[33]

Eaton, in the meantime, had in 1631 and 1633 visited Elbing and Danzig in an unsuccessful effort to save the privileges of the Eastland Company from the threat of continental warfare. When finally in 1635 Eaton disclaimed the Massachusetts Bay Charter before the Court of King's Bench, Davenport found him ready to organize a new plantation company. Drawing heavily for members and funds on their home parish of St. Stephen, Coleman Street, the group chartered the *Hector* of London and early in May, 1637, set sail for New England. Thus step by step the Baltic merchant and London preacher had undertaken the leadership of a new colony.[34]

Like the New Haveners, Hartford and New London settlers sought their leaders among the landed gentry, the Puritan ministry, and the legal profession. From the towns founded by John Winthrop, Jr., lawyer, naval secre-

30. New Haven Hist. Soc., *Papers*, VII, 5.
31. Calder, *The New Haven Colony*, p. 17.
32. *Ibid.*, p. 10.
33. *Ibid.*, pp. 15, 29.
34. *Ibid.*, pp. 30–31.

tary, and world traveler; by Thomas Hooker, yeoman's son and Puritan preacher; by Ludlow the lawyer and Haynes, "the gentleman of great estate," came the lesser towns of the Connecticut coast and river valleys. These men crystallized widespread discontent, not only in England but also in Massachusetts, and outlined the colony's future geographical exploitation as surely as they drew up its laws or its confessions of faith.

Once under way, the colonization movement continued to draw upon the talents of its founders for leadership. The most important decision facing any small company of colonists was the selection of sites for the new towns. Chance might play a part in such a choice, but taken together the colonial towns of Connecticut present an orderly pattern created by the economic demands of the settlers, and these demands in turn directed the flow of architectural change and the development of town planning.

Connecticut's earliest settlement had three distinct phases: eastern, central, and western. In the east colonists first laid out New London and Norwich near the coast and Plainfield, Windham, and Woodstock farther north. From these centers colonists settled all the late seventeenth- and early eighteenth-century eastern towns. The watershed of the Thames River and its tributaries defined the western area of east Connecticut settlement; the New London and Windham county line divided the Massachusetts settlers moving south from the New London and Norwich men pushing inland from the coast.[35]

The clear line of separation between the settlement of eastern and western Connecticut is still evident in the dialectal characteristics of the two areas. The short "o" in such words as "coat," "road," and "home" is common, for example, in eastern Connecticut and eastern New England but rare in the western parts. The term "round clam" is common in western Connecticut but in the east the traditional word "quahog" is still used. Of eight typical eastern New England words only one is found beyond the western boundary of Tolland and New London counties.[36] Inhabitants of eastern and western Connecticut occasionally use different words for the same concept even when both words are found side by side throughout the rest of New England. For example, in western Connecticut "lowland" describes "the low-lying land

35. Information on settlement, widely scattered in town histories, is briefly summarized and grouped in gazetteer fashion in Florence S. Crofut, *Guide to the History and the Historic Sites of Connecticut* (New Haven, Yale University Press, 1937), 2 vols. The most reliable and useful local accounts are: Benjamin Trumbull, *A Complete History of Connecticut . . .* (New Haven, 1818); John W. Barber, *Connecticut Historical Collections* (New Haven, 1836); Ellen D. Larned, *History of Windham County* (Worcester, 1874–80); Charles H. Levermore, *The Republic of New Haven* (Baltimore, 1886); Frances M. Caulkins, *History of New London, Connecticut* (Hartford, 1852).

36. Hans Kurath, *Handbook of the Linguistic Geography of New England* (Providence, Brown University, 1939), pp. 26, 28, 29.

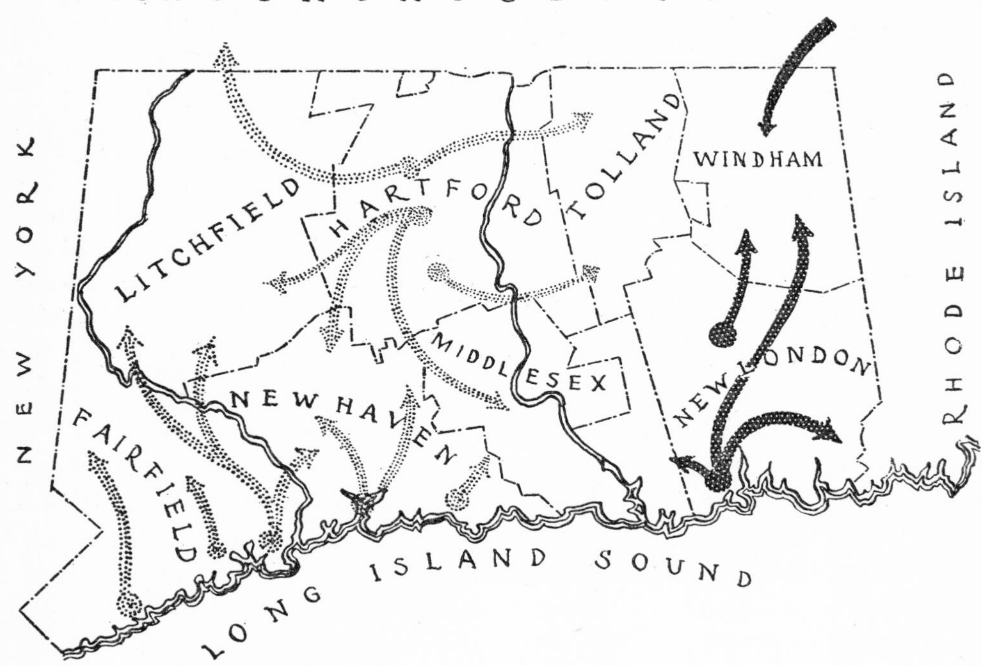

4. Direction of colonial settlement in Connecticut

along rivers . . . except meadows," but in the eastern part of the state "intervale" or "interval" denotes the same kind of land.[37]

Two different avenues directed the settlement of central and western Connecticut. One led south from Massachusetts down the Connecticut and Farmington River valleys [38] and included the towns of Windsor, Hartford, Wethersfield, and Middletown. The other route was Long Island Sound; along it were planted Fairfield and Saybrook and the towns of the New Haven colony—New Haven, Milford, Guilford, Branford, Greenwich, and Stamford. The New Haven towns expanded northward and the Connecticut River towns spread outward in all possible directions. Thus their people occupied during the late seventeenth and early eighteenth century the area which afterward

37. Hans Kurath, *Linguistic Atlas of New England* (Providence, Brown University, 1939), map 28. See also map 41, river; 123, furrows. The Farmington River formerly reached the sound at New Haven but had its course altered by the glacier.

38. W. R. Rice and H. E. Gregory, "Manual of the Geology of Connecticut," *Connecticut State Geological and Natural History Survey, Bulletin 6* (Hartford, 1906), pp. 251–254, map and discussion.

became Middlesex and Tolland counties. Settlers thrusting westward for new lands finally reached Litchfield County in the mid-eighteenth century.

Rivers and the coastline of Long Island Sound afforded perhaps the easiest method of travel but if the shores had not been suitable for immediate settlement the emigrant would have pushed inland. Actually the choice of exact location for the first settlement was determined only partially by the course of rivers and the coastline. The colonists' large flocks of animals could not survive even a year without adequate pasturage; to drive them inland away from natural marshes and meadows would have doomed the animals to starvation and upset the agricultural unity of the town group.[39] (Fig. 4.)

One can only guess the extent and exact location of the seventeenth-century meadowland which nourished the first settlers' flocks, but certain relationships can be established between the areas settled and the distribution of present-day soils in Connecticut.[40] Connecticut's topography falls naturally into four regions: an eastern highland, a western highland, a central river basin which divides into two branches at Middletown with one mouth at New Haven, the other at Saybrook. The fourth natural region is the narrow strip of coastline bordering Long Island Sound.

Within the 50 by 100 mile rectangle of Connecticut five soil groups predominate. First, natural meadow and silt lands lie along the shore and river beds. Second, the terraces (Merrimac, Hartford, and related soils) are found chiefly in the central valley and to a lesser degree along the banks of other streams. No rocks and few stones make the terraces ideal for both crop and pasture agriculture.

The third soil type, the red sandy central valley loam (Wethersfield, Cheshire, and so forth), is more stony but still an excellent all-purpose soil. The fourth soil group includes the Drumloids (Charlton and related soils). These soils are fairly rocky but still supply good grass and orchards. The fifth group, the Highland sandy loams (Gloucester and so forth), are more rocky and stony and support only fair grass, corn, and rye crops.

First settlements were generally made in the vicinity of what are today tidal marshes or river lowlands. Thus, out of eighteen towns founded before 1650 twelve were located in areas of tidal marshes and Merrimac loam, still

39. Archer B. Hulbert, *Soil: Its Influence on the History of the United States* (New Haven, Yale University Press, 1930), pp. 85–86.

Brands and brand marks occupy a large section of the early records. Occasionally they are sketched in town records, see reproduction, William H. Wilcoxson, *History of Stratford* (Stratford, Stratford Tercentenary Commission, 1939), p. 347.

40. Terminology of the Connecticut Agricultural Experiment Station has been adopted. A wide variety of nomenclature exists, see Mont F. Morgan, *The Soil Characteristics of Connecticut Land Types* (New Haven, Connecticut Agricultural Experiment Station, 1939). See also *Outline Soil Map of Connecticut.*

considered Connecticut's richest soil, supplemented by terraces of excellent all-purpose soils. Moreover, the land claimed by these twelve towns included an estimated 80 per cent of such soils within the colony.[41]

Of the remaining six settlements, four had large areas of good Podunk silt often combined with other rich soils.[42] Middletown, alone among the river towns, seems to have had a small proportion of silt-covered lands. Together the five river towns included almost 95 per cent of Connecticut's silt and other rich river lands. In the judgment of Eaton and Davenport the value of New Haven's harbor apparently outweighed the quality of its soil. Dissatisfied with Watertown in Massachusetts "since a boat could not pass from the Bay thither, nearer than 8 or 10 miles distance," they could not see that it "was compatible with our conditions." They "sent letters to Connecticut for a speedy transacting the purchass the parts about Quillypicate." [43] When the purchase was completed New Haven became the only town founded before 1650 on land enriched by neither Merrimac loam nor Podunk silt. Even the Hartford sandy loam, typical of New Haven County, was much reduced by trap rock and salt marshes. A well-protected harbor seemed more important than agricultural considerations.

From 1650 until 1700 less easily reached but still fertile soils attracted settlers. The towns founded in this period tapped the last of the meadows and terraces; colonists began to settle upon the central valley loams, and east of the Connecticut River were drawn to the rew remaining areas of Charlton soils. In this period the settlement of the western branch of the central valley, including Wallingford, Meriden, and Durham, was virtually completed.

Roughly twenty-two additional towns laid out and settled between 1650 and 1700 resulted from migrations or separations from older Connecticut communities. Only Woodstock, Windham, and Plainfield in Windham County were founded by settlers from Massachusetts. Of these twenty-two towns fourteen have a considerable area of Charlton or Merrimac loam.[44] Of the remaining eight Simsbury and Glastonbury have Podunk silt, and two towns to the north of New Haven have the improved soils of the former bed of the Farmington River, the choicest of which is the Wethersfield loam.

41. Includes the following towns: New London (1646), Groton (1649), Stonington (1646), Saybrook (1636), Norwalk (1649), Branford (1644), Guilford (1639), Milford (1639), Stratford (1639), Fairfield (1639), Stamford (1641), Greenwich (1640). Wherever practical, date of first settlement is used.

42. Hartford (1636), Windsor (1635), Wethersfield (1634), Farmington (1640), Middletown (1650).

43. *Letters of John Davenport,* ed. by Isabel MacB. Calder (New Haven, Yale University Press, 1937), p. 67.

44. Haddam (1663), E. Haddam (1685), Woodbury (1673), Windham (1688), Pomfret (1691), Canterbury (1697), Plainfield (1671), Preston (1686), Norwich (1689), Lebanon (1692), Colchester (1698), Mansfield (1695).

After 1700 Gloucester and Charlton loams were the best still available in the colony, and they controlled settlement after the earlier towns had exhausted the Podunk and Merrimac land.

Woodstock, Danbury, Suffield, and Enfield were settled before 1700 but on soils of uneven quality. It is easy to explain the settlement of such a remote site as Woodstock in terms of the soil available at the time it was settled and the rich vein of Charlton loam which runs across the town.[45] (Fig. 4.) Danbury likewise has a large area of Charlton loam. Suffield and Enfield have good but late soils.

After 1700 settlers in numbers reached the last considerable area of Gloucester loam in western Windham and Tolland counties. Colonists had opened this land earlier at their own risk of title pending settlement of the claims of Capt. John Mason and under such conditions few had come. Finally in 1705–8 the Assembly divided among 180 volunteers of the Narragansett War the mediocre Voluntown lands and completed the allotment of lands east of the Connecticut River.[46] (Fig. 4.)

The initial settlement of the colony ended in the second quarter of the eighteenth century with the laying out of Litchfield County. A combination of hilly terrain and poor soil made this land the last to be settled but here as elsewhere in the colony the site of the town first settled points like a magnetic needle to the best agricultural land available. Bantam, now Litchfield, was planted squarely on the largest piece of Charlton loam in the county, which in terms of the rocky and sandy soils in which the county abounds is excellent soil. Once again migration from older Connecticut towns supplied the bulk of the inhabitants, but a sprinkling of settlers came southward from Massachusetts. The western boundary of the county and the southern limits of Sharon, Kent, Goshen, Torrington, and Harwinton framed the last frontier.

Only speculation in western lands could develop so barren a county. The Assembly sold the townships of Sharon, Salisbury, Canaan, Norfolk, Kent, Goshen, and Cornwall to individual purchasers, and the proprietors of Hartford and Windsor sold the seven eastern towns, Harwinton, Torrington, Colebrook, Barkhamstead, Winchester, New Hartford, and Hartland on a speculative basis. When all the towns of Litchfield were taken up the settlement of virgin land had ended in Connecticut. After 1750 her slowly growing population was content with more crowded lands or migrated to other colonies

45. The term "late" means the soil holds its moisture and is unsuitable for cultivation until late in the spring.

46. Benjamin Trumbull, *A Complete History of Connecticut; P.R. Col. Conn.*, I, 196, 356–361; IV, 186, 335–336; V, 47, 419–420. Proprietors Map of Voluntown, MSS, Connecticut State Library.

or to Westmoreland, Connecticut's holdings in what is now eastern Pennsylvania, and other colonies.[47]

Only a few thousand settlers peopled Connecticut, but the colony, however small, provided one of the myriad adjustments to rapidly changing society which Englishmen made in the late seventeenth century. No single class and no single county alone made the plantation. Discontent with enclosure and with the Established Church were linked; Puritanism and the increase of wealth went hand in hand. Technical skill and the knowledge of far places helped protect the yeoman from the wilderness, and to the plan of his town and church the Connecticut settler brought all the English life of his day. New England might have been settled fifty years later; it could not have been settled fifty years earlier; until 1620 no class of Englishmen had emerged that had the youth, wealth, and high connections to win favors from the Crown or Parliament and that at the same time shared with husbandmen and yeomen their religious and economic unrest. Migration to New England offered the dispossessed countryman a home and land, the merchant a market, and the exile asylum. In the first three decades of the seventeenth century wealth and church combined for the first time with a host of new skills to make the New England plantation possible as well as desirable. Not for many decades, if indeed ever again, would small segments of so many classes of English society be able and willing to venture abroad.

The knowledge which they applied to navigation and naval architecture, the plans of their towns, the division of land, and the erection of their homes was a unique new combination of tradition and experiment. The homogeneity of Connecticut's population, the poverty of much of its terrain, and its tardy growth accidentally combined to preserve at least the external features of that Puritan experiment in town design for nearly a century and a half.

47. Crofut, *Guide to the History . . . of Connecticut,* I, 388 ff. The subject of secondary migration is summarily dwelt with in Lois K. M. Rosenberry, *Migrations from Connecticut Prior to 1800* (New Haven, Yale University Press, 1934), pp. 7–13; and by the same author, *The Expansion of New England* (Boston, Houghton Mifflin Company, 1909), pp. 354–459.

II. The Towns

Connecticut buildings and plans, essentially derivative in their nature, reflected the process of the colony's settlement. Radical changes in colonial style depended chiefly upon fresh immigrations, usually of persons familiar with European fashion or, more rarely, upon the importation of books illustrating new trends in European design. The colony's architecture, town plans, and land division were like its settlers—rural, Protestant, and English. Like its population, the colony's buildings and roads elaborated a seventeenth-century stock of ideas. From the economic, religious, and social patterns of Stuart England the colonists derived a style which, although first developed and now best preserved in Puritan meetinghouses, penetrated to some degree every Connecticut dwelling, sermon, and town plan. Based upon practical adjustments of seventeenth-century life, the long retention of that style led to its idealization as an aesthetic standard in the eighteenth century. Although well known as a symbol of protest throughout the English-speaking world after 1600, the Plain Style in isolated Connecticut had an almost uncontested development for a century and a half. Streets, homes, meetinghouses, and land allotments came to represent a humble but orderly answer to the challenge of Catholic cities in New Spain and New France; in time a counter-baroque style of architecture and planning evolved.

Yet the primary problem which faced the settler was not aesthetic. The practical need of existence in a wilderness came foremost; to survive he fell back upon the experience of his own generation in the planning of streets and the allotment of property; he believed that only an orderly town plot could guarantee him military and economic security.

Once the title had been cleared, the seventeenth-century Englishman, whether he lived in Ireland, New England, East Anglia, or Bermuda, surveyed his land. In so doing he followed the custom of his times because by 1600 the survey had become an indispensable weapon in the hands of soldiers and a priceless tool for large landowners. In America the survey alone could review the extent of the colonist's land claims and sketch the roads, churches, and future property holdings of the utopia he visualized in the New World.

Town surveys were, of course, more elaborate than the familiar town plans. The latter had evolved in Europe simply as maps or views of an urban growth at any point in its career. They indicated primarily the street plan of the town, and secondarily, either by implication or actual drafting, they showed the location of buildings within the town; even main routes to other settlements rarely appeared beyond town limits. Such printed plans aided the traveler and whetted the curiosity and interest of the reading public during the fifteenth, sixteenth, and seventeenth centuries. They illustrated only famous cities; small towns seldom appeared. And by an unforeseen accident the maps have become primary sources for the student of historical town planning despite their original purpose—to publicize travel, national trade, or empire building.[1]

Town surveys, on the other hand, from their beginnings gave full descriptions of the contemporary scene upon which social action could be based. Since they were seldom published, their value as artistic reproductions became incidental to their main purpose, and, since accuracy was always paramount, the surveyor made every effort to describe each detail beyond question of doubt. Surveys achieved a wide variety of purposes, military, economic, and political, but in every instance accurate description rather than idealization of the area in question dominated their design. Thus in the Netherlands Charles V and Philip II had careful plans drawn of over two hundred towns in order to simplify tactical problems of the Duke of Alba's administration.[2]

In England economic considerations rather than military necessity dictated the majority of the surveys. A necessary preliminary to the enclosure of common fields and the dissolution of copyholds was the construction of an accurate terrier and a complete map of the area in question.[3] Therefore, after the sixteenth-century enclosures had spread widely, the art of the surveyor became commonplace, and the surveyor himself came to be noted as the paid tool of the large landholder, the English copyholder's symbol of the destruc-

1. The best early English collection of such plans is found in John Speed, *The Theatre of the Empire of Great Britain* (London, 1611), hereafter abbreviated to Speed, *Theatre . . . Great Britain.*

2. These have been largely reproduced from the manuscript maps. *Atlas des villes de la Belgique au XVIe siècle, cent plans du géographe Jacques de Deventer . . .* (Brussels, Institut National de Géographie, 1884–1924). *Nederlandsche Studen . . . Plattegronden von Jacob van Deventer* (The Hague, 1884–1924).

3. Howard L. Gray, *English Field Systems* (Cambridge, Harvard University Press, 1915), pp. 14–15. The author gives an excellent account of this source material. See also Richard J. Tawney, *The Agrarian Problem in the Sixteenth Century,* Appendix II.

tion of customary land rights.[4] Many of these sixteenth- and seventeenth-century enclosure surveys, both in written and in graphic form, still exist and form the basis of modern property rights in those parts of the British Isles which they describe.[5]

In Ireland, the city of London and the Crown used the surveyor as a weapon in their quarrel over the distribution of land holdings and the administration of Ulster. Each side drew elaborate surveys to indicate the failure or success of the Irish plantation and its ability to fulfill the commitments made. Although many of these plans and maps burned in the eighteenth- and twentieth-century fires at the Irish Record Office, one complete set has survived and illustrates the artistry of its author, Sir Thomas Phillips.[6] (Figs. 7, 8, 31.)

The poverty of information about unsettled colonial areas made early surveys of Connecticut mere sketches. After exploration the town proprietors did draw more elaborate maps as guides for new settlers, and the expansion of a town often closely followed such plans. In other instances surveys have survived that were drawn by travelers fully cognizant of the European tradition of the survey. One type of town map for which I have found no European precedent is the ecclesiastical survey. Congregations in newly settled areas used such surveys to influence the Assembly to effect a separation of towns, and their maps stressed the road system and distribution of houses within the then existing boundaries.[7]

A critical examination of both European and American surveys may eventually reshape our concept of society in the seventeenth century. In Europe the surveyor felt bound to record with minute artistry the teamwork of a village harvest, the tiled roofs and geometric gardens of a Dutch fortress city, the graceful hull of a river craft, the crumbled tower of an Ulster church, the rough walls of a Yorkshire cottage, the ambling curve of an open-field road in Sussex.[8]

In America the haste of the moment made such labors of love rare, but still the surveyor has left us many of our best records of early settlement: John White's colorful water color of the fort at Roanoke painted for all to see the settlement's tragic weakness; Richard Norwood's survey of the Somers Islands recorded the curious land distribution of the Bermudas; in

4. John Norden, *The Surveyors Dialogue* (London, 1607), pp. 1–7.

5. George Hill, *An Historical Account of the Plantation in Ulster* (Belfast, 1887), p. 200, is an Irish example. Hereafter this is abbreviated to Hill, *Plantation in Ulster*.

6. Sir Thomas Phillips, *Londonderry and the London Companies, 1609–1629* (Belfast, H. M. Stationery Office, 1928), p. 92, hereafter called *Phillips MSS*.

7. These surveys are now found chiefly in the Connecticut State Library, the Yale University Library, and local town halls.

8. For a particularly complete example, see Charles S. Orwin, *The Open Fields* (Oxford, Clarendon Press, 1938), Appendix, Laxton map of 1635.

October, 1607, a few weeks after English colonists had landed at Sagadahoc, John Hunt sketched the church, storehouses, garrison buildings, and fortress as Capt. George Popham hoped they would look some day; John Underhill, in his survey for John Knowles completed in 1664, sketched some eight Jamestown houses whose foundations alone remain; the abortive fort at Saybrook was recorded in the surveying tradition by John Winthrop, Jr., during the seventeenth century and by Ezra Stiles in the eighteenth century; the meetinghouses, cemetery, and brightly painted homes of colonial New Haven appear best in the Wadsworth map or survey of 1748. Such fine examples of the surveyor's art were rare but far from unknown in colonial America; less handsome surveys exist by the hundreds. (Figs. 17, 18, 26–30, 56.)

Both colonial and English surveys indicate that, before 1630, only trading companies and colonists in newly conquered territory concerned themselves with town planning. At home conditions both in the larger towns and in villages were critical, but until the Great Fire of London no one advanced a comprehensive solution to the problems of either town or village. Rather, in the early years of the seventeenth century, towns altered their street plans rapidly and in piecemeal fashion and maintained, side by side, both new and old institutions. The English city, town, and village were in flux, but each had solved its problem momentarily without regard for any over-all principle. Thus no domestic school of town-plan design had arisen in England before 1635 and the settlement of Connecticut.

The planning problems of London and of the bigger towns did not resemble those of the agricultural village. The growth of urban population, a slowly increasing security from attack, and a vastly enlarged commerce had rendered the traditional walled town archaic. To face their new needs townsmen had made three rather obvious adjustments: they built beyond the defensive walls of the town; they enlarged docking facilities for water-borne commerce; and in a few instances they designed an orderly street plan to serve future building needs. The Elizabethan and early Stuart Englishman left untouched the overburdened complexity of his city's medieval inheritance.

The largest of English cities, London, when John Speed engraved it in 1610 (Fig. 5), extended for 2½ miles along the Thames. The ruined town walls no longer constricted the city's growth and now stood surrounded by built-up areas. River vessels docked and unloaded at numerous quays and basins which had good access to warehouses and shops. A single bridge which spanned the Thames led to a shallow but equally long urban development on the south bank of the river which promised, in time, to double the shipping facilities of the town.[9] London, however, lacked a flexible plan of street development

9. Speed, *Theatre . . . Great Britain*, p. 29.

to care for its increasing population. The existing pattern was logical only in its broadest sense. It radiated north from the river, its main axis, in an irregular manner, but the individual streets were crooked and narrow. Moreover, the blocks on which buildings had been erected were so small that they were nearly covered by construction. Building on the outskirts seemed scarcely more logical and it too stood compressed on small irregular pieces of land separated by narrow streets. Westminster alone presented a more orderly appearance, due in large measure to the effect of the palaces and mansions fronting the Thames, but farther back from the river even Westminster had as confused a street pattern as London proper.[10] Although town walls had not seriously hindered the growth of London and although shipping facilities had improved, there is no evidence that by 1610 any direct street plan had been devised to serve the city's new population and wealth. (Fig. 6.)

Twenty years later, in 1630, on his own land north of his house on the Strand the 4th Earl of Bedford began the development of Covent Garden by securing royal permission to plan an Italian piazza framed with arcades. By 1635 Inigo Jones had almost completed the task of design and building. As pictured by Colin Campbell before the disastrous fire of 1795, the piazza must have been magnificent (Fig. 66), but even by 1738, if Hogarth is to be believed, it had become encrusted with temporary shacks and its open market was abused by pimps, prostitutes, and beggars. Three hundred feet wide and 360 feet long, the square had wide avenues entering on two sides; on the south a low terrace separated it from the Earl of Bedford's gardens; on the northern and eastern sides of the square Jones built arcades which shaded the entrances to the three-story houses above them and which the earl let at a good price. On the western end of the square stood St. Paul's Church, flanked by two small gates and two larger houses. At a later time the square was completed on the south side by matching arcades with houses above.[11] With the exception of Bloomsbury, no area in Stuart London so effectively combined keen business acumen, royal concern for the Church of England, and a sophisticated taste for Italian design as did Covent Garden. Although the piazza made a lasting contribution to English architecture, English urban planners disregarded its lessons for nearly a century.

English shire and county towns provided a less imaginative street plan for their enlarged populations. Often their systems of communication seemed totally incapable of rational expansion. None of the forty-eight towns illustrated by Speed in 1610 shows the advent of any effective solution. In the few towns which had had a sound street plan at their foundation, such as

10. *Ibid.*, p. 28.

11. John N. Summerson, *Georgian London* (New York, Charles Scribner's Sons, 1946), pp. 13–17. Colin Campbell, *Vitruvius Britannicus* (London, 1717), I, 20–22.

5. London in 1610

6. The Thames waterfront in 1647

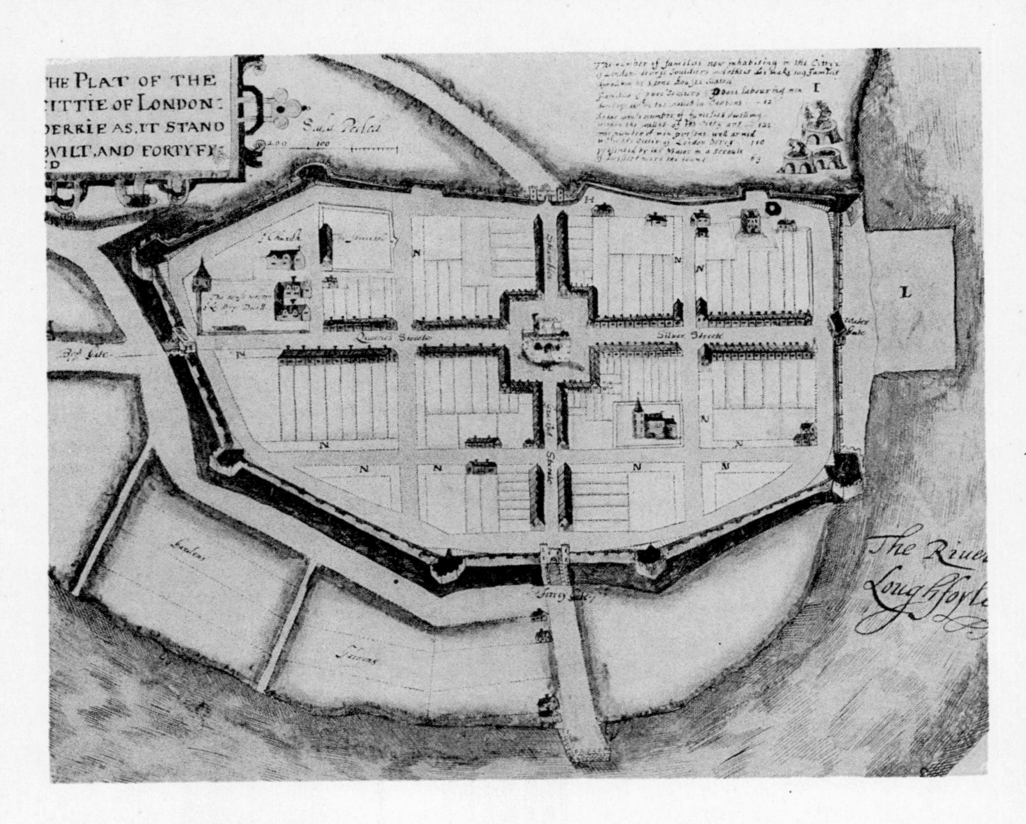

7. Londonderry in 1622

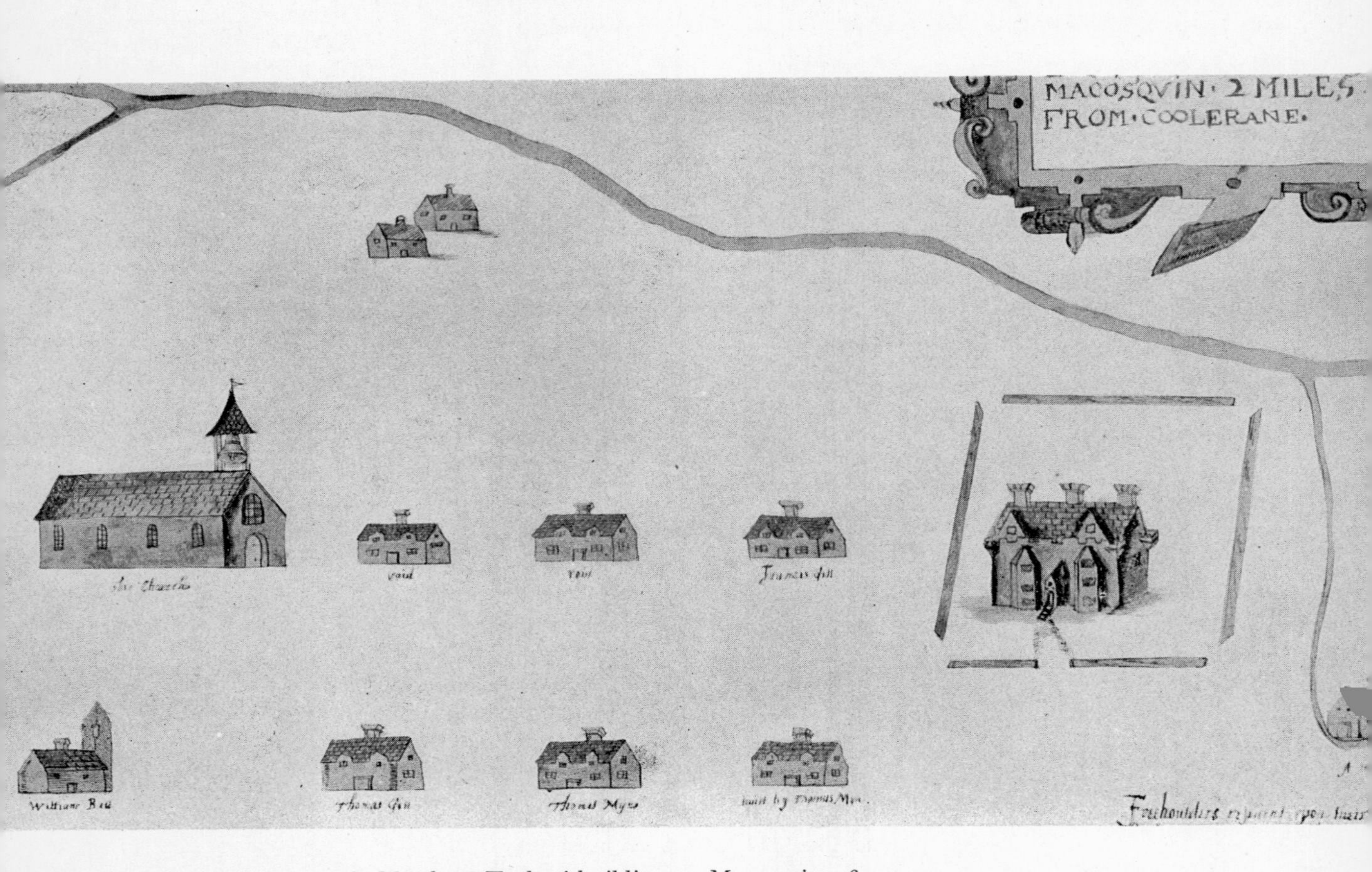

8. Merchant Taylors' buildings at Macosquin, 1622

Salisbury, Chichester, or Winchester, seventeenth-century additions lacked the symmetry of the original plans.[12]

Some eighteen of the towns illustrated by Speed in 1610 were walled, and of these only three had even the simplest fortifications. In each of these other fifteen examples a long wall of stone, broken only by round towers and gates, encircled or partially encircled the town. The wall itself consisted of a series of shallow planes which permitted it to follow a gentle curve. Artillery had made such walls indefensible by 1610; their great length, their lack of bastions, and the absence of strategically placed towers were doubtless considered archaic by the military.[13] In 1610 they symbolized that relative internal security of England under the Tudors and early Stuarts which permitted towns to neglect the construction of new defenses like those that characterized the landscape of the Netherlands and to ignore the advance of continental military engineering.

Within the walls towns varied in the disposition of their buildings. A few, like Chichester, had not yet exploited all their intramural sites, but most had breached their defenses in one manner or another; in Shrewsbury streets and houses stood upon the foundations of unused fifteenth- and sixteenth-century fortifications. Sometimes only the name of former gates recalled the site of the wall; occasionally, as at Chichester, a town retained a relatively complete though unused installation. Everywhere that the seventeenth-century English town had grown past its defensive walls, it had expanded without apparent plan despite the fact that within the town a Roman or late medieval street pattern might still remain inviolate.[14]

Water determined much English town life, since without a reservoir system nearby streams had to furnish water for all purposes. Although Speed apologized for his omissions, among the forty-eight towns he illustrated in 1610, forty-two stood on the banks of streams. Of these, twelve bordered navigable rivers. Along their waterfronts an occasional quay jutted out into the current but docking facilities were in most cases still limited, and the persistent failure of the towns' road systems to accommodate river-bank commerce reduced their usefulness.[15] Towns at the mouths of rivers or on open water still had the character primarily of a fortress and had found it difficult to adjust themselves to the commercial demands of their now busy harbors.

Town streets and village lanes suffered another serious handicap. Perhaps as much as any other single factor the narrow gauge of roads and streets had

12. Speed, *Theatre . . . Great Britain*, pp. 10, 14, 26.

13. Newcastle was a typical town with archaic town walls. Cf. Berwick, *ibid.*, pp. 89–90.

14. Chester, *ibid.*, pp. 73–74. Salisbury, *ibid.*, p. 26. Pierre Lavedan, *Histoire de l'urbanisme* (Paris, H. Laurens, 1926), I, 382–383, 391–393.

15. A case in point is Newcastle. J. Speed, *Theatre . . . Great Britain*, p. 90.

slowed the introduction of logical town plans. The most direct commentary on the conditions of travel is the type of transport used in the early seventeenth century. Lanes were so narrow that nowhere but in London might a traveler see carts or wagons wide enough to accommodate a pair of horses. Elsewhere the average carter used either a narrow two-wheeled cart or a four-wheeled wain. To either he hitched horses or oxen in tandem, a difficult way to pull a cart since the leading animal will not stay up in his traces without constant urging; yet the tandem permitted the use of a much narrower cart than a team could pull. Tandem harness prevailed both in the city and in the country and made use of collars much like those used today. Pack horses still plodded along isolated roads and within the smaller towns after seasonal rains had made the streets too muddy for carts. Although individual horses adapted to the poor narrow roads of the time more easily than the small tandem cart, they carried less. Light country travel contrasted with the press of coaches on the streets of London. There Sir Sanders Duncombe had been given letters patent to use and let for hire covered or sedan chairs in the hope of easing the city's traffic.[16]

The English agricultural village of the seventeenth century had other problems quite distinct from those of London and lesser towns. It faced not a rapid increase in population (indeed often a decline was to be noted) but a fundamental reorientation of its economy. Village life was in flux, midway between the open fields of the late medieval period and the enclosed pastures of the eighteenth century. The issue had not yet been settled, and both types still existed incongruously side by side.[17]

Had a knowledgeable traveler been able to venture in a balloon over the counties of England in 1630 he could have told at once whether he floated over enclosed or open country. Not only hedgerows but the plan of the villages below him revealed the way in which land was divided. Near open fields he would see nucleated villages.[18] These villages consisted of two or more roads with cottages on either side. Stretching out behind each cottage was a narrow homelot between 2 and 6 acres in extent, upon which the cottager had built his barn, hayrick, and any other shelter or outbuilding which he

16. Gervase Markham, *Farewell to Husbandry* (London, 1631), p. 145. David Loggan, *Oxonia Illustrata* (London, 1675), Plate XI. Moreover, the cost of carts was still very high. James E. T. Rogers, *A History of Agriculture and Prices in England* (Oxford, 1887), V, 676–677. Henry Peacham, *Coach and Sedan* (London, 1636), reprinted facsimile (London, F. Etchells and H. Macdonald, 1925).

17. Henry Best, *Rural Economy in Yorkshire in 1641,* Surtees Society, Publications, vol. XXXIII[e] (Durham, 1857), 100. William H. R. Curtler, *A Short History of English Agriculture* (Oxford, Clarendon Press, 1909), p. 105.

18. Gray, *English Field Systems,* p. 274. The only exception to the nucleated village illustrated is in Kent where the open-field system did not obtain.

9. Laxton in 1635.

needed. The parish church stood at one end of the principal street or in the center of town and by its size and careful workmanship dominated the adjacent buildings.[19] A little way off he would see a manor house, sometimes completely isolated,[20] sometimes commanding the village proper, but always surrounded by well-kept park or trimmed garden.[21] (Fig. 9.)

Many different factors had contributed to the creation of the nucleated village, but no single one was more important than the open fields. Harrison noted as early as 1577 that in champion (open-field) country the houses stood close together, while in wooded country, where the open-field system was not practical, they were widely separated on individual plots of land.[22] The vast open fields, cultivated in strips and after harvest opened to the flocks of the entire community for common grazing, forced the people to live close together in a compact village, since isolated farm buildings could not service the many widely scattered holdings of each copyholder. As the proportion of enclosed land increased, street plans changed. The nucleated settlement which had formed the sole pattern of rural life gave way to the isolated farmhouse surrounded by its owner's pasture and set apart from its neighbors.[23]

The position and type of the village mill gave an index of the changing times. Formerly windmills were the most common sort and stood in the center of open fields equally accessible to all holders in the field. With the development of the enclosed village water mills became more common, and their site often provided one of the axial roads of the village. The small size of the windmill was no longer offset by the convenience of its location, since scattered pastures had replaced the large arable fields which the windmill had formerly served.

Lanes and ways ran in the seventeenth century as they had for centuries without adjustment to the practical needs posed by new enclosures. All paths had led to the edge of open fields and then cut across them at intervals about a furlong apart and at right angles to the direction of the plowing.[24] This arrangement gave maximum access to individual strips of land but broke

19. Basil Oliver, *The Cottages of England* (London, B. T. Batsford, Ltd., 1929), Plate III. Charles R. Smith, *The Antiquities of Richborough, Reculver and Lymne* (London, 1850), p. 192.

20. Sussex Archaeological Society, *Collections,* XLIV, 147. Seventeenth-century survey of Atherington Manor.

21. *A History of Northumberland,* ed. by Edward Bateson (London, 1893), II, 452.

22. Raphael Holinshed, *The Chronicles of England, Scotland and Ireland* (London, 1577), "Description of Britaine," p. 85.

23. Gray, *English Field Systems,* p. 272. See his discussion of Kent. Sussex Archaeological Society, Collections, XLIV, 154.

24. Osbert G. S. Crawford, *The Strip Map of Littlington* (London, H. M. Stationery Office, 1937), p. 4. An excellent study employing the aerial photograph as a source.

down under the new demands of enclosed pastures. After enclosure laborers replaced the boundary stones with quickset hedges, and the long narrow furrows of arable land became square pastures filled with grazing cattle. The shift changed the character of the road. Before enclosure it had been only a way from the village to the large open fields, used at sowing and harvest time as a road and during the rest of the year for grazing. After enclosure the road first became a means of daily communication to and from each isolated pasture. As a result open-field roads no longer served the whole village and many villages found their holdings cut off from the road by a neighbor's hedge and field. In 1641 Henry Best recorded how often he had to load his wain, as it stood in a stream, by passing hay over strong quickset hedges, since no road led to his pastures.[25] Ogilby, writing for travelers as late as 1675, felt obliged to distinguish in all his sketches between open-field roads and those passing through enclosed country. Enclosure almost entirely remade the English country-road system; only the nucleated village with its church, manor, green, and cottages has lingered until the present day, changed but not destroyed.[26]

Although ignored at home the English town planner had left his mark overseas. A strong colonial tradition, beginning with the bastides of Edward I in France, continued during periods of English expansion until the early seventeenth century. The western frontier of English colonization in 1600 lay in Ireland only 500 English miles from London. To the east, Calais, lost to France in 1557, was but a day's sail from Dover. Soldiers still garrisoned the unchanged Welsh bastides, Flint and Carnavon, which had been built by Edward I in the thirteenth century, although they were less than 200 miles from London.[27] Scotland sturdily maintained an independent crown some 300 miles north of London, while northern Ireland stood outside the pale of English dominion. (Figs. 10, 11.)

Within this narrow empire England had developed a traditional technique of control for frontier communities. At its base stood the bastide fortress, essentially a garrison town designed to give English minority groups protection from numerically superior but largely unorganized native populations.[28]

25. Best, *Rural Economy in Yorkshire in 1641,* p. 40.

26. John Ogilby, *Itinerarium Angliae or a Book of Roads of England and Wales* (London, 1675), facing title page. "The road is all the way bounded with two parallel black lines if inclosed or hedged in on both sides, or else if open, with two parallel dotted lines or lastly if bounded or hedged on one side and open on the other with a black line and a dotted line parallel to it."

27. Speed, *Theatre . . . Great Britain,* pp. 122–123, Flint and Caernarvon.

28. Bastide fortifications were not impressive when compared with establishments designed to withstand siege. England's share in the development of the thirteenth- and fourteenth-century bastide is stressed in Caroline Shillaber, "Edward I, Builder of Towns," *Speculum,* XXII (1947), 297 ff. An authoritative general discussion of the bastide is found

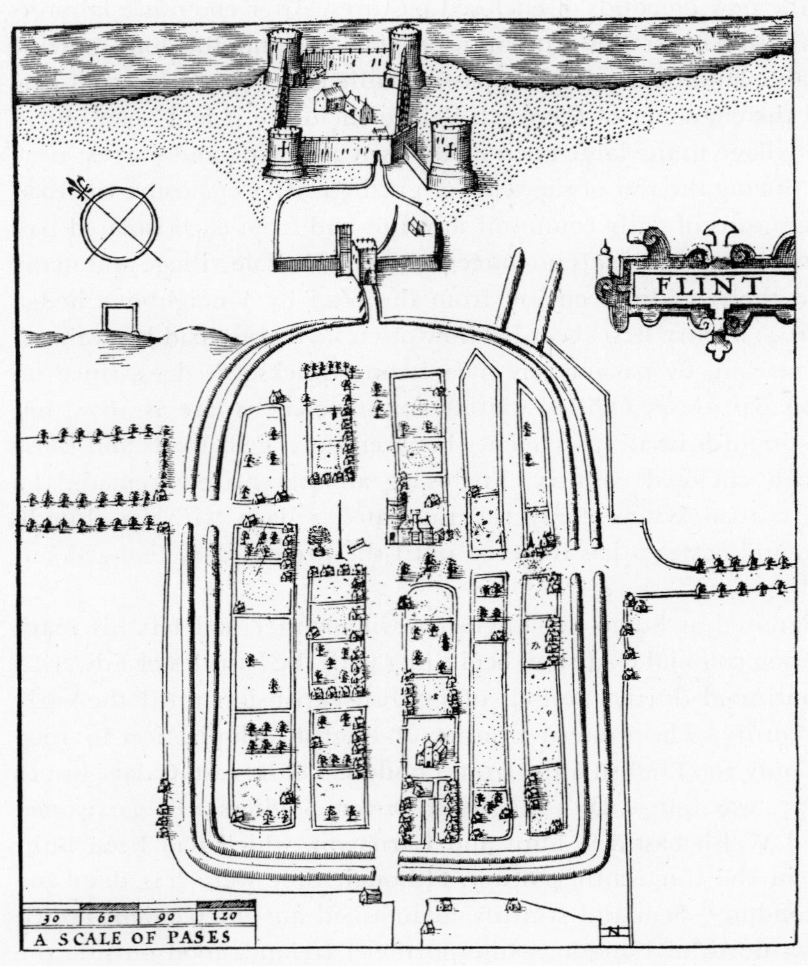

10. Seventeenth-century Flint

Developed in southern France by Edward I and the Count de Poitiers, Eustache de Beaumarchais, from earlier ecclesiastic *salvetates* or towns of refuge, the bastide had two important aims: its design guarded against external attack and at the same time served to suppress internal rebellion. To these ends the founder laid out a square or rectangle on an isolated strategic site. He then completely walled the town and divided it into a grid pattern with the central market place commanding all streets. On this central square the town hall, barracks, and other administrative buildings stood ready for use in crushing riots with cavalry or artillery. Although a few common pastures were retained, the founder allocated land both within and outside the

---

in Lavedan, *Histoire de l'urbanisme,* I, 309 ff. Thomas F. Tout, *Medieval Town Planning* (Manchester, Manchester University Press, 1934) is also useful.

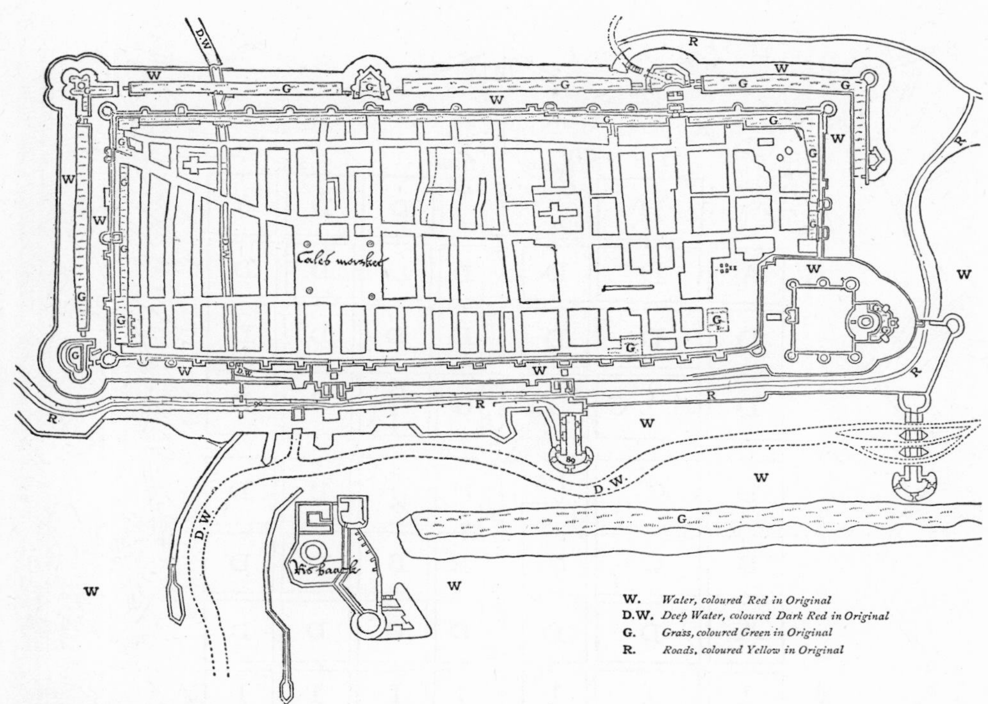

11. Calais about 1557

walls by lots and limited building to sites within the wall.[29] Such towns withstood large-scale siege by well-organized armies only indifferently, since their founders had designed them as frontier posts to give a limited security to colonists in time of anarchy.[30] (Fig. 11.)

During the sixteenth century continental military engineers and theorists had built many real and visionary cities which followed the bastide tradition. Deriving essentially from the rediscovery of the Roman military camp and its application to everyday warfare, these cities had large open squares from which artillery could be trained down any street at will.

English engineers seemed little moved by the elaborate radiating streets of such continental writers as Philibert de l'Orme or Du Cerceau but they did adopt for their armies the Roman camp as known on the Continent. In 1598 Robert Barret's *Theorike and Practike of Moderne Warres* showed a large camp measuring 750 paces to the side, with a strict zoning of function into rectangular blocks and a central market place near which the general's tent stood (G, Fig. 12), an almost exact rendering of the plan used by Francis I to rebuild, strengthen, and refortify Vitry-le-François and very close indeed

29. The 1556 plan of Calais, England's last continental bastide, illustrates the type perfectly. Harold A. Dillon, "Calais and the Pale," *Archaeologia,* LIII (1893), 302.

30. *La Grande encyclopédie* (Paris, 1886–1902), A. Giry, "Bastide."

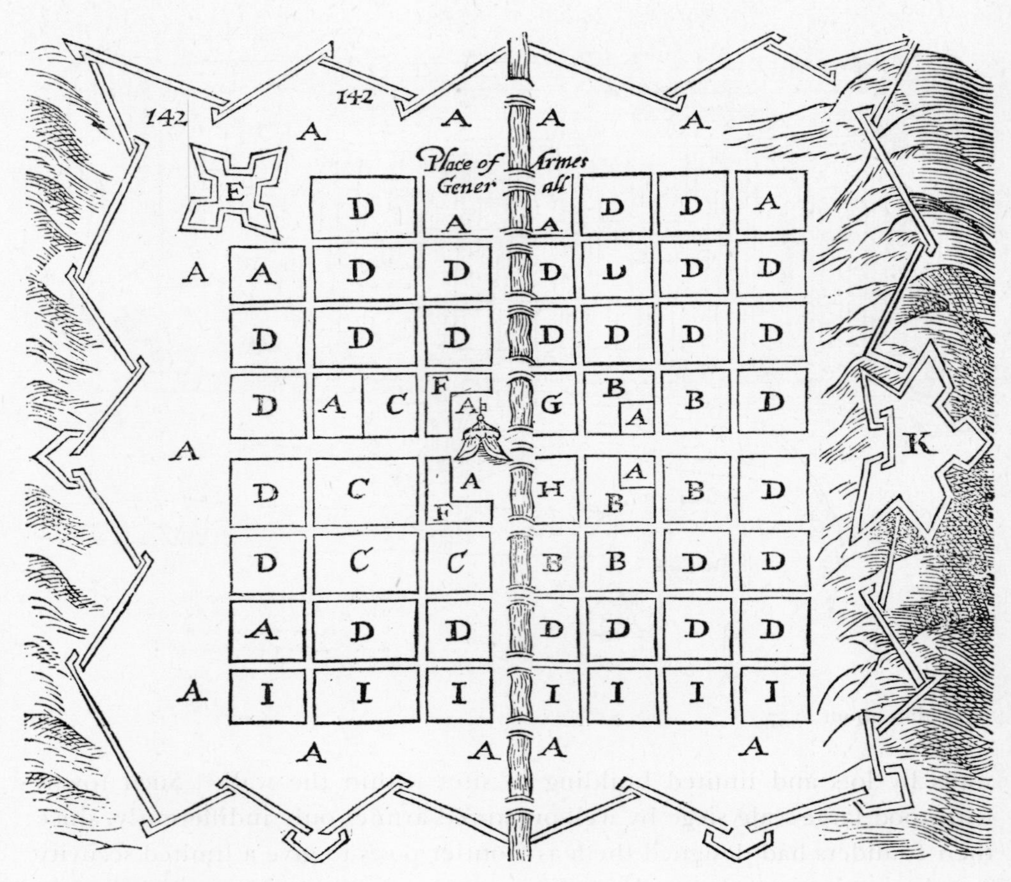

12. Robert Barret's camp, 1598

A. Cavalry and infantry with the general's tent and parade ground; B. lancers and light-horse troops; C. men-at-arms; D. infantry, pikes, and shot; E. artillery ammunition; F. officers and noblemen; G. market place; I. pioneers, artificers, and cattle; K. fort on a small hill.

to the popular conception of Caesar's encampments in the Gallic war.[31]

In 1600 English frontier colonies had begun a westward trend. Pushed off the European continent by the fall of Calais, England wished to consolidate her conquest of Ireland, but Ulster still remained independent. It was only in 1603 that Hugh O'Neil, Earl of Tyrone, submitted to Elizabeth, and even this submission was tempered by his pardon and the return of most of his lands. Before 1609 no comprehensive plan for Irish colonization took effect. Numerous rebellions, culminating in Sir Cahir O'Doherty's capture and the

31. I am indebted to Turpin Banister for this suggestion. Lavedan, *Histoire de l'urbanisme,* II, 14–21. Robert Barret, *Theorike and Practike of Modern Warres* (London, 1598), *Julius Caesar* (London, 1630), n.p.

destruction of Culmore and Derry in 1608, had delayed establishment of an English plantation in Ulster, and until that time Tyrone, O'Cahan, and other Irish earls exercised a share of political control. Their flight to Brussels late in 1607 cleared the last obstacle to a thorough resettlement of Ulster.[32]

Chief responsibility for the broad outlines of the Ulster settlement rested with Sir Arthur Chichester, Lord Deputy of Ireland from 1604 to 1616, whose instructions for Sir James Ley and Sir John Davies stipulated most of the conditions found in the later "Articles of Plantation." In their final form the articles offered many economic privileges for accepted English and Scottish planters.[33] Their land was to be held in "free and common soccage as of the Castle of Dublin." In return the articles outlined certain duties for the adventurers. The undertaker of a holding of 2,000 acres had to build a castle with a strong fortified courtyard, or, as it was called in Ulster, a bawn; an estate of 1,500 acres must have a strong house and bawn, and one of 1,000 acres had to have at least a bawn. Near each fortified place homes for settlers were to be built. Every holding, whether of 1,000, 1,500, or 2,000 acres, had to provide its parish with a church and 60 acres of glebe land for a Church of England pastor. Finally the number of tenants was fixed, and a plan for the segregation of Irish natives laid down. Beyond this point, the adventurers were free to set up such plantations as they chose.[34]

For one of the escheated counties of Ulster a different sort of contract was drawn up. In Londonderry the contracting parties were the Crown and the City of London rather than individual adventurers, and they agreed in January, 1619, upon the rights of the City in the County of Derry and the sums that should be expended in Londonderry. Only in the construction of Derry and Culmore was the City's duty specifically defined. Derry was to be laid out with sufficient space for five hundred houses of which forty were to be built by November, 1610; and Coleraine should be planned for three hundred houses of which forty should be built by November, 1610.[35] Moreover, both places were to be sufficiently fortified.

32. Hill, *Plantation in Ulster,* p. 57. Theodore W. Moody, *The Londonderry Plantation, 1609–1641* (Belfast, W. Mullan & Son, 1939), pp. 29–30. *Calendar of State Papers, Ireland, 1606–1608,* pp. 259–556, 609.

33. Institute of Historical Research, *Bulletin,* XII, 178–183. Chief among these privileges was the cancellation of all rent for four years, free export of produce, duty free import of tools, and use of the king's timber for building.

34. The 1609 conditions of settlement specified that each proportion was to have a strong court or bawn which either stood alone or was to be built around a masonry house or "castle." The undertakers in practice often built their houses into one, two, or even three walls of the bawn so as to make bawn and stone house indistinguishable parts of a single complex. Moody, *Londonderry Plantation,* pp. 34–35. *Phillips MSS,* Plates XXVII, XXXI.

35. *Phillips MSS,* pp. 13–16, Articles 2, 4, 27.

These terms of the Crown's contracts with the adventures and with the City gave the Ulster plantation a distinctive character. By 1622 some fifteen towns had been laid out and more or less successfully established.[36] Derry in 1622 had 218 houses; [37] Culmore had had perhaps £1,500 spent on her buildings.[38] Even Phillips, who viewed the efforts of the City to colonize Ulster with such disgust, estimated the county's English population at one half the native.[39] The settlement of Englishmen in northern Ireland had made a firm if cruel beginning.

This growth of the English population had produced two distinct types of town plan: on the one hand the large military establishment closely resembling Calais, the continental bastides, and military camps, and on the other the "tenant village," built by the twelve companies in conformity with their charters for the exploitation of their holdings and the protection of their English settlers from the native Irish.[40]

Fortunately there exists a rather complete record of the actual progress Ulster made in town planning and house construction during the first two decades of the seventeenth century. Differing widely from the English town or village, the Ulster plantation was an experiment in the foundation of a colony. Here Englishmen had the opportunity not merely to alter existing towns but to plan and build new ones. The survey conducted by Sir Thomas Phillips in 1622 on the eve of the founding of New England therefore gives clear evidence of the development of English town planning and architectural opinion. His sketches recorded contemporary planning without the confusion of earlier work completed before the seventeenth century.

These maps and plans show the broad divisions of the country into the twelve proportions of the London companies,[41] how each proportion was allotted,[42] and how the chief towns within each holding were laid out.[43] The survey does not, however, make clear the actual allotment of land to individual tenants and consequently cannot be used to determine field systems.[44]

36. *Ibid.*, pp. 18, 147–148.

37. *Ibid.*, p. 143. Coleraine had 159 houses.

38. The Londoners had spent £27,197 on buildings and fortifications at Derry. *Ibid.*, p. 142.

39. The returns for the proportions of the twelve companies gave 947 British and 2,283 Irish natives. Londonderry and Coleraine had an additional 465 British but it is not clear that the Irish natives were all listed. *Phillips MSS,* p. 139.

40. Cf. Culmore with Ballykelly, *Phillips MSS,* pp. 17, 49.

41. "A General Plat of the 12 Proportions," MS map, *Phillips MSS,* Plate I.

42. "Plat of Lands Belonging to the Company of Goldsmiths," MS map, *Phillips MSS,* Plate V.

43. "The Buildings Belonging to the Company of Drapers at Monnemore," MS drawing, *Phillips MSS,* Plate XXIX.

44. Occasionally some home lots are shown. "The Plat of the City of Londonderry," MS map, *Phillips MSS,* Plate III.

Here alone it is inadequate. In other respects it provides a unique cross section of the military and civil town planning of the English colony in the early seventeenth century. It was, in its day, a direct precedent for the New England experiment.

Some seventeen towns were illustrated in Phillips' survey, of which perhaps three were primarily military establishments. Among these latter Londonderry was by all odds the most important. The explosion of a powder magazine in 1568 had destroyed most of the original Irish settlement, which was not again garrisoned until 1600, when Sir Henry Docwra retook the town. Its destruction had been so complete in 1568 that only ruins of the abbey, bishop's house, two churches, and the old castle remained.[45] No other dwelling houses of any sort still stood, and timber had to be fetched from great distances. Stones from the ruins, a nearby slate quarry, and plentiful cockle shells served the masons well.[46]

Docwra hurriedly adapted the ruins of the sixteenth-century fortress to the requirements of his garrison. Within the walls two main streets leading from each of the two gates made a simple crossing from which an occasional lane led to individual buildings. The most interesting feature of his plan was its proposed extension to the south. Here he sketched a grid pattern modified only by the bastions. Six large blocks would then have been added to the town, safely remote from naval bombardment. (Fig. 13.) From a modern view the document gains importance because it represents an English scheme for urban development drawn more than half a century before Sir Christopher Wren's project for the reconstruction of London. Docwra's interesting plan for the southward extension of Derry was unfortunately never carried out. In 1608 the Irish under Sir Cahir O'Doherty once more besieged and destroyed the town, and although the revolt was quickly subdued, it was necessary to completely rebuild Derry after the English had recaptured the place.

The plan from which the modern city developed is generally attributed to Thomas Raven, a surveyor of considerable note in the employ of the city of London.[47] In 1616 the city sent him to Ulster and entrusted him with the task of erecting walls and fortifications for Derry in accordance with the 1609 compact of the city with the Crown.[48] The walls were finished in 1611, and the block plan of the new town laid out, but no new permanent dwellings

45. Ordnance Survey, *Memoir of the City and North Western Liberties of Londonderry* (Dublin, 1837), pp. 98–99, hereafter called *Ordnance Survey Memoir.*

46. *Ibid.* and Moody, *Londonderry Plantation,* p. 55.

47. *Ordnance Survey Memoir,* p. 99. A divergent view attributes this design to Sir Edward Doddington and believes Thomas Raven was only entrusted with surveying technicalities. Moody, *The Londonderry Plantation,* p. 275.

48. *Ordnance Survey Memoir,* p. 99.

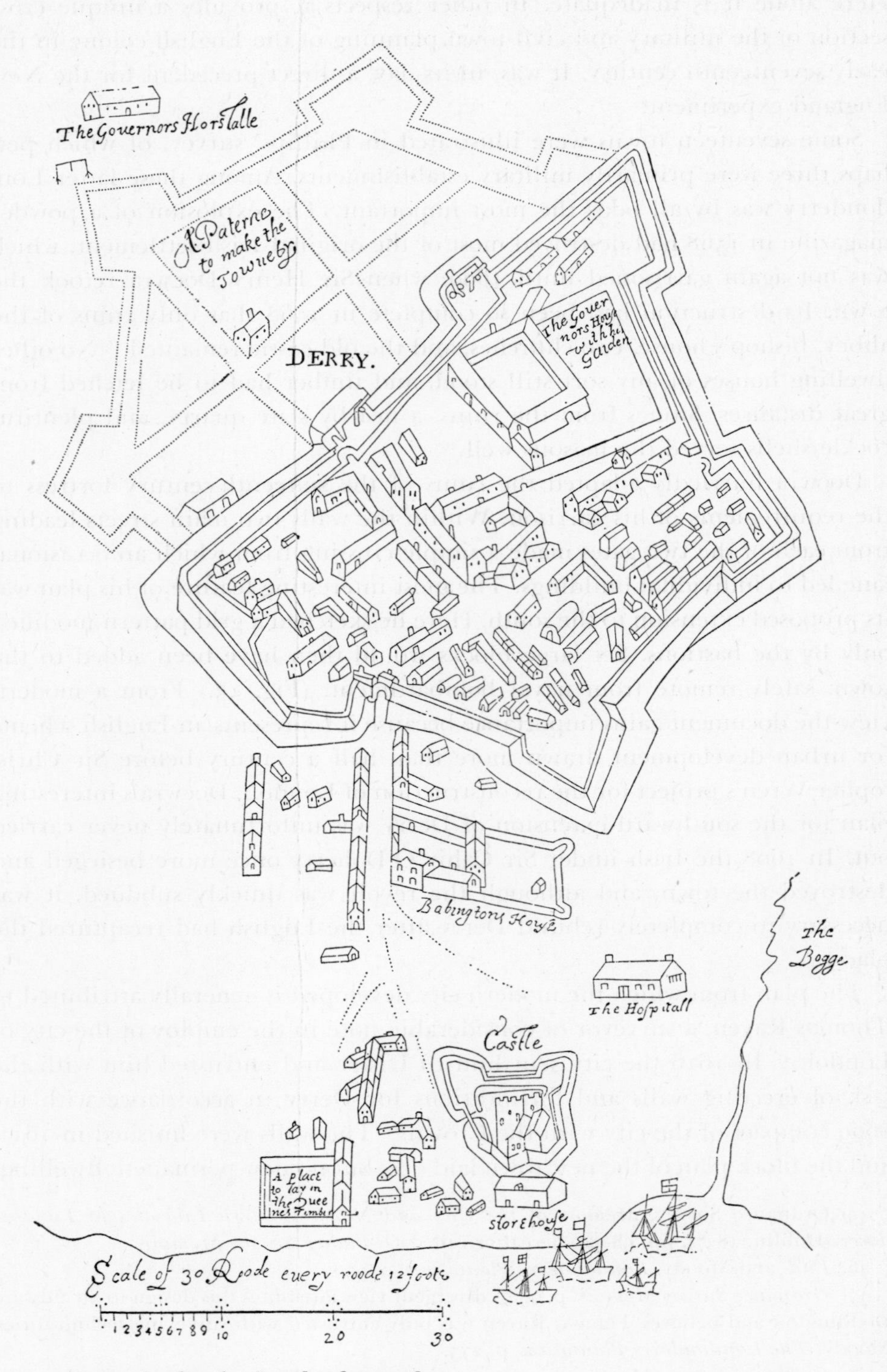

13. Docwra's plan for Londonderry, 1600

were built in that year.[49] In 1619 most of the central avenue had buildings stretching along both sides of its full length.[50] By 1625 the city had built a market house, and perhaps half of the available sites within the walls had been used for new construction.

Raven's plan for Londonderry reflected continental, colonial, and military traditions adapted to the peculiar social conditions of the Ulster plantation. Like the bastides it was a walled city, but the rudimentary bastions of the early seventeenth century replaced medieval round towers.[51] From the military camps of the sixteenth century it drew a grid of streets parallel to the principal cross axes of the four gates. As on the Continent, the large market square lay athwart the city's streets. Like Calais the houses were laid out with large gardens and back lots in part to reduce the population within the walls and in part to provide food in time of siege. (Fig. 7.)

That Raven conceived Derry chiefly as a stronghold for the English he made clear in the details of his plan. Not only did he wall the city against external attack, but he provided against internal rebellion of the Irish as well. To this end he destroyed the old castle, because he feared it might provide a safe refuge for rioters within the town's walls. In 1618–19 the city carried on his ideas and placed cannon in the market place, which commanded the main streets of the town.[52] Late in 1622 Sir Thomas Phillips designed a square fort, to be located on the central square, which mounted heavy cannon both above and below a handsome classical arcade—a fort that Phillips felt would be "a greate strength to the cittie." [53] (Fig. 7.)

In their plans for smaller villages the Londoners showed the same concern with defense from native rebellion. Every town illustrated by Sir Thomas Phillips in his survey of 1622 had three parts: the cottages of the tenants, the lot for the Established Church building, and the bawn. (Figs. 8, 14, 31.) The last stood apart from the tenants' cottages, its stone walls often furnishing one or more sides of the planters' strong houses. Defenses were simple, but they gave some security to Englishmen living among discontented Irish natives. George Canning, an agent for the Ironmongers, perfectly described the feelings and modest hopes of his fellow Englishmen when he wrote in his

49. See plan of 1611. Moody, *Londonderry Plantation,* Plate III.

50. Nicholas Pynnar, "Plan of Londonderry," MS map, Trinity College. Reproduced in two versions. Moody, *Londonderry Plantation,* Plate VI. *Ordnance Survey Memoir,* p. 98.

51. It was sharply criticized for faulty military engineering. Moody, *Londonderry Plantation,* p. 276. This plan, unlike Culmore, lacked effective bastions for artillery.

52. Pynnar, "Plan of Londonderry," MS map. Moody, *Londonderry Plantation,* Plate VI.

53. *Ordnance Survey Memoir,* p. 114. *Phillips MSS,* pp. 5, 148.

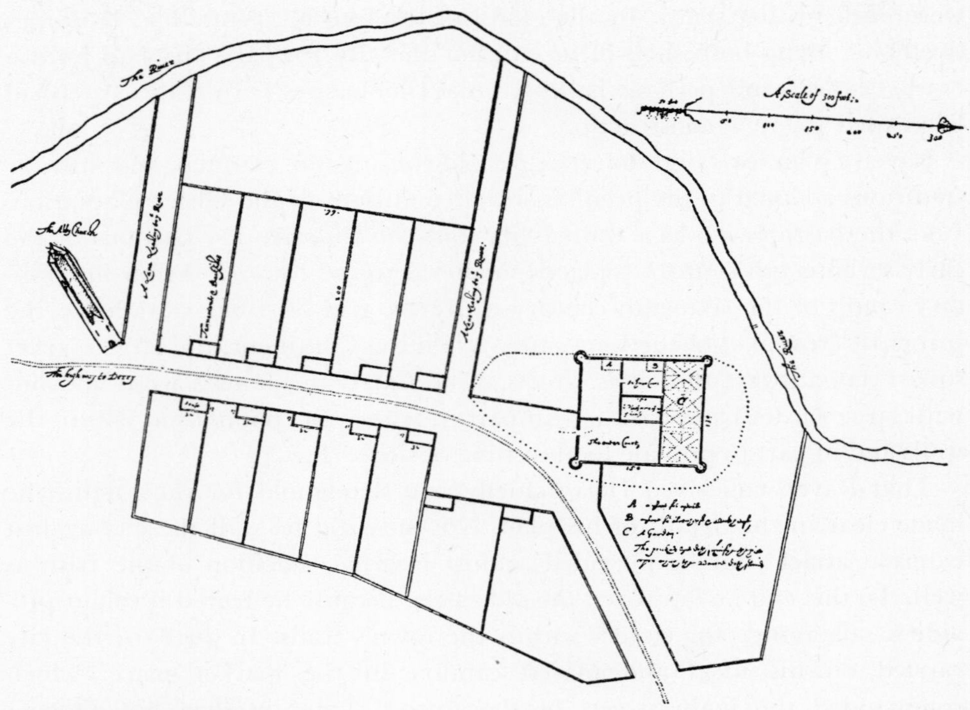

14. Plan of Macosquin

report of May, 1616, that "when the second floor is laid on your castell, I hope it will be a secure place against one hundred men." [54]

Dwellings of the tenants stood a little apart from the bawn and clustered about a small square or stood compactly together on a single long street. Behind each cottage stretched the familiar home lot assigned to each tenant. (Fig. 14.) The larger holdings farmed by the Irish and English cottagers did not lie in open fields but in enclosed parcels of 60 to 120 acres for which the London companies exacted a rack rent.[55]

Close by the cottages a large lot was reserved for an Established Church building. In some villages the settlers had by 1622 already erected a handsome stone church; in others they had laid only a foundation; and in a few they had been too poor to do even this.[56]

But such communities were rare. The ideal and most common village in

54. John Nicholl, *Some Account of the Worshipful Company of Ironmongers* (London, 1866), p. 396; plan of this "castell," p. 392.

55. They were to use the agricultural methods of the English Pale. Moody, *Londonderry Plantation,* pp. 26, 33–34. One hundred and twenty acres was ideal but 60 acres often was the reality. *Phillips MSS,* pp. 151, 165. This is in contrast to the Irish custom of gavelkind. Moody, *Londonderry Plantation,* pp. 48–49.

56. For a small but completed church, see Merchant Taylor's village at Macosquin. *Phillips MSS,* pp. 101, 156. Moneymore was a fine village without any church. *Ibid.,* pp. 152, 161.

Ulster slavishly followed the aims of the Crown for the Irish plantation. Its bawn defended the English settler, its church symbolized the conversion of the Irish, and from its cottages rents returned to the coffers of the London companies.[57]

Inevitably the experiments in town planning of the Ulster plantation became well known in London and surrounding counties. Not only were fifty-five livery companies of London assessed for its support but in 1635 they, together with the Irish Society, had to stand trial in the Star Chamber for an alleged breach of contract with the Crown.[58] Less spectacular but equally important, a series of seven assessments between 1610 and 1616 had tapped virtually every merchant and artisan purse in London to a greater or lesser degree. From the more than £6,000 paid by the merchant tailors to the £30 assessment of the woolmen a wide range of sums totaling some £60,000 had underwritten the initial cost of Ulster's settlement.[59] As he had paid for the Virginia Company, the individual member of the livery company paid for colonial miscalculations in Ireland.

Knowledge of Ulster had even spread beyond the confines of London. The system of apprenticeship which drew people chiefly from the surrounding counties disseminated an awareness of the plantation widely.[60] Those persons to whom the Ulster plantation began to pay dividends after 1616 and those who became involved in the Star Chamber trial of 1635 must have made it their business to know some details of Irish settlement. Moreover, although the plantation was divided into nine great manors and these deeded to the nine large livery companies, each of the latter had many small companies joined with it for the management of some one particular manor. Thus associated with the salters were the dyers', saddlers', cutlers', joiners', and woolmen's companies.[61] Virtually all members of any of the great livery companies had come in contact with the Ulster experiment.

57. A satisfactory plan nearly completed by 1622 is given by Moody, *Londonderry Plantation,* Plate XII.

58. Charles Welch, *History of the Cutlers' Company of London* (London, Cutlers' Company, 1923), II, 146 ff.

59. Moody, *Londonderry Plantation.* Appendix C lists the companies and their fines. It should be remembered that by 1620 the London livery companies were no longer composed solely of men devoted to the calling of their guild. Membership in the companies was largely hereditary and the skilled apprentice admitted to the freedom of the company was relatively rare. Robert J. Blackham, *The Soul of the City, London's Livery Companies* (London, S. Low, Marston & Co., Ltd., 1931), p. 60. Arthur H. Johnson, *The History of the Worshipful Company of Drapers of London* (Oxford, Clarendon Press, 1922), III, 89–97. In 1629 only 14 of the 420 Draper's Company freemen were drapers by profession.

60. *Records of the Worshipful Company of Carpenters* (Oxford, Carpenters' Company, 1913), I, Apprentice Entry Books, 1654–94. M. Campbell, *The Elizabethan Yeoman,* pp. 277–278, Appendix II.

61. London Salter's Company, *Short Particulars of the Manor of Sal* (London, 1838), p. 6. The Ulster experiment is a virtually indispensable chapter in every history of the

The connection between the Ulster plantation and the beginnings of settlement in America is known to have been close. Among the leaders Sir Thomas Smith, Sir John Popham, and Sir Francis Bacon were all interested in both projects. Smith was for many years the head of the Virginia Company of London; Popham was one of the principal promoters of the simultaneous but abortive settlement at Sagadahoc in Maine. The Virginia Company like the Ulster enlisted the aid of the livery companies, and many Virginia settlers had had experience in Ireland before coming to America.[62] The drapers, to name one group, whose proportion included much of southwestern Ulster, contributed heavily to American colonizing ventures. By 1609 no fewer than 4 men who later became wardens of the Draper's Company had invested in the Virginia Company, together with 7 other less prominent drapers. Some 51 additional members of the Draper's Company in all probability subscribed in one way or another to the Virginia Company before 1624. In addition Johnson lists 16 persons, members of the company, as settlers in Virginia. The company's connection with Bermuda was scarcely less close, since 13 masters, liverymen, and apprentices supported that venture.[63]

New England's relation to Ulster seems somewhat less direct but nonetheless certain. Among the members of both the Dorchester and the Massachusetts Bay companies there was a generous representation from the London guilds and livery companies which had underwritten the Ulster experiment. Of the 121 members of the Dorchester Company 22 were mercers, drapers, tailors, goldsmiths, grocers, or connected closely with some branch of the clothing business.[64] The New England Company adventurers included at least 22 persons who belonged to one or another of the guilds.[65] Some 4 haberdashers subscribed to the company. Neither were the Massachusetts Bay adventurers devoid of subscribers from the guilds; almost 40 persons out of a possible 110 were members of guilds which had taken part in the Ulster plantation.[66]

In addition to regular subscribers the New England Company's lists of adventurers included many prominent ministers whose parishes bordered on the Coleman Street ward in London. Perhaps the most famous of these was

---

livery companies. See also: Arthur C. Stanley-Stone, *The Worshipful Company of Turners of London* (London, Lindley-Jones & Brother, 1925), pp. 163 ff.; Nicholl, *Some Account of the Worshipful Company of Ironmongers,* pp. 375–418.

62. Charles M. Andrews, *Colonial Period,* I, 70 n., 71–72.

63. A. H. Johnson, *History of the Drapers,* IV, 83–89.

64. Frances Rose-Troup, *John White* (New York, G. P. Putnam & Sons, 1930), pp. 448 ff.

65. Frances Rose-Troup, *The Massachusetts Bay Company and Its Predecessors* (New York, Grafton Company, 1930), pp. 19–20.

66. *Ibid.,* pp. 130–162.

John Davenport of St. Stephen's, whose parishioners included Theophilus Eaton and Sir Richard Saltonstall.[67]

A few men were prominent in both Ireland and New England. The founder of Saybrook, the Connecticut town which most resembled the Ulster plantation, Lord Saye and Sele had extensive Ulster holdings in Oneilan which he sold to Sir Anthony Cope.[68] Such men were rare because a conscientious Puritan could scarcely act as undertaker for a plantation which had as one of its avowed aims the establishment of the Anglican Church in Ireland.[69] On the other hand, as a member of a guild such a man could not ignore Ulster, since he had to pay an extraordinary fine assessed upon him individually by his Court of Assistants to maintain English settlements there.[70]

Before the settlement of Connecticut in 1635 Englishmen in Virginia had tried to apply their traditional military town plan on American soil. At Roanoke the small garrison built a simple triangular fortification to enclose their camp.[71] The Jamestown settlers were luckier. After they landed on the shore of the Chesapeake Bay "the Counsel was sworn and the President elected, which for that year was Maister Edm.-Maria Wingfield," a soldier who had seen service in Ireland. Wingfield, after a surprise attack upon his first weak fort, strengthened it into one of triangular shape with semicircular bastions, which he secured with palisades or stockades. In its final form the fort closely resembled an Ulster bawn erected at a short distance from the town.[72] The plan of Jamestown, which has been revealed by excavation and by the discovery of several seventeenth-century surveys of the settlement, was essentially that of a company town in Ireland.[73] Built on a low isthmus, the homes of the settlers huddled closely around the church and its lands. (Fig. 15.)

67. Andrews, *Colonial Period,* II, 145–147 and note.

68. George Hill, *Plantation Papers* (Belfast, 1889), p. 7.

69. Moody, *Londonderry Plantation,* p. 97.

70. A large-scale investigation of persons whose interests were involved in both the Ulster plantation and the New England colony is not indicated, since religious differences would cause different men in the same guild to invest differently. Thus an Anglican could scarcely be expected to support Puritan New England, or a Nonconformist, Anglican Ulster. Comprehensive lists of guild members are rare, and lists of masters and wardens include too few names to be of use. An outstanding exception to this rule is the Shipwrights Company. C. H. Ridge, *Records of the Worshipful Company of Shipwrights* (London, Phillimore & Co., Ltd., 1939–46), 2 vols. Henry L. Phillips, *Annals of the Worshipful Company of Joiners of the City of London* (London, privately printed, 1915), pp. 92–130.

71. Stephen Lorant, *The New World* (New York, Duell, Sloan, & Pearce, 1946), pp. 185, 188.

72. For a reconstruction of the fort, see Henry C. Forman, *Jamestown and Saint Mary's* (Baltimore, Johns Hopkins Press, 1938), pp. 38–39. Semicircular bulwarks were used instead of more advanced triangular bastions.

73. Most important of these "plats" are the Ambler MSS, including a survey made by John Underwood for John Knowles in 1664 and that made in 1680 for William Sherwood by John Soane. Forman, *Jamestown and Saint Mary's,* pp. 116–120.

As in the Ulster plantation, London companies specified the design of the settlers' houses, allotted small bordering home lots, and granted additional fields to each settler outside his village. As at Ulster, the palisade, church, and storehouse were the principal concern of the settlers.[74]

The New England colonies, like Virginia, retained the traditional colonial town plan during their first years of settlement. Bradford's sketch shows the home plots of Plymouth lying along a single street near the Common House. Other researchers have found that a fort of some sort stood on a hill within the stockade and that it was used as a meetinghouse. Similarly, although the earliest engraved plan of Boston is that of 1722,[75] the town land records and earlier manuscript charts indicate that in 1635 it was a small nucleated village overlooking a sheltered harbor and significantly protected further by the usual independent fort constructed on one of the town's three hills.[76] The settlers of Connecticut in 1635 had, therefore, a well-established tradition to guide them in their policy of land settlement and town planning. It remains to be seen how they altered this pattern in the seventeenth and eighteenth centuries.

Settlement in Connecticut at first closely followed English precedent set at Jamestown and in Ulster. In every town planted before 1645 the settlers laid out nucleated villages. Such settlements grouped the home lots closely together regardless of the disposition of property throughout the remainder of the town land. Thus the several square miles of the town's land naturally divided into a central nucleus of dwellings and a land system that extended from that nucleus to the bounds of the town grant. Only in Ireland, Wales, and on the Continent, where the English had found themselves in a minority and feared the native inhabitants, had there been such universal agreement as to the ideal town plan. In Britain itself individual counties varied widely from the isolated farmhouse of Kent or the Devon fishing town to the manorial village of East Anglia surrounded by open fields. Although each of these types had some points of similarity to the Connecticut town, the Ulster adventurer town provided the colonist his only complete prototype.[77]

The plan of the early Connecticut villages contributed little that was new

74. Accounts of George Percy and Capt. John Smith. Lyon G. Tyler, *Original Narratives of Early Virginia 1606–1625* (New York, Charles Scribner's Sons, 1907), pp. 15, 19, 35, 151.

75. John Bonner, *The Town of Boston in New England* (Fra. Dewing Eng.) (Boston, 1722). See I. N. Phelps Stokes, *American Historical Prints* (New York, New York Public Library, 1933), p. 20.

76. Some outline of the field system has been drawn up as well. *Memorial History of Boston,* ed. by Justin Winsor (Boston, 1880), I, 532 and frontispiece. See also description of Wells's 1687 chart of the harbor. *Ibid.,* II, Introduction, L.

77. I do not wish to imply that no English villages had features in common with Connecticut settlements.

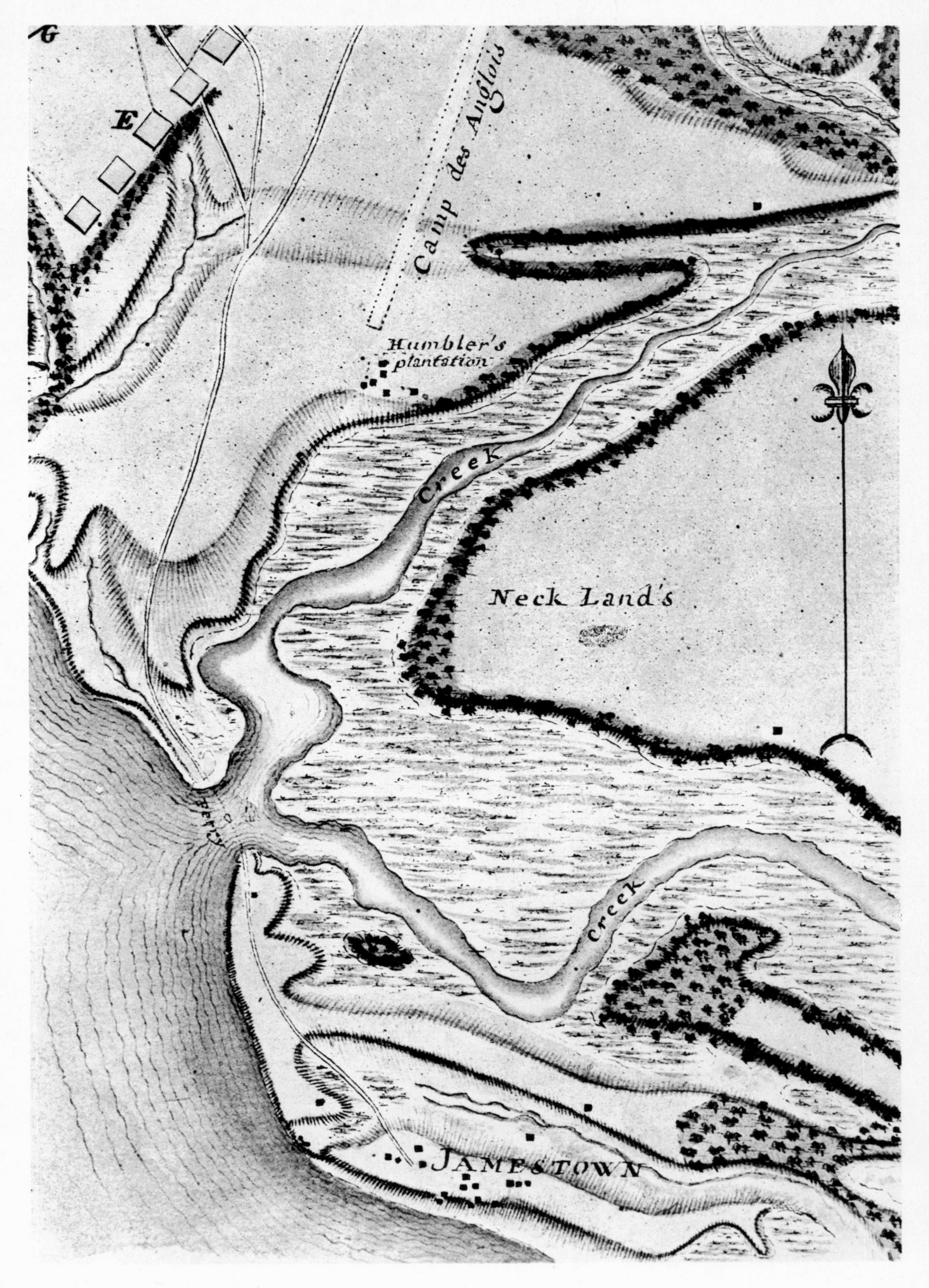

15. Jamestown in 1781

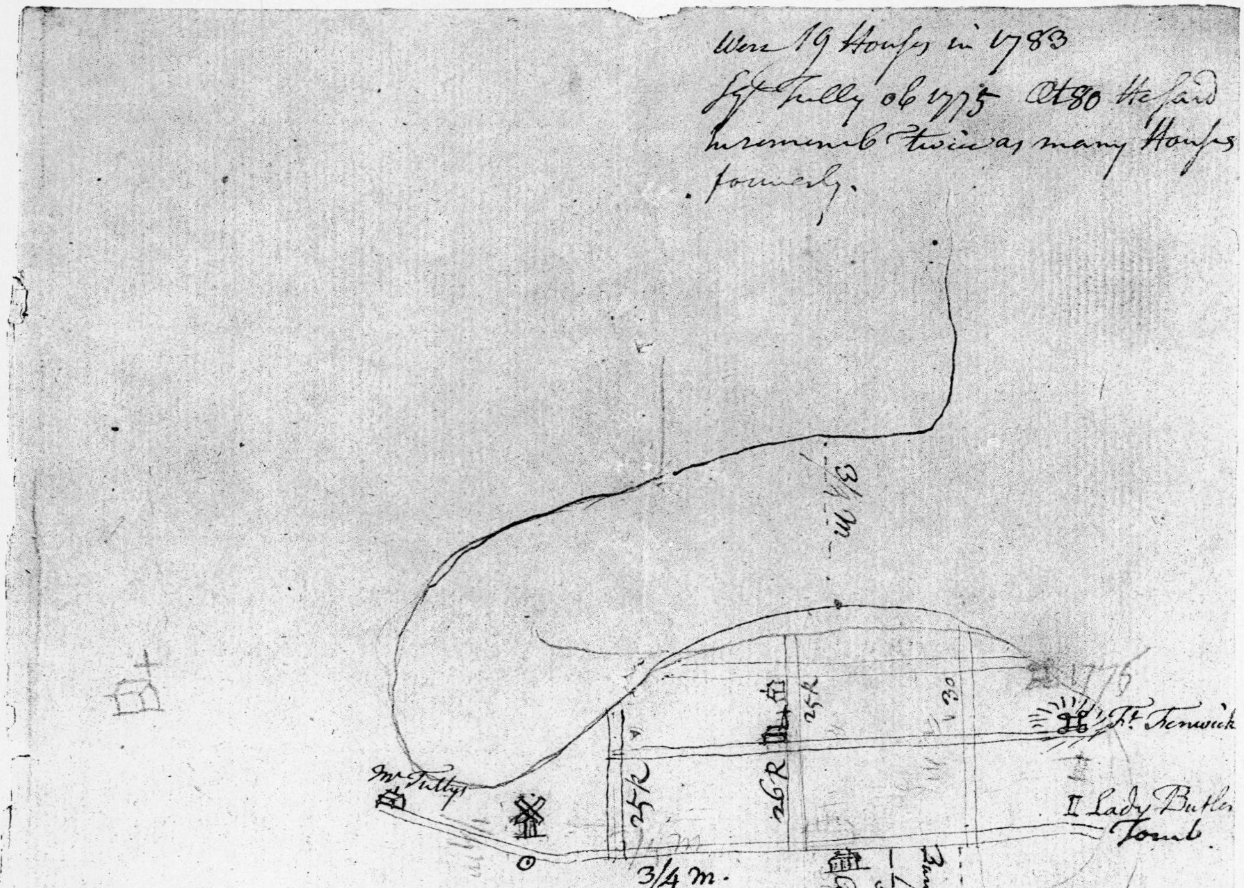

Were 19 Houses in 1783
Esq Tully old 1775 Aet 80 he said
remembd twice as many Houses
formerly.

3/4 m.

1776

Ft. Fenwick

Lady Butler Tomb

Mr Tullys

25 R

26 R

30

3/4 m.

College

Burying Ground

50 R

The Oval fr. Windmill to fort
3/4 M. More than half M. wide
but not 3/4. Fr. Head So. Cove
to End Lynd pt. 2 M. wc is due S fr. fort

30

⊙ 1 1/3 M to Meetg W 2p N
1 M. measured fr. Mr Tullys
to the Fort. Abot 3/4 M fr.
Windmill to Fort
17 Dwellgs May 17 1793 counted

10 R 30

College

Burying Ground laid 1731

17. Saybrook in 1793

16. Fairfield about 1780

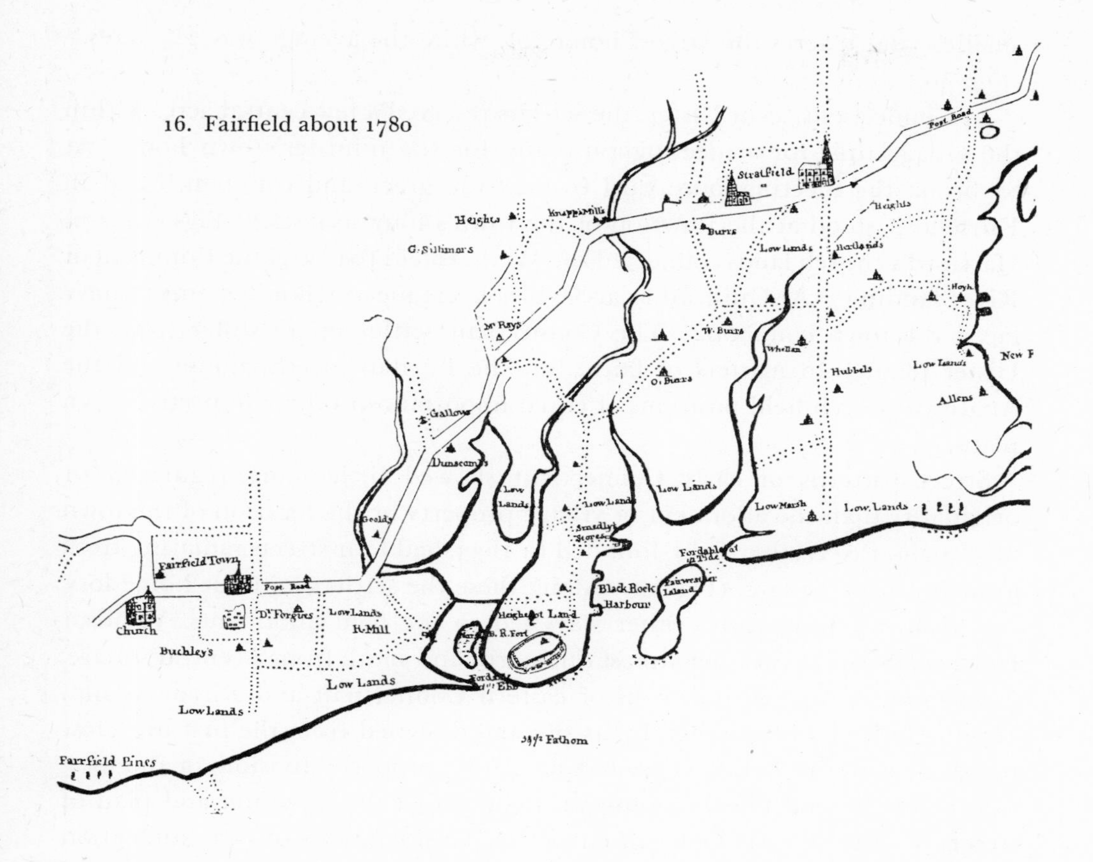

to the Ulster scheme. The colonists chose sites with an eye both to defense and to pasturage. Fairfield, Milford, Branford, Guilford, New London, and Saybrook first built on the banks of streams or near salt marshes.[78] Many of these towns stood on narrow points jutting out into Long Island Sound, which they easily fortified with a palisade.

The selection of such sites was not the only similarity between Ulster and Connecticut towns. Property allotment within the nucleus of settlement followed Irish precedent. Until 1650 home lots in Connecticut were roughly uniform and allowed to vary only within relatively narrow limits. Thus the average Milford planter's home lot ranged from 2¾ to 7 acres.[79] (Fig. 21.) At Guilford about 3 acres seems to have been the rule. Fairfield house lots on the original four squares, although variously shaped, usually contained about 2½ acres.[80] At Saybrook, with the exception of the Fenwick lot, 1½ acres was the

78. See above, Chapter I.

79. Leonard W. Labaree, *Milford, Connecticut; The Early Development of a Town as Shown in Its Land Records* (New Haven, Yale University Press, 1933). Connecticut Tercentenary Pamphlets, XIII, 4.

80. Elizabeth H. Schenck, *The History of Fairfield* (New York, 1889), I, 64 ff.

smallest and 5 acres the largest home lot, while the average was 2½ acres.[81] (Fig. 56.)

In Connecticut, as in Ulster, the settlers reserved a few central acres within the village unit for a meetinghouse and for the minister's own house. At Saybrook the meetinghouse yard fronted the green and common,[82] and in Fairfield it stood at the junction of the town's four squares.[83] (Figs. 16, 17.) Hartford's church lands connected the Wethersfield road and the Connecticut River landing.[84] At Guilford as at Saybrook the meetinghouse seems to have faced the town common.[85] The Connecticut settler might differ from the Ulster planter in matters of faith, but the Puritan meetinghouse and the Anglican church held positions of equal importance in their respective town plans.

Street patterns of early Connecticut showed little more regularity or originality than the allotment of village property or the location of the town meetinghouse. Wethersfield, founded in 1633, had four streets radiating from a small central square. (Fig. 22.) Along these the settlers laid out home lots, and from their junctures other ways led to the field allotments. Windsor had a single street running almost due north and south from a central square. New London, like many towns of eastern Connecticut and Rhode Island, appears to have been shaped by its site and designed from the first to follow the shore contours.[86] Elsewhere factors of site, property division, or the location of the central meetinghouse yard controlled the direction and plan of streets. In all the early Connecticut towns considerations of communication for its own sake did not matter; the ways which were laid out represented an embodiment of the right of each property owner to get free access to his property. The manner in which towns surveyed home lots and more distant land divisions determined the length and direction of roads and outlying streets. The surveyor gave no thought to the possibility of settlement along the borders of these more remote roads nor did he seriously consider communication by land with neighboring towns. When both these eventualities were realized in the early eighteenth century, the clear-cut, often symmetrical planning of streets near the meetinghouse center contrasted sharply with the

81. Gilman C. Gates, *Saybrook at the Mouth of the Connecticut River* (New Haven, Wilson H. Lee Company, 1935), pp. 152–153.

82. *Ibid.* See also Ezra Stiles, "Itinerary," MSS, Yale University Library, I, 510.

83. See 1779 map of Fairfield, MS map. Reproduced by Louis F. Middlebrook, *Maritime Connecticut during the American Revolution* (Salem, Essex Institute, 1925), I, 57.

84. N. Porter, *Hartford in 1640,* "Map of the Allotments" (Hartford, 1850). A "Plan done at the direction of the Town of Hartford."

85. Joel Tuttle, MS map of Guilford. A reconstruction of the central village area with all owners of plots. Copies in Yale University Library and the New Haven Historical Society.

86. Ezra Stiles, "Itinerary," MSS, I, 510; VI, 69, 71. Some very fine sketches of the town.

wandering, haphazard lanes which bordered the first decentralized building sites. By the nineteenth century the retention of these old streets was a serious problem; in twentieth-century traffic their inconvenience has become intolerable. The modern planner does not threaten the village green and meetinghouse yard but he likes to annihilate the ring of streets that lie just outside the town's first nucleus.

In the design of his defensive measures the Connecticut settler showed himself well aware of English colonial tradition and probably of the English villages in Ulster. Often temporary, these fortifications disappeared, with one exception, during the eighteenth and nineteenth centuries. Yet something is known about them. At Milford a strong tradition of a "palisado" exists, although there is some question as to its exact use and extent. Both Windsor and Guilford had "strong places" or stone houses provided with some means of defense. That at Windsor, which was destroyed about 1809, seems to have been simply a heavily built, rectangular stone house of two stories with a gable roof and minimum fenestration.[87] The Whitfield House at Guilford, which remains today, also followed Irish precedent and stood at some distance from the town green. The house could not defend the town of Guilford but only harbor its inhabitants in time of Indian trouble. To do this it was built, as were the Ulster strong house and bawn, a little removed from the village, so as to insure that natives who might have access to the village would not also have access to its refuge.[88] (Fig. 60.)

Saybrook was probably the Connecticut town most closely connected with the Ulster plantation. Lord Saye and Sele, its patron, held some 3,000 acres in the County of Armagh as one of the undertakers for Ulster,[89] and he was fully aware of the scheme used in many adventurer towns in Ireland. He employed Lion Gardiner, an engineer thoroughly trained in continental European military practice, to lay out the town and fort.[90] Gardiner planned Saybrook as a grid running parallel to the long axis of a point of land that commanded the mouth of the Connecticut River. (Fig. 17.) He laid out the fort overlooking the sound, near the tip of this peninsula.[91] Like the Whitfield House at Guilford, this fort was isolated from the houses of the settlers.[92]

87. Henry R. Stiles, *History of Ancient Windsor* (New York, 1859), pp. 155–156.

88. J. Frederick Kelly, *The Henry Whitfield House* (Guilford, Henry Whitfield State Historical Museum, 1939) gives the best account of the restoration of the house. For details of its origin, see below, Chapter IV.

89. Hill, *Plantation Papers,* p. 7.

90. *Dictionary of American Biography,* "Lion Gardiner"; Lion Gardiner, *Relation of the Pequot Wars,* p. 8 (from Curtis C. Gardiner, *Lion Gardiner and His Descendants* [Saint Louis, Whiple, 1890]).

91. Ezra Stiles, "Itinerary," MSS, I, 67. Gates, *Saybrook,* pp. 102–103, 98–99.

92. See map. Gates, *Saybrook,* p. 153. Ezra Stiles, "Itinerary," MSS, VI, 69, 71.

Of the first defenses on this site, laid out by Gardiner in 1636–37,[93] nothing remains above ground; but a later fort built by Major Mason in 1647 stood almost intact until 1870, when the Connecticut Valley Railroad was extended to the Point.[94] Views of Mason's fort taken at the time of its destruction indicate that it was built on a considerable eminence without elaborate ramparts.[95] Ezra Stiles had sketched Saybrook fortifications a century earlier in 1760 as an L-shaped bastion on a hill south of the town.[96]

The best clues to Gardiner's intentions are three sketches in the Winthrop Journal. Two of them show the fort as a small rectangle of 20 x 30 feet. In each sketch the four corners of the central rectangle are flanked by a bastion whose outline varies from sketch to sketch. In the most detailed view the bastions are four-sided, irregular polygons. The third sketch, which best corresponds with the descriptions of the Saybrook "Hall," might have been drawn in Ireland, so closely does it resemble Ulster work. (Figs. 31, 56.) If this plan was strictly followed it would indicate that the Hall at Saybrook resembled many fortified administration buildings of the various London companies in Ireland. These structures included a central courtyard about which a number of buildings with only roughly related purposes were grouped. This was a typical business practice of the London companies before the fire of 1666 and naturally they followed it in Ulster. Fully to utilize the deep London blocks, then thought admirable for town homes and gardens, these companies had devised a courtyard plan which gave maximum space for the Guild Hall and subordinate buildings with a minimum frontage. In Ulster the buildings had heavy stone walls built into walled courts to complete the bawns required of each plantation.

Such simple military works were adequate for the defense of the Connecticut River mouth only because the channel off Saybrook Point was narrow, and the Indians innocent of European engineering. After playing its role as a place of refuge during the Pequot War, the fort itself became an empty symbol of English authority and lingered only as a picturesque reminder of the colony's early years.

Among the earliest settlements founded by the English in Connecticut one town, New Haven, had antecedents quite distinct from the traditional pattern of English colonial towns in Ireland and on the Continent. Its plan, the first of the English Renaissance, antedated Christopher Wren's studies for London by some three decades. The classical roots of New Haven's street

93. Mention is made of this fort which appears to have been a fortified house. Gardiner, *Pequot Wars,* p. 11.

94. Coast and Geodetic Survey (1892, first issued 1853), scale 1/20,000. No. 360; United States Geological Survey, Connecticut (1877), *Saybrook,* scale 1/62,500.

95. Gates, *Saybrook,* p. 96.

96. Ezra Stiles, "Itinerary," MSS, I, 67. Certain of his later plans indicate that the fort had at one time been completed as square with four bastions. "Itinerary," MSS, VI, 69, 71.

layout do not appear at first glance. The town would seem to have been principally a development of the bastide or military town, a Calais, a Londonderry, or Ville-Franche without fortified walls. (Figs. 7, 11.) Like these it had a grid pattern with a large central square left open as a common or market. As in European models, its surveyor permitted no deviation of the street directions to include a diagonal axis, nor did he alter the rigid outline of the nine squares to allow for topography or for possible connecting roads to nearby fields or distant towns. (Fig. 18.)

Moreover, although the elaborate arcades found at Calais fronting the central square are missing in New Haven, it is possible that they were omitted solely because the demands of an essentially rural economy differed from those of a continental port. The use of very deep blocks (the original nine squares are each 52 rods or 286 yards on a side) insured the maintenance of open areas within the town. These open areas, free from housing, were part of the bastide tradition and, as has appeared, provided food during a siege regardless of how closely buildings were placed on street frontages. In all these things New Haven resembles the tradition of Calais and Londonderry.

Where New Haven's resemblance to the bastide city ends is where it makes its most significant contribution to the art of town planning. The very choice of site is clearly not the choice of a military engineer familiar with the part played by maritime fortress towns in Europe. Not only is there no provision for walls or protecting works, but the town is laid out at such a distance from water that its nearest point (the southern corner) could not command the mouth of the harbor with the limited range of seventeenth-century artillery.[97] Moreover, although New Haven was intended to be a port, its original plan did not cater to maritime needs.[98] None of the earliest streets ran parallel to the shore; indeed, most of the town stood at some distance from the harbor. Even the position of the nine squares on a wedge between two streams had little maritime significance, since the streams themselves were too shallow either for shipping or for docks and in the seventeenth century had different beds which cut into the nine squares at two points. The western fork of the larger stream actually traversed one of the nine squares to reach the corner of Church and Chapel streets. Its other branch ran through what was in 1641 the property of Samuel Eaton, William Tuttle, Mrs. Eaton, and David Yale, and crossed what is now Grove Street.[99] Clearly in orienting the town John Brockett, who is said to have been its surveyor, had some

97. The shore line has now been extended quite far into the harbor. In 1748 the distance between the nearest corner of the nine squares and the harbor was 32 rods or 176 yards. James Wadsworth, "Plan of the City of New Haven taken in 1748," MS map, Yale University Library.

98. Andrews, *Colonial Period,* II, 146.

99. Brockett map of 1641. MS map. Copy made by Mrs. Sarah D. Woodward, Yale University Library.

object quite distinct from the use of the streams or the natural harbor front. (Fig. 20.)

The curious site and orientation of New Haven can only be explained by the assumption that Brockett or those responsible for the town's plantation were fully aware of Vitruvius (the Roman writer on architecture whose manuscripts were discovered in the fifteenth century) and his maxims for town planning.[100] In Book I Vitruvius lays down his rules for the ideal site of a city. Reflecting his Mediterranean background, he was quick to point out the problems of southern exposure and heat.[101] Yet, on the other hand, he admitted the value for defense of well-drained meadows and salt marshes near the sea, an advantage which New Haven enjoyed together with almost all Connecticut towns of the littoral.[102]

Having chosen the site and fortified his city, the Roman architect next concerned himself with the direction his streets should run. Primarily he sought to prevent a free passage to any prevailing wind, as he believed that winds were not only chilling but carried disease.[103] Hence he planned to have none of his streets run directly toward a prevailing wind. "The lines of houses must therefore be directed from the quarters from which the winds blow, so that as they come in they may strike against the angle of the blocks and their force thus be broken and dispersed." [104] (Fig. 19.)

The direction of the winds at any given site therefore determined the orientation of the town at that site. But Vitruvius did not find the direction of the prevailing winds by observation and comparison with known directions. Rather, he arbitrarily reduced the number of possible quarters for

100. Although the first English translation of Vitruvius was not published until 1692 it is certain that his work was well known in England in 1635. John Shute in *The First & Chief Groundes of Architecture* indicated an acquaintance with the writings of Vitruvius as early as 1563. Henry Wotton's *Elements of Architecture* (London, 1624), while not a translation of Vitruvius, shows a familiarity with *The Ten Books on Architecture* and an effort to apply them. Numerous editions of Vitruvius had appeared on the Continent both in translation and in Latin. The French edition of J. Martin (1547), the German edition of W. Ryff, or Rivius (1548), and the Spanish edition of M. Urrea (1587) are among the most renowned. Italian editions are very common, no fewer than four issues (1556, 1567, 1584, 1629) being listed for the Barbaro edition alone. The extent to which Vitruvius was known by builders is made uncertain by Moxon who at the end of the seventeenth century listed the "Titles of Some Books of Architecture, Sebastian Serlio in Folio, Hans Bloom's Five Collumns in Folio, Vignola in Folio, and Vignola or the Compleet Architect in Octavo" but omitted Vitruvius' own works. J. Moxon, *Mechanick Exercises* (London, 1703), p. 156.

101. Not a serious problem in New England. Vitruvius, *The Ten Books on Architecture,* trans. by Morris H. Morgan (Cambridge, Harvard University Press, 1926), Book I, chap. iv, p. 18. All my page references are to the Morgan edition. This work is hereafter called Vitruvius.

102. Vitruvius, Book I, chap. iv, p. 20.

103. *Ibid.,* Book I, chap. vi, pp. 24–26.

104. *Ibid.,* p. 27.

18. New Haven in 1748

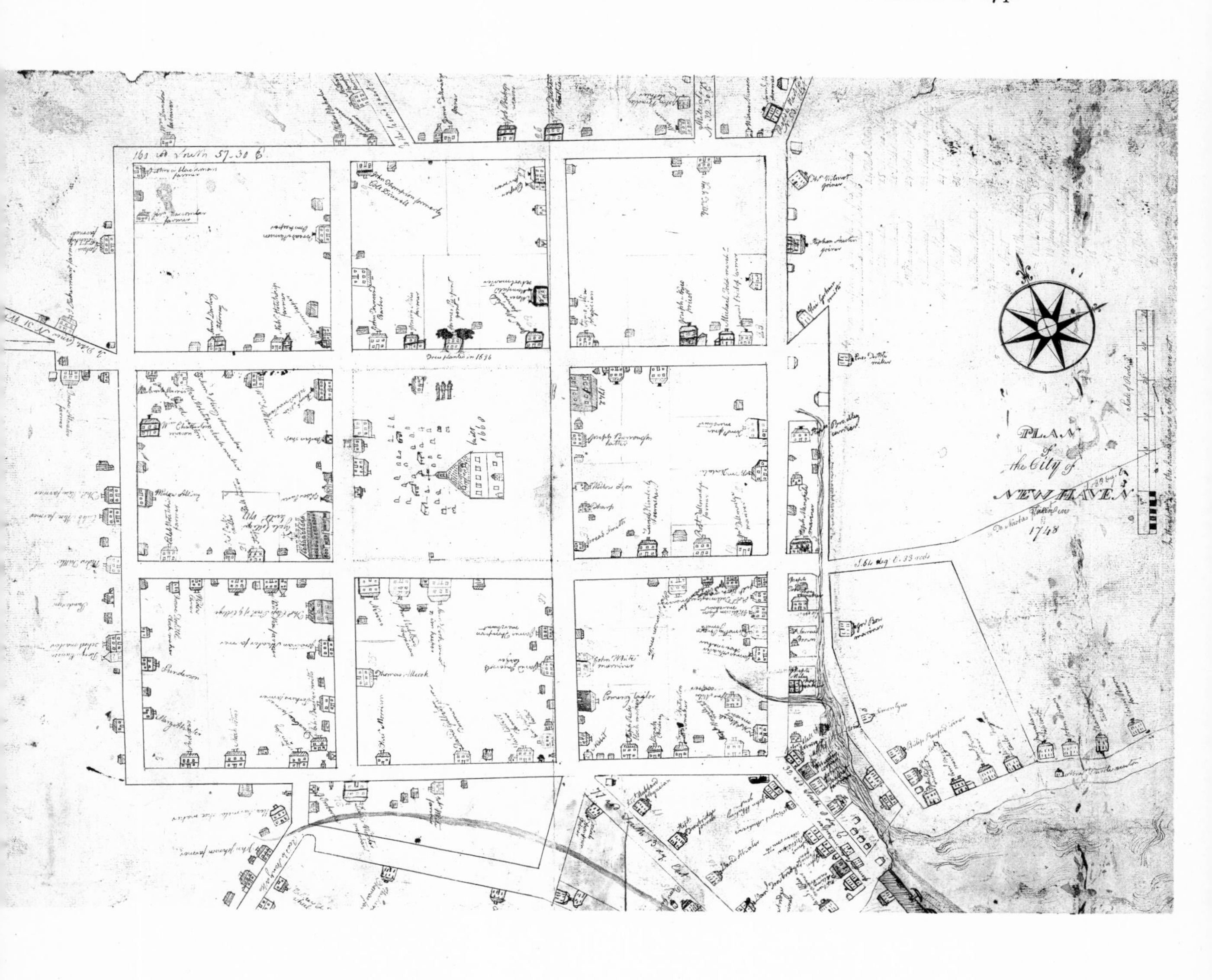

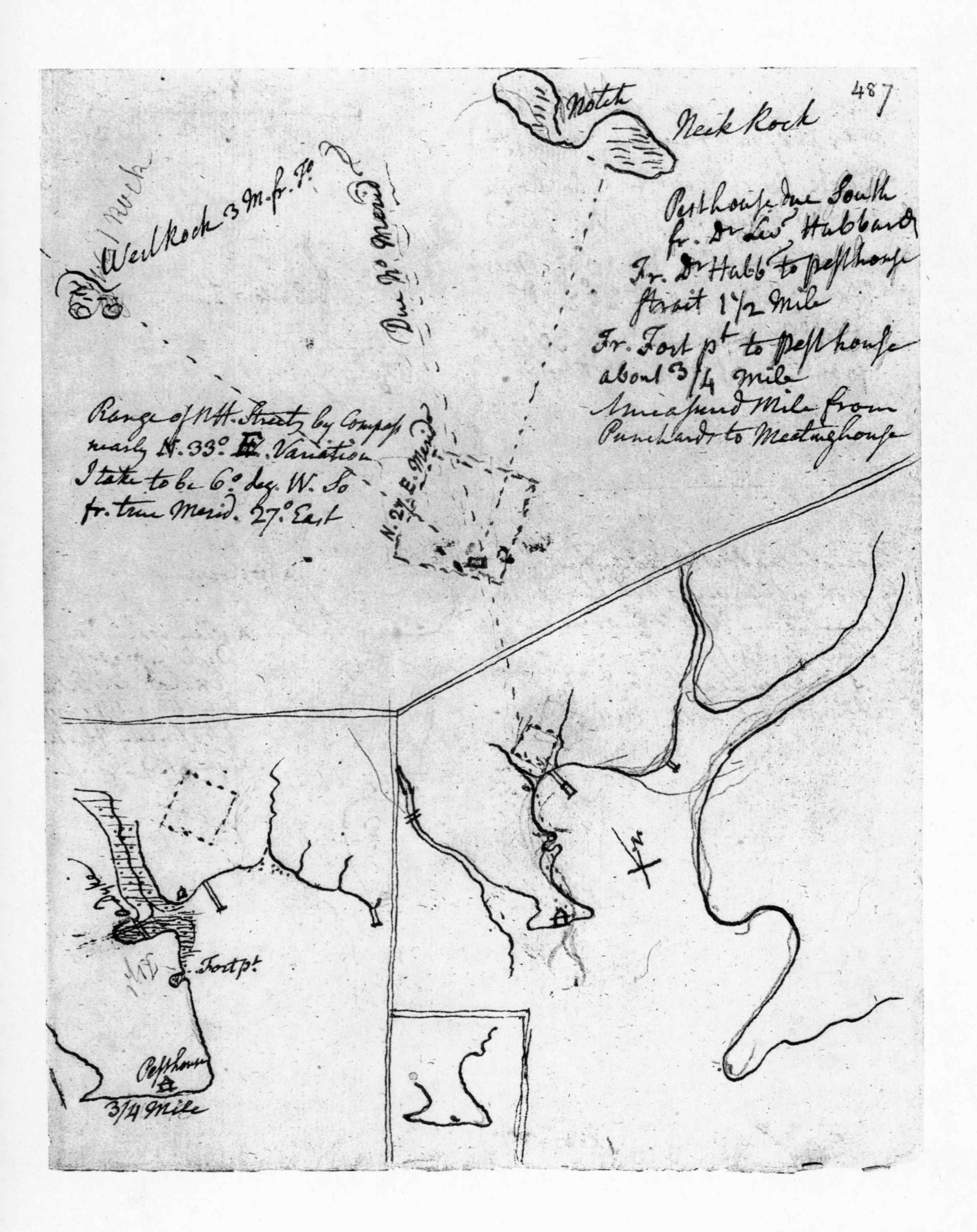

20. The orientation of New Haven

19. Vitruvian town orientation

winds by assuming that any wind came from one of eight different directions. These points were 45° apart, commencing with the north or zero degrees. Thus a wind was presumed at 45°, 90°, 135°, and every 45° thereafter up to 360°.[105] (Fig. 19.)

Therefore in order to lay out an ideal city with none of its streets pointing directly into a wind, half its streets should run either at 22° 30′ or 22° 30′ in addition to any multiple of 45° up to and including 337° 30′. The other half should run at right angles to those already laid down, and would also be free of any prevailing wind, since they too must lie midway between the 45° points from which Vitruvius assumed all winds came.

To lay out the streets of his city with these principles in mind Vitruvius found *true* north from the sun and then laid off the sixteenth part of a circle or 22° 30′ from each side of north.[106] Within the 45° thus laid out the north or "Septentrio" wind was considered to lie.[107] The final step that he advised was

105. *Ibid.*, pp. 27–31.
106. *Ibid.*, pp. 29–31.
107. *Ibid.*, p. 30.

to "let the directions of your streets and alleys be laid down on the lines of division between the quarters of two winds." [108]

At New Haven most of the steps outlined by Vitruvius seem to have been taken. The streets of nine major squares meet at right angles, and the large square formed by the nine smaller ones is not oriented due north but 118° 53′ east of north; or, if Chapel Street be taken as a base line instead of Church Street, the town plan can be considered to be oriented at an angle of 28° 53′ west of north. In either case there is an error of only 6° 23′ from the multiples of 22° 30′ which Vitruvius considered ideal.[109] (Fig. 20.)

In all probability this error represented the difference between true and magnetic north in 1638. Certainly it would have been far simpler for Brockett, a practical surveyor presumably experienced in the survey of English enclosures, to work with magnetic north.[110] The procedure recommended by Vitruvius was clumsy, complicated, and depended for its accuracy on dividers or measures of large size.[111] Although the 6° 23′ may represent a small error inherent in the practical application of Vitruvius' method, it is possible that John Brockett and the planters of New Haven were unaware of the difference between true and magnetic north.[112] Ample literature had been published in England before 1638 on the subject of magnetic declination or variation, but the extent of its circulation is problematical.[113] The works of Robert Norman and William Borough had described magnetic declination and dip, and William Gilbert had tried in 1600 to explain magnetic phenomena by the concept of the earth as a single great magnet. Public interest in magnetic observations grew with the commerce and explorations of the New World, but public knowledge of magnetic phenomena in 1638 is hard to assay.[114]

108. *Ibid.*, p. 27. Or again, "This done apply a gnomon to these eight divisions and thus fix the directions of the different alleys." *Ibid.*, p. 31.

109. This bearing was obtained by actual survey. No true orientation of the city's streets exists in the office of the city surveyor—only relative bearings. Courtesy of Alexander Cahn, surveyor, 839 Chapel Street, New Haven.

110. John Norden assumed the use of magnetic north. *The Surueyors Dialogue* (London, 1618), p. 128.

111. Vitruvius, Book I, pp. 26–27.

112. Columbus is generally credited with the first positive observation of a ship passing through a point of zero variation (declination) west of the Azores in 29° west longitude. Previously any variation had been interpreted as a failing of the individual compass and was corrected with lodestones. Samuel E. Morison, *Admiral of the Ocean Sea* (Boston, Little, Brown & Co., 1942), p. 204, gives a clear account of the events of the night of September 13, 1492.

113. "Declination" is the term preferred by geodetic journals for the natural angle between true and magnetic north while "variation" describes the same angle for mariners. "Inclination" is the dip of a magnetic needle from the horizontal.

114. Robert Norman, *The Newe Attractive* (1581, 1589, 1596, 1614), to which was added in 1581 William Borough's *A Discourse of the Variation of the Compas or Magneticall Needle*. William Gilbert, *De Magnete* (1600).

In any event, it appears that the magnetic declination at New Haven in 1638 was between 6° and 8° west of true north.[115] Therefore if Brockett laid out the city on a Vitruvian ideal line 22° 30′ west of magnetic north in 1638, it would lie between 28° 30′ and 30° 30′ west of true north today, after passing through a cycle of even greater declination. Within these limits falls the contemporary surveyed street direction of 28° 53′ W. It seems safe to conclude that Brockett or the founders of New Haven oriented the city's nine squares according to the maxims of Vitruvius but used magnetic north.[116]

Certainly the application of Vitruvius' ideas to the town plan of New Haven was the most radical urban innovation introduced by the first generation of Connecticut settlers.[117] Apart from this development the streets of seventeenth-century towns reflected not so much American conditions as English precedents, well tried in Wales, Ulster, and France. As yet no new pattern had been invented, because English traditional urban designs fitted the aims of the Puritans. Thus these same plans, clothed with a new symbolism, became the New England villages of the eighteenth century.

Yet colonial ingenuity and adaptation were not altogether lacking. For the larger problem of organizing the many square miles of virgin land which ran from the tiny cluster of houses at the center of the settlement to the boundary of the township no European precedent existed. Here the colonial surveyor and proprietor laid out original and important designs whose influence upon American planning has never quite been lost.

115. Hermann P. H. Fritsche, *Atlas der Erdmagnetismus für die Epochen 1600, 1700, 1780, 1842, und 1915* (Riga, Müllersche Buchdruckerei, 1903), Plates I, II. This work indicates a theory of world changes from 1600 to 1915. Edmund Halley's equal variation chart, "A New and Correct Chart Shewing the Variations of the Compass in the Western and Southern Oceans as observed in the Year 1700," is reproduced in *Terrestial Magnetism,* I, No. 1. Assuming that Connecticut had a cycle of magnetic change that paralleled New Jersey as it did in the eighteenth century, then in 1638 Connecticut's declination would be between 6° and 8° west, because New Jersey experienced a steady increase in its westerly declination in the seventeenth century and had a declination of 8° 18′ in 1650. Louis A. Bauer, *United States Magnetic . . . Charts for 1902* (Washington, Government Printing Office, 1902), p. 109. "The greatest change in magnetic declination and therefore the one of most importance to the surveyor is the so-called secular change. . . . This change appears to be of periodic character like the motion of a pendulum that is—the compass needle after moving continuously in one direction for a long term of years gradually comes to a standstill and then begins a motion in the opposite direction." *Ibid.,* p. 99. See also pp. 103, 109.

116. Apart from the difficulty of appraising the exact magnetic north in 1638, compass cards would be hard to read closer than 6° or half a point.

117. The deep blocks of New Haven were only bisected in the late eighteenth century. "Plan of the City of New Haven June 6th A Domini 1802." Anonymous MS map, Yale University Library. This is the first map to show all the squares divided; otherwise, though not extended outside the nine squares, Brockett's plan remained untouched.

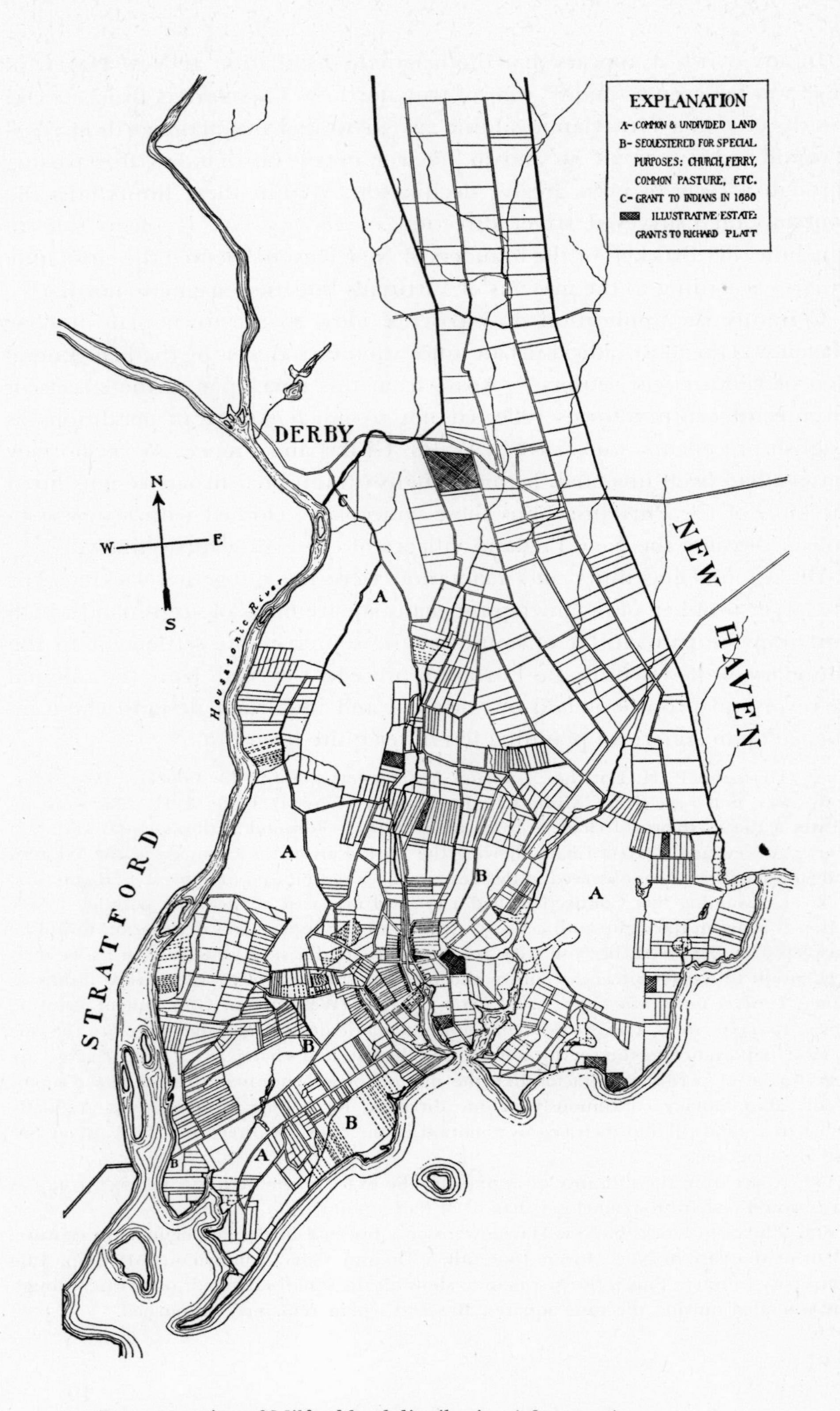

21. Reconstruction of Milford land distribution (1639–1700)

III. The Lands

The neat avenues, treeless squares, and generous meetinghouse lots of Connecticut villages masked the colony's real wealth: this lay north and south, east and west of the home lots. Beyond the village proper, ownership of land (so much owned by so few) materialized in the walls, fields, and wastes of outlying land divisions which were physical reflections of the fact that a proprietary of about fifty families held title to some 30 square miles. These first-comers and their descendants had only to retain their interests to see the value of their holdings increase, since as the population grew its appetite for fresh land sharpened. By 1790, at the end of the colonial period, when the opening of the trans-Appalachian west and the exhaustion of the colony's acres halted the spiral of speculation, Connecticut had a population of 49.1 persons per square mile.

In consequence a plan of land division for each town came to be a necessary corollary of the colony's street plans.[1] During the seventeenth century the twin needs of suitable home sites on the one hand and of equitable land allotment on the other were dealt with separately, but by the mid-eighteenth century land allotments and home lots had merged. Between 1630 and 1750 almost all the elements of the western township, so skillfully blended in the Land Act of 1796, had been tested in one or another of the Connecticut towns. In less than a century area or township planning had replaced the European traditions of village home and dispersed, distant fields.

1. Street layouts are generally called "town plans"; in the New England sense the "town" covers perhaps 36 square miles in extent and includes what is now more generally considered an area, region, or township. This chapter deals with the Connecticut town in this larger, more extensive sense of outlying lands that lay beyond the nucleated settlement but within what has come to be known outside New England as the township. "A Map of the Colonies of Connecticut and Rhode Island Divided into Counties and Townships from the Best Authorities" by Tho. Kitchin, Geogr. (London, 1758) is the earliest complete survey of Connecticut showing town lines. Edmund B. Thompson, *Maps of Connecticut before the Year 1800* (Windham, Hawthorn House, 1940), p. 30.

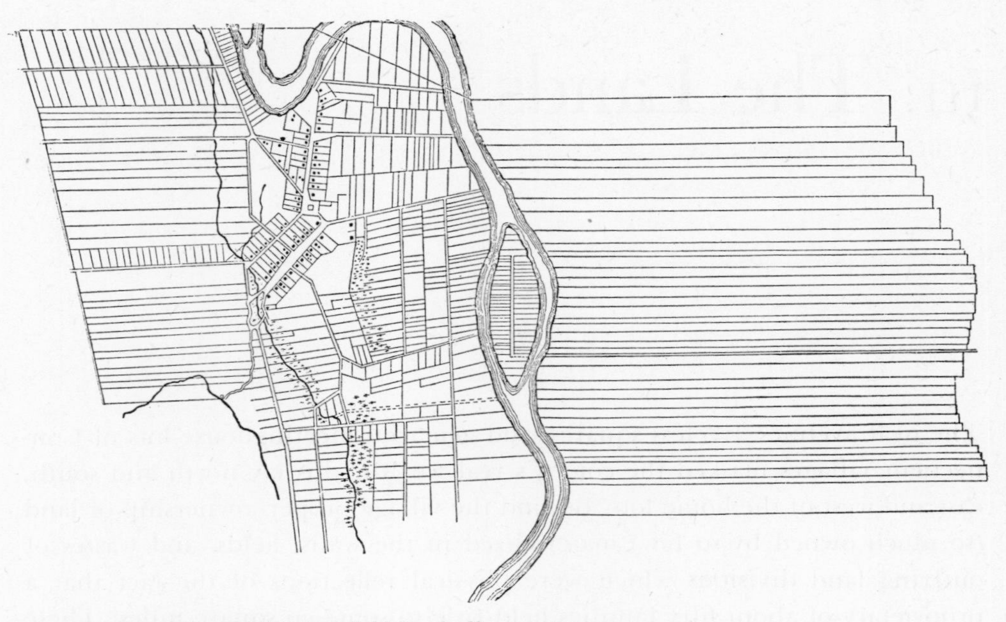

22. Reconstruction of Wethersfield land allotments

In land division the settlers abandoned the conservatism which had characterized their street plans. The allotment of wilderness seemed to ridicule humble European field systems. Since neither inherited rank nor traditional holdings had much meaning, the unworked land was the only outwardly visible asset of the settlers; the first surveyed division lines had to reflect either the size of each settler's contribution to initial expenses of the plantation or the extent of his personal property. Thus the way the land was distributed at the foundation of a town only a few weeks' sail from England might make the yeoman and husbandman either proprietor, first settler, or late-comer.[2]

After the land had been justly distributed was time enough to lay out highways and roads to reach each piece of property. The complete record of this process has been traced in only two instances, but the findings of those who investigated have been generally accepted. Charles M. Andrews completed the less detailed of these studies in 1889. Illustrating his research with a simple map, he concluded that the Wethersfield land division determined

2. Roy H. Akagi, *The Town Proprietors of the New England Colonies* (Philadelphia, University of Pennsylvania Press, 1924), pp. 103–109. This work is still the most effective general account of the foundation of New England towns though the physical aspects of town planning are not stressed.

its road system on both the east and west banks of the Connecticut River.[3] (Fig. 22.)

Leonard Labaree went further and not only attributed the road system of Milford to land division but concluded that successive land allotments over a period of fifty years had produced a ladder of independent road networks which became sites for the daughter towns of Orange and Woodbridge. (Fig. 21.) In order to prove his contention he constructed a complete town survey from the land records, which clearly showed the subordinate function of roads as the secondary manifestation of property divisions.[4]

More recently Glenn T. Trewartha used these materials to stress the importance of land division in New England townships when he compared New England to other British colonies. By using reconstructed plans of other students he showed that when the New England planter with his unique economic and religious aims was absent community settlement was also absent. Thus in colonies where the proprietary grant replaced the town grant, individual, isolated land settlement prevailed with an altogether different road pattern. For many years land ownership, not commerce on land or sea, made the New England township practical.[5]

A full interpretation of New England regional plans will have to await many studies like those of Andrews and Labaree, but much can be learned from existing manuscript surveys of Connecticut. Such remains combined with carefully reconstructed plans of recent date and the evidence of aerial photographs give a fairly detailed picture of the colony's progress in regional planning which may be indicative of New England towns generally.

In every town founded before 1640 the settlers chose low open ground for their site. Wethersfield, Milford, and Fairfield typified the land policy which was followed. At Wethersfield the banks of the Connecticut River furnished the meadowland considered vital for the pasturage of the village herds. At Milford the marshes framing the mouth of the Wepawaug served the same purpose. Beyond a central area of home lot and common the proprietors of

3. Charles M. Andrews, *The River Towns of Connecticut* (Baltimore, 1889), pp. 4, 61. The sketch map of Wethersfield is regarded as a standard illustration of a New England village. Charles O. Paullin, *Atlas of the Historical Geography of the United States* (New York, Carnegie Institution of Washington and American Geographical Society of New York, 1932), p. 25, Plate 41D. One additional far less detailed map deserves mention—Irene Rice's study of Enfield (MS in Yale University Library), reproduced by Thomas J. Wertenbaker, *The First American's 1607–1690* (New York, Macmillan Company, 1929), p. 58.

4. Leonard W. Labaree, *Milford, Connecticut; The Early Development of a Town as Shown in Its Land Records,* pp. 12, 18–20.

5. Glenn T. Trewartha, "Types of Rural Settlement in Colonial America," *Geographical Review,* XXXVI (1946), 568, 595–596.

Milford and those of Wethersfield laid out a series of lots which together comprised the first division. At Milford these lots varied in length but averaged 10 acres in area. At Wethersfield they were in general a trifle larger and a few proprietors even held 100 acres in a single piece. Apart from the grant of land for home lots Milford voted the town's first division in 1646, and before 1687 seven such divisions of upland, together with two of meadowland, had been granted.[6] (Figs. 21, 22.)

Fairfield's first two divisions occurred in 1668, and the divisions of 1671, 1682, and 1688 followed the already traditional pattern. Each time ribbons of lots were allotted to some fifty proprietors who qualified to share in these divisions as freemen and purchasers of Indian lands. The lots varied in size and shape but each proprietor had a given position in the rotational order in which lots were allotted.[7]

By 1700 almost all the land in the seventeenth-century townships had been divided. The award of this land in successive ladders had had a permanent effect on the road system and had affected the choice of building sites outside the original nucleated village. Throughout the seventeenth and indeed well into the eighteenth century, in order to follow property divisions, almost all colonial highways were local dead-end roads which simply provided access to new lots within each town. They were not lanes of commerce between towns but connected the settlers' houses with their lands: [8] intertown travelers used Long Island Sound and the various rivers. As late as 1700 only one road linked New York and Rhode Island via Connecticut. The Lower Post Road and no more than five highways served as country (or intertown) roads. Plainfield in 1712 had no road passing through the town from east to west, and apart from the shore towns only Hartford and New Haven shared any regular travel.[9]

At Fairfield seventeenth-century division of colonial property has permanently affected the town's road system which is still divided into three parts, each created by the original purpose of the land it served. The town's grant was a rectangle approximately 7 miles wide which ran some 15 miles inland from the coast. At the base of the rectangle Roger Ludlow's four squares overlooked Long Island Sound. (Fig. 16.) Around these squares nineteenth- and twentieth-century "developments" have obscured the bound-

6. Andrews, *River Towns of Connecticut,* pp. 4, 47. Labaree, *Milford, Connecticut,* p. 11.

7. Elizabeth H. Schenck, *The History of Fairfield* (New York, 1889). Appendices IV–XXII reproduce the list of planters and their allotments. See also Labaree, *Milford, Connecticut,* p. 69.

8. This is shown by the wide variety of road maps in the Connecticut Archives. For example, "Bounds of North Fairfield, 1762," MS map, Eccles., XII, 97.

9. Isabel S. Mitchell, *Roads and Road Making in Colonial Connecticut* (New Haven, Yale University Press, 1933), pp. 9, 20. Connecticut Tercentenary Pamphlets, Vol. XIV.

ary between colonial home lots and the "Half-mile of Common" just north of the village, but formerly this common extended north to the Hull's Farm Road. Within its limits modern roads meander as the swine and cattle of the seventeenth-century common herd wandered. Roads twist about from hillside to stream and follow contours in sharp contrast to the rectangular squares and straight streets of the first home lots.

Some 2 miles north of the village the tortuous lanes of the Half-mile of Common disappear, and after one crosses the Hull's Farm Road parallel highways run almost due northwest to the original Fairfield town line, now the Redding boundary, roughly 9 miles away. This curiously regular road system was laid out to serve the Fairfield Long Lots which began at the Hull's Farm Road and extended "into the country to the end of the bounds." Each narrow Long Lot could be reached by the Hull's Farm Road at its base, and the occasional straight town highways gave access to the north.[10] (Fig. 24.)

Between the eastern and western Long Lots the town proprietors chose to reserve the Half-mile of Common which they did not divide until later. As one might expect, the roads even today in the Half-mile of Common follow the contours of the common and radiate along irregular spokes from the hub of Greenfield Hill, an eighteenth-century settlement.

When the proprietors of a town decided to retain a large tract of land as a common, they modified the town's road system and limited available sites, since land undivided or held in common could not be used for homes. At Fairfield during the early seventeenth century settlers built only in the vicinity of the four squares. The Long Lots were not distributed until 1682 and owing to their inconvenient size and shape were probably held for speculative purposes and not used for house sites until late in the eighteenth century. Since the proprietors held the Half-mile of Common until 1688, no houses stood there much before 1700, and only some decades after the Half-mile of Common was divided in 1700 did settlers move to Greenfield Hill. Fairfield was not unique: land, not roads and houses, sketched the earliest Connecticut townships.

The origin of such seventeenth-century land plans remains obscure. The resemblance between the small community settlement at the hub of a series of divisions and an English seventeenth-century unenclosed village surrounded by two or three open fields is suggestive. This resemblance Charles M. Andrews was quick to notice, and more recently Glenn T. Trewartha indicated parallels in New England and England, although with the important reservation that the seventeenth-century agricultural village already partially

10. Schenck, *History of Fairfield,* I, 1. Modern traffic has tended to follow these late seventeenth-century roads and strikingly illustrates their utility. Connecticut State Highway Department, *General Highway Map of Fairfield County,* Sheet 5, 1938.

enclosed best explained the origin of such towns as Milford, Wethersfield, and Fairfield.[11]

A first examination of the pattern of holdings in such villages seems to confirm this hypothesis. Certainly the English strip system roughly corresponds with the assignment of land within a division. In both, long, rectangular lots were allotted in regular order to various owners and in both a plan of the land brings out the familiar ladder pattern.

But here the resemblance ends. Just as the village proper was no slavish copy of the English village but a development of colonial practice in Ireland and on the Continent, so the organization of Connecticut lands varied in important respects from the open-field system of England. These differences emerge when a careful comparison is made between surveys of English and Connecticut villages. Fundamental to such a comparison is the reduction of both maps to the same scale. When this is done, their resemblance becomes remote because the average holdings in Connecticut are much larger than the average holdings in an English open field such as that at Cambridge. The illusion of resemblance was partly fostered by the original omission of a scale on the map of Wethersfield reproduced by Andrews.[12] (Fig. 22.) Thus the holdings at Wethersfield appear small and narrow like those of an English village because the cartographer used a small scale. But if compared on the basis of the same scale with English field surveys, it is at once clear that the New England village strips are much larger. A few strips at Wethersfield were ¼ mile wide and nearly 3 miles long. The apparent resemblance may have led to Andrews' bold although not unqualified hypothesis concerning the Germanic origin of the New England system.[13]

The holdings of selected individuals give a most graphic index of the wide gap between the English and American land systems. English writers do not agree as to what constituted an average copyhold. It seems that before enclosure a man's holding might reach 50 acres, widely distributed in many narrow strips little more than 2 rods wide and perhaps a furlong or 660 feet in length. After enclosure a copyhold of 50 or 100 acres was no longer exceptional, but the new pastures were made from many small strips each a furlong in length, and therefore were generally bounded by roads or ways that were a furlong apart.[14] Edgeware in 1597, although completely enclosed, had pastures of only 4 to 11 acres, and the length of these pastures tended to re-

11. Andrews, *River Towns of Connecticut,* p. 43. Glenn T. Trewartha, "Types of Rural Settlement in Colonial America," *Geographical Review,* XXXVI, 572.

12. Andrews, *River Towns of Connecticut,* p. 4.

13. *Ibid.,* p. 43.

14. Richard J. Tawney, *Agrarian Problem in the Sixteenth Century,* p. 163.

23. Deeping Fen, 1662

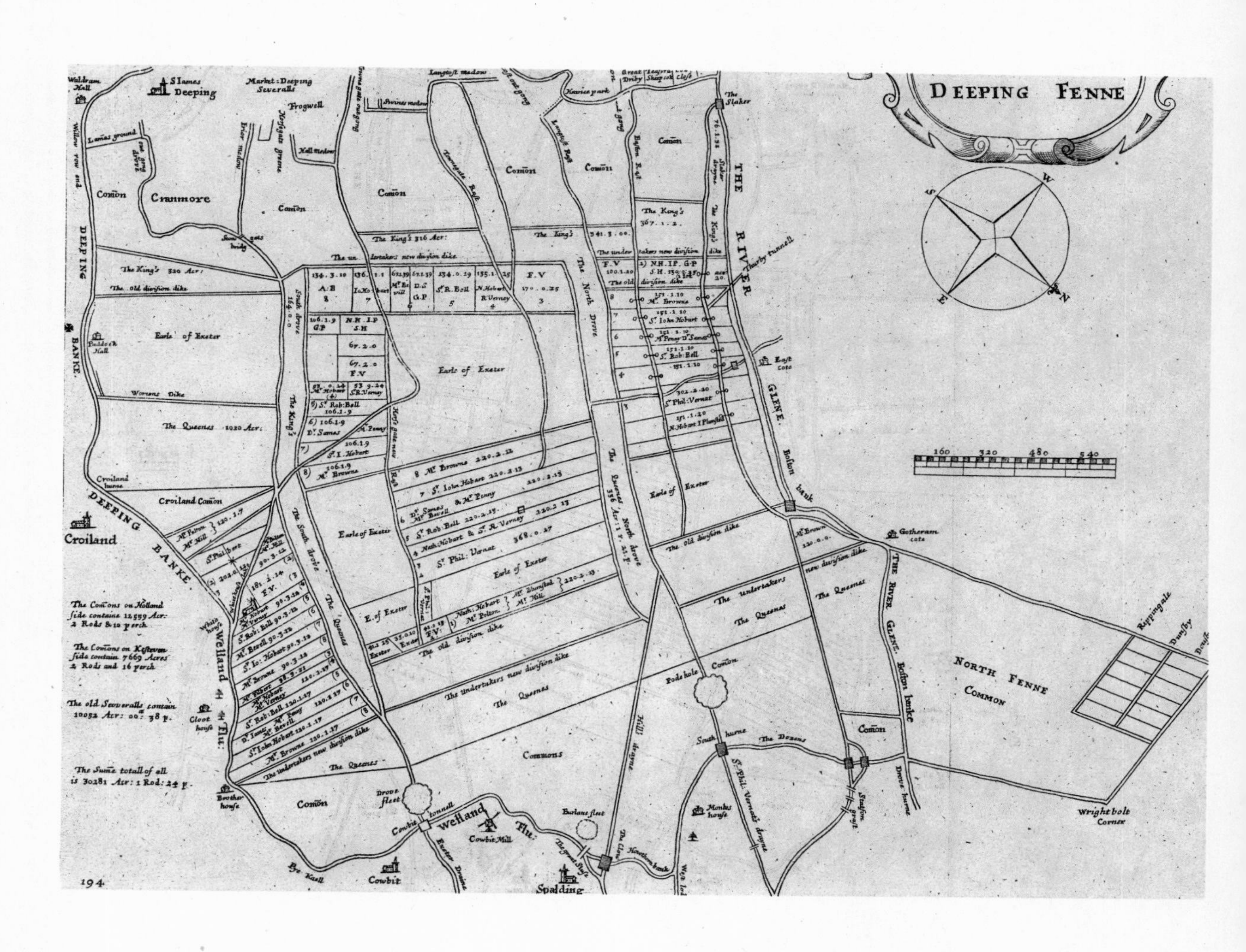

24. Section of the Hull's Farm Road with Fairfield Half-mile of Common above and beginning of Long Lots below it

25. Nathaniel Webb's survey of Lebanon, 1772

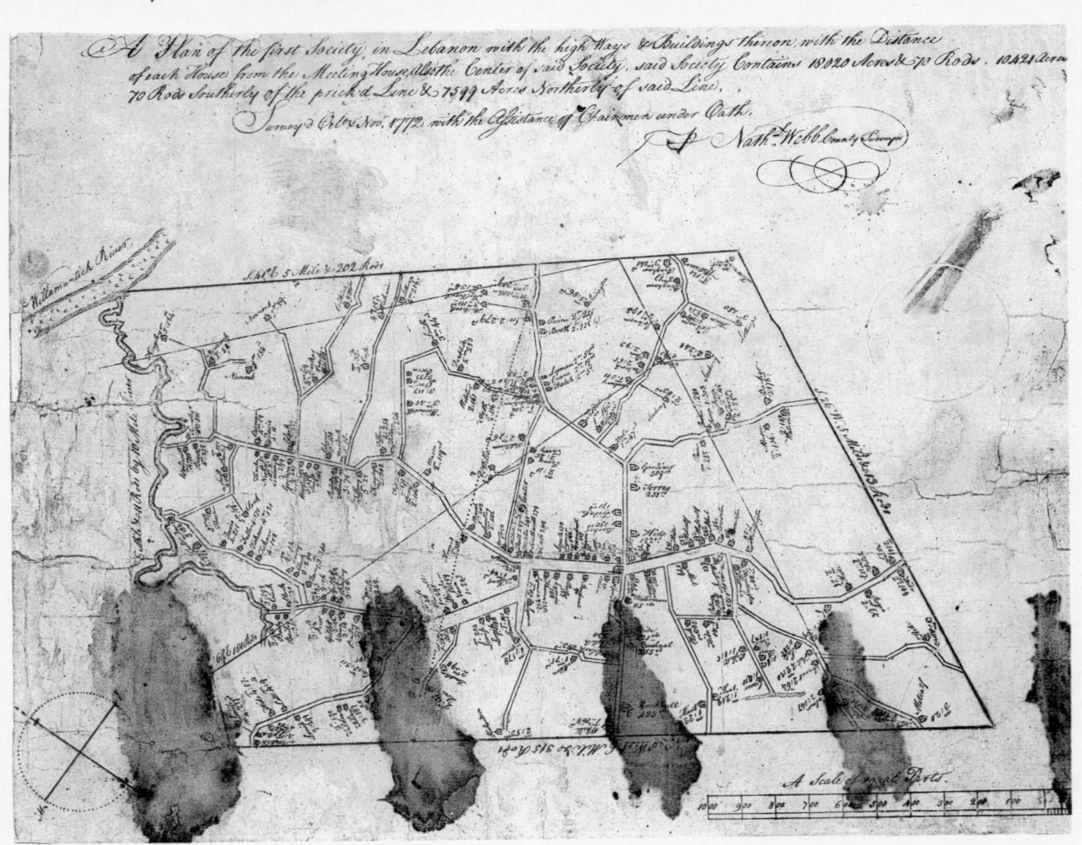

main constant, since enclosure had merely converted a number of narrow strips into a few square fields.[15]

Neither English strips nor enclosed pastures approximated the size of New England allotments. Connecticut strips were often so long and wide that despite their proportions they could include several more nearly square English pastures. The Long Lots at Fairfield, laid out in 1682, comprise the most famous and best preserved seventeenth-century land division. (Fig. 24.) As we have seen, the Half-mile of Common separated them from the town on the south; each lot ran straight northwest from the Hull's Farm Road to the Redding boundary, a distance of several miles.[16] In part because of their distance from the village, the boundaries of the lots became confused, a situation which in 1757–58 led to an order of the town proprietors requiring anyone owning Long Lots to mark his land by a stone wall. For this purpose surveyors appointed by the town surveyed each lot and laid it out afresh. To indicate each property line stone markers were placed on the Hull's Farm Road from which stone walls were to be built northwest to the Redding town line.[17]

The surveyors in 1758 found that the lots corresponded only roughly with those laid out in 1682, and they uncovered many discrepancies.[18] Nonetheless, tradition apparently carried more weight than the ruling of the committee, and the remains of the boundary walls that exist today lie along seventeenth-century allotments rather than along the corrected eighteenth-century boundaries. The traces of the walls, still plainly visible from the air, lie in long parallel lines separated by distances that correspond exactly to the allotment as recorded in the minutes of the town meeting. (Fig. 24.)

These Long Lots extended some 10 miles north and although the narrowest was 3 rods and the widest 59 rods, they averaged about 22 rods in width. When the long lots were included with the other holdings of such a man as Thomas Staples, the extent of his landed property became truly enormous. In 1681 his estate included 1,128 acres of pasture and woodland in the commons, 26 acres of building lots in addition to his home lot, and 20 acres of distributed pasture in the other divisions of the town. With his Long Lot, Staples' total acreage probably came to over 1,400 acres. Similarly Maj. Nathan Gold possessed title to some 1,500 acres, while no fewer than 58 persons each held more than 400 acres.[19] While most extensive holdings belonged

15. *Ibid.*, p. 172. An excellent example showing parallel conditions is "Plan of the Manor of Walworth and Parish of Newington, Surrey, in the Year 1681," London Topographical Society, Publications, Vol. LXV (1932).

16. Fairfield Town Records (Votes), Book B, pp. 41, 66, 67, 68.

17. Fairfield Land Records, XIII, 110; XIV, 554.

18. Cf. Fairfield Town Records (Votes), Book B, pp. 67–68.

19. *Ibid.*, p. 66.

to "proprietors" or dividend holders, Fairfield in this same year had only 184 taxable persons; hence nearly one third of the property owners held more than 400 acres apiece. Since land was almost the only real asset of the village, the right to share in a dividend laid the basis for the Connecticut town's social stratification and distribution of wealth.[20]

The physical appearance of the town land arranged in a checkerboard of tiers reflected the scheme of town division. The division represented for the town, as it did for the joint stock company, a liquidation of the claims of the investing partners by a division of their real assets. The term "division" had inherent validity,[21] and although the use of the division as a primary unit of land allotment in the late seventeenth and eighteenth centuries was in the main American, the New England settlers did not lack precedent for it.

Scott indicates that from their earliest beginnings joint-stock enterprises had resorted to the division of assets, at first after every voyage, later at longer intervals. These assets included both capital subscribed and profits.[22] When such companies came to underwrite colonial ventures, the tradition of the division remained, but the chief asset was not treasure but land which was similarly divided among the shareholders. The Bermuda Company's division of the Somers Islands in 1617 is probably our best documental seventeenth-century precedent for the procedure used to divide large areas of land in English colonies.[23] The steps taken by the "Undertakers for the Plantation of the Somers Islands" are familiar ones. In 1616 Governor Tucker was instructed to survey the islands and prepare a plot of them showing a division into eight "tribes." [24] He was to subdivide these tribes into fifty shares of 26 acres each. The shares were then to be allotted to the adventurers on the basis of their investment in the company.[25] The Bermuda Company entrusted

20. Akagi, *Town Proprietors of the New England Colonies,* pp. 4–5. An interesting case is the Fairfield land division. Sixty-seven persons held land but were not proprietors. Schenck, *History of Fairfield,* pp. 67–68.

21. *New English Dictionary on Historical Principles.*

22. William R. Scott, *The Constitution and Finance of English, Scottish and Irish Joint-stock Companies to 1720* (Cambridge, University Press, 1910–12), I, 153.

23. Settlement of Bermuda began with the wreck of Sir George Somers and 150 settlers in 1609 on their way to succor Jamestown, and thereafter the Bermuda colony was closely bound with the development of Virginia. Wesley F. Craven, *An Introduction to the History of Bermuda* (Williamsburg, 1938; reprinted from *William and Mary College Quarterly,* N.S., XVII), pp. 15 ff.

24. Instructions to Governor D. Tucker, 1616, Article 7. Sir John H. Lefroy, *Memorials of the Discovery and Early Settlement of the Bermudas or Somers Islands,* 1515–1685 (London, Longmans, Green & Co., 1877), I, 108. *The Journal of Richard Norwood,* ed. by W. F. Craven (New York, Bermuda Historical Monuments Trust, 1945), p. 58; Scholars' Facsimiles and Reprints, I.

25. Nathaniel Butler, *The Historye of the Bermudaes or Summers Islands* (London, Hakluyt Society, 1882), p. 104–105.

the task of making the survey to Richard Norwood, a mathematician and inventor. He took the liberty of reducing the size of the shares to 25 acres [26] in order to insure their equal size and thus created an additional difficulty of an unassigned "overplus." [27] Norwood surveyed and numbered the holdings in narrow strips, many of which ran the full width of the main island. The company distributed the strips and followed by lot the principle of rotation. Certain land, and the income from it, was kept undivided for the defense of the islands and to cover the general and public charges of settlement. Ireland, St. George's Island, and St. David Island, together with the lesser islands, made approximately an additional two "tribes" of such reserved land. Most of the Bermuda adventurers resided in England and not in the colony, and the islands were only large enough to permit one division, but the procedure the Bermuda Company followed in the award of the land dividend provided a precedent for the Connecticut proprietors just as elaborate as the Irish Society's street plans for the Ulster plantation.[28]

Promoters of the New England plantation and the settlers themselves did not need to look abroad for a model of land allotment which might be adapted to American conditions. Many of them had seen and a few had invested in the reclamation of the Fens which lay between Boston in Lincolnshire and King's Lynn in Norfolk. In order to facilitate the drainage of these and other tidal marshes Parliament in 1600 had passed a General Drainage Act which authorized the lords of manors and the majority of commoners in any common fen to deliver a portion of their lands to such persons as might undertake their drainage and reclamation.

The task though still not completed today led to the opening of thousands of new acres of rich land. The undertakers shared this land in proportion to their individual investment in the cost of digging and maintaining the drainage ditches. Since the risk was great the expectation of reward was also high: Francis, Earl of Bedford, a moderate Puritan, the builder of Covent Garden,

26. Twenty-six acres per share is asserted to have been the ideal of the company. *Journal of Richard Norwood,* Introduction, p. xxviii. Norwood felt that 25 acres would be nearer correct but apparently in the course of the actual survey a further reduction was necessary, in many cases to 24 acres. Richard Norwood's "Book of Survey of 1662–63," in Lefroy, *Memorials . . . of the Bermudas,* II, 657 ff.

27. Butler points out in the *Historye . . . Bermudaes,* p. 104, that the "overplus" from which Governor Tucker's share was to be taken fell in a very fruitful valley due to a shift in the order of the survey. Norwood's own account of the "overplus" is given in "The Book of Survey of 1662–63," in Lefroy, *Memorials . . . of the Bermudas,* II, 706.

28. Note cases of George Smith and Richard Edwards. Rotation was largely by tribes. No fewer than eight persons were to have ten shares apiece in each tribe. Butler, *Historye of the Bermudaes,* pp. 105–106. Some common land, though little, was reserved within the tribes. Lot 19 of the Hamilton Tribe is a case in point. *An Introduction to the History of Bermuda,* ed. by Craven, pp. 29–30.

and a patient promoter of drainage schemes, received 40,000 acres out of a promised 95,000 acres as his share of the Bedford Level.[29]

Some of the surveys upon which the promoters based their hopes have survived. Sir William Dugdale in 1662 reproduced a typical large-scale survey of the allotment of shares in the newly recovered land. At Deeping Fen in Lincolnshire (Fig. 23), 20 miles southwest of Boston, the shares in each division varied from the 1,020 acres of the Queen to "F.V." 's 67-acre, 2-rod lot. Although the acreage in the allotments ran large, the survey gave every undertaker a share in each part of the drained terrain. Since in many cases the works of Vermuyden and other engineers aroused widespread resentment, the knowledge of the undertakers' land practices spread throughout the adjacent counties of Lincolnshire, Norfolk, and Cambridge. A few men like Sir William Brereton and Sir John Popham invested in both the drainage of the Fens and the settlement of New England; many more New England settlers in 1640 knew the Fens by their reputation in their own time as the most radical English merger of Puritan investment and land division.[30]

American settlement closely resembled the drainage of the Fens in some respects. In both by virtue of corporate enterprise vast new acreages were made available to investors free or virtually free of any conflicting title or encumbrance. Under such conditions the ladder of large lots, the rotation of persons by lottery, and the early division of land assets simply and directly answered all the needs of the investors, whatever hardship they might have wrought upon the Fen commoners or the American aborigines.

Most seventeenth-century Connecticut towns have prospered, and, unlike Fairfield, their suburban growth has submerged all traces of colonial planning. A nearly continuous belt of suburban houses now links Hartford, Farmington, and Wethersfield.[31] New London in 1940 was a city of over 30,000. New Haven's mushroom growth during the early eighteen forties and the prosperity of neighboring Milford, Branford, and Guilford after 1880 as summer resorts and minor manufacturing centers have made an almost continuous and fairly wide ribbon of settlement along Long Island Sound.[32] Stratford is now a suburb of Bridgeport, while Stamford's proximity

29. William Dugdale, *The History of Imbanking and Drayning of Divers Fenns and Marshes* (London, 1662), p. 413. H. C. Darby, *The Draining of the Fens* (Cambridge, 1940) gives an excellent account of the whole project.

30. Dugdale, *The History of Imbanking,* p. 194. See also the allotment of land by Vermuyden at Hatfield, *ibid.,* p. 142 and the facsimile of the Acerlebout MS which shows lot numbers, in George Dunston's *The Rivers of Axholme* (London, 1909), p. 32; and surveys of Lindesey and Axholme levels, in Dugdale's *History of Imbanking,* pp. 150, 419.

31. Connecticut State Highway Department, *General Highway Map of Hartford County,* No. 6, Sheets 3, 4, 1938.

32. The tracks of what is now the New York, New Haven & Hartford Railroad were the primary factor in this development. By 1852 the whole Long Island Sound route

to New York has made it grow to a city of over 60,000 inhabitants.[33] Somewhere in the backyards of these endless suburban developments the boundary walls of most seventeenth-century property divisions lie buried.

The Connecticut town as an experiment in land division had three stages: the nucleated village, the transitional town, and the colony town. The first, the nucleated village, was gradually abandoned by the proprietors of new towns at the end of the seventeenth century. Its cluster of small home lots, its multiple divisions, its ladder road system, its reservations of land for public purposes, the religious orthodoxy it expected of its proprietors all seemed anachronistic to the land speculators of the eighteenth century. They wanted a quick opening of the wilderness which would assure them an immediate return from their investment, and to this end they devised a new sort of town plan.

Fortunately for present purposes many eighteenth-century settlements have not prospered. Isolated from good shore and river routes by their sites, the towns of Litchfield, Tolland, and Windham counties have grown erratically, and for periods of their existence many have had declining populations.[34] Ample documentation for the design of many later towns still exists. Plans and surveys both in trial and final form shed light on the aims and decisions of their proprietors. Reinforcing such contemporary material are a few late eighteenth- and early nineteenth-century reconstructions of town allotments made within a generation of the founding of the town and based upon relatively complete land records. The thorough familiarity of such cartographers with local topography makes their work substantial.[35] (Fig. 30.)

In their fundamental mechanics these later town schemes changed but slightly from seventeenth-century models. Both illustrated the concept of equal division for equal contribution.[36] In both the location of any particular

---

from Stamford to Kingston was complete except the Groton-Stonington link, which was opened in 1858. Sidney Withington, *The First Twenty Years of Railroads in Connecticut* (New Haven, Yale University Press, 1935), map, p. 16. Connecticut Tercentenary Pamphlets, no. 45.

33. *State of Connecticut Register and Manual* (Hartford, 1947), p. 387.

34. Harwinton's population varied as follows: 1736, 100; 1737, 161; 1756, 250; 1774, 1,015; 1782, 1,215; 1790, 1,367; 1800, 1,481; 1810, 1,718; 1820, 1,500; 1830, 1,516; 1840, 1,201; 1850, 1,175. Richard M. Chipman, *History of Harwinton* (Hartford, Williams, Wiley & Turner, 1860), p. 97. Cornwall's population in 1790 was 1,475; in 1850, 2,041; in 1900, 1,175. United States Bureau of the Census, *A Century of Population Growth* (Washington, Government Printing Office, 1909), pp. 71–73.

35. Most spectacular of such plans is Eben North's map of Colebrook done as if the surveyor were flying on an oblique angle over the town. "A Plan of Colebrook" (1816), MS map, Connecticut State Library.

36. A wide variety of methods were used to measure this contribution. Ministers in general were rated high in all land allotments. Other persons were rated on the basis of their

holding was determined by the identity of the person by whom its lot was drawn. Thus in final analysis choice of site was based on chance.[37] In almost all seventeenth- and many eighteenth-century plans certain parcels of land were withheld for the use of the minister and his church. All of these factors shared in common were sufficient to create a basic similarity between colonial Connecticut towns of any period; thus they obscured the existing real differences and created the illusion of an unchanging style of town plan. Actually two elements were far from static, and their development accounts for such changes as appear in later Connecticut towns. On the one hand the size of the home lot was enlarged, and on the other hand the area included in the primary division grew and eventually came to embrace the whole town grant. Immediate speculation, not long-term value, dominated the proprietor's thinking.

The increase of the size of the home lot came gradually and did not at once destroy the tradition of seventeenth-century town planning. In the eastern part of the colony this tendency appeared as early as 1647, when the New London home lots were first recorded. Even at this early date lots of 6 acres were not uncommon.[38] Of the thirty-five original proprietors of Norwich in November, 1659, only one had a home lot of less than 6 acres. Though 6 acres would have seemed a large first allotment to the settlers of Fairfield or Wethersfield, the proprietors of Norwich assumed that it would be supplemented by other divisions of upland and meadow.[39] At New London these additional divisions of common and undivided land continued until the early eighteenth century, and as a result settlement spread from the town's first center, just as it did at Milford and many other towns of western Connecticut.[40]

In Windham County the home lot became large enough to affect later settlement. At New Roxbury, later Woodstock, the first planters in 1685–86 allotted themselves home lots which averaged 16 acres. Although the smallest building lot contained only 10, some were as large as 30 acres. In order to give each man fair treatment, the proprietors grouped the home lots on three favored sites, since at any one location good building land became quickly exhausted. Additional assignments of pasture and upland were made after this other allotment, but the size of the home lot at Woodstock sufficed to disperse settlement and isolate its three parts. Moreover, roads were provided not as part of the town plan but as makeshifts after lots had been laid

---

estate, size of family, contribution to the settlement, and so forth. Schenck, *History of Fairfield,* I, 69, 154.

37. Akagi, *Town Proprietors of the New England Colonies,* pp. 107–109.
38. Frances M. Caulkins, *History of New London, Connecticut,* p. 60.
39. Frances M. Caulkins, *History of Norwich, Connecticut* (Hartford, 1866), pp. 60–61.
40. Caulkins, *History of New London,* p. 263.

out. Only in that part of the town which the Roxbury proprietors sold did any semblance of the hitherto traditional Connecticut town plan obtain.[41]

Woodstock was by no means an exceptional town in Windham County. In 1686 Windham was surveyed and laid out to some fifteen proprietors. Each proprietor had a home lot of 31 acres and a nearby, although often not contiguous, pasture of 20 additional acres. Furthermore, within the township two other groups of home lots were granted, one at Ponde Town or Mansfield and the other at Willimantic, almost contemporaneously with the survey of Windham Center.[42]

Such a system had one disadvantage: inadequate communication. Dispersed home lots meant that many additional miles of roads had to be cut and maintained. With a small population these were generally neglected, and, as a result, each home lot became an isolated farm.

Such extensive first settlement resulted not in a series of well-integrated although separate towns splitting off from the parent town over a period of years but in a single discordant unit which spread over all the township's land. Congregations disputed endlessly over the choice of a minister or the location of the meetinghouse, and even after a vote minorities seldom abandoned their stand. Without stores, harbors, or main roads the location of the town's center became a devious religious question upon the solution of which each settler's attendance on the Sabbath depended. As towns grew, only direct, divine intervention could have kept the town's population center near its meetinghouse site, and this seldom happened.[43]

Lebanon in Windham County, which happens to be better documented than the average, had most of the difficulties that towns without nuclear settlement experienced in adapting radical Protestantism and Congregational church government to their dispersed condition. First settled about 1697 by New Londoners, the town immediately adopted a policy of large home lot grants of 42 acres and large secondary divisions. Most of these properties were located in two chief grants north and south of a line running

41. Larned, *History of Windham County,* I, 25–26, 27–29.

42. A recent reconstruction was done by E. Thompson, *A Map of Windham, Connecticut* (Windham, 1932). *Windham, Connecticut, a Memorial Volume of the Bi-centennial Celebration* (Hartford, New England Home Printing Company, 1893), p. 23.

43. A variety of ways were used to determine the town's center. Usually its geographical center on one axis was located on its main road or simply at the crossing of its two axes. Almost any system worked hardship through the winding nature of the roads and the consequent length of trips to and from the meetinghouse. These disputes became so frequent that the Assembly was forced to act. In 1731 and 1742 it enacted rules for the choosing of meetinghouse sites. These acts provided that a committee of the Assembly (1731) or the County Courts (1742) fix the site. Thereupon the new society must build or be taxed for the cost of the meeinghouse. No exceptions to these laws were allowed even in the case of mutual agreement. *P. R. Col. Conn.,* VII, 334–336; IX, 398–400.

about 3 miles southwest of Windham. About 1700 the settlers in both grants agreed that they would build a common meetinghouse somewhere on the center line of the two tracts, a highway 30 rods wide, laid out in 1697.[44] (Fig. 25.)

All went relatively smoothly until 1724, when repairs of the fabric became necessary. The violent objections of distant settlers made it clear that the old meetinghouse was no longer a convenient one and the matter was dropped. In 1727 Goshen was set off as a separate society to the south of Lebanon, a separation which by 1769 had caused the population center of the remaining First Society in Lebanon to move 1¾ miles to the north.[45] From 1727 on the northern society remained divided on the choice of a meetinghouse site until in 1804 a Superior Court ruling, confirmed by the Court of Errors, declared that the meetinghouse should remain on its traditional site. At a later time the village to the north was permitted to build a new meetinghouse for the northern inhabitants.[46] These ecclesiastical quarrels symbolize the total inadequacy of the Lebanon town plan: in one township the proprietors tried to combine the incongruous elements of large home lots, Congregational church government, and one ecclesiastical society for the township, and they failed. Lebanon's town plan resembled eighteenth-century work, but her institutions looked only to the seventeenth century.

At Lebanon the communal village had almost disappeared. (Fig. 25.) Only the form remained without reality, for the town's inhabitants who lived and quarreled on home lots scattered over a wide township. Roads did not lead directly to successive divisions but ran like erratic footpaths from house to house. A survey of the road system made in 1779 showed only a pattern of black lines without any more logic than the frozen tracks of animals in the snow. Before the introduction of the automobile such dispersion did not prove of value; only the Norwich road upon which the pre-Revolutionary prosperity of Lebanon was built still bears heavy traffic. Unlike the logical system of Fairfield most of the colonial roads are abandoned and no longer

44. F. S. Crofut, *Guide to the History and Historic Sites of Connecticut,* II, 605. Orlo D. Hine, *Early Lebanon* (Hartford, 1880), pp. 11, 71 ff. Hans Kurath, *Handbook of the Linguistic Geography of New England,* Plate I. J. W. Barber, *Connecticut Historical Collections,* p. 324. See Nathaniel Webb, "Plan of the First Society in Lebanon with the Highways & Buildings thereon with the Distance of each House from the Meeting House Surveyed 1772," MS map, Yale University Library.

45. *Ibid.* Also Nathaniel Webb, "A Plan of the Third Society in Lebanon called Goshen surveyed 1769–1770," MS map. Photostat in Connecticut Historical Society. Not to be confused with Goshen in Litchfield County.

46. This "Village" is still designated as the Village Hill on contemporary maps. United States Department of the Interior Geological Survey, *Willimantic* (1945), scale 1/31,680. Hine, *Early Lebanon,* p. 72.

even qualify as dirt or third-grade roads.[47] Property division, which at Lebanon overruled all other considerations, left the township for two centuries an amorphous area without adequate road and house-site planning.[48]

In November of 1705 some 160 veterans or their representatives met to consider the division of the Voluntown land awarded to them as soldiers of King Philip's and other colonial wars. Although originally the boundaries of their land had run some 6 miles to a side, by 1705 the Assembly reshaped it into a rectangle of 37 square miles, which was only a little over 2 miles broad at its base.[49] The spring of 1706 saw this division completed and all the lands given to their owners. The town plan as drawn on parchment and preserved today is noteworthy because for the first time in Connecticut all the town's land was laid out and allotted to the proprietors without any reserved common or lands left undivided for roads, meetinghouse, or parsonage. The "town" no longer existed except in name. The veterans had replaced it with 150 farms of nearly equal size.[50]

Settlers came slowly to Voluntown, perhaps because of the handicap of its land division, but its plan added one principle to Connecticut town-planning practice which the eighteenth-century colonists of the area seldom disregarded. For the first time the whole area of a township was laid out, divided, and allotted prior to settlement. The village and township plans were now a single unit, planned, surveyed, and assigned together. By a judicious distribution of lots it was still possible to create a nucleated village, but after 1715 the over-all concept of a single plan for the whole township area almost without exception replaced the earlier seventeenth-century series of opportunistic land allotments. In this respect the eighteenth-century town was closer to the early nineteenth-century townships of the familiar Northwest Ordinance than to its seventeenth-century predecessors.[51]

47. Compare Connecticut State-wide Highway Planning Survey, *County Traffic Flow Maps,* Fairfield No. 5 and New London No. 1. United States Department of the Interior Geological Survey, *Willimantic,* scale 1/31,680 (1945).

48. It should not be supposed that after 1700 communal villages of the traditional sort were no longer laid out. Durham's final plan as adopted by the legislature and the original grantees of land provided for a central village of homeplots and successive divisions of much of the remaining land. James Wadsworth, "Map of Durham," MS map (*ca.* 1790). A north-south street 8 rods wide was indicated as the main axis and on it homeplots were laid out—this as late as 1707. William C. Fowler, *History of Durham* (Hartford, 1866), pp. 20, 30.

49. Largely due to the settlement of Rhode Island boundary claims. E. D. Larned, *History of Windham County,* I, 240–242.

50. In 1718 there were 119 in 18 families. The town did not pay taxes until 1741. *P. R. Col. Conn.,* VIII, 429.

51. Voluntown Proprietors Map, MS map, Connecticut State Library. This map indicates nearly square allotments of 40 acres. Amelia C. Ford, *Colonial Precedents of Our National Land System as It Existed in 1800* (Madison, University of Wisconsin, 1910),

At the turn of the century opinion was still divided between the merits of a nucleated village like Fairfield and the virtue of an initial complete allotment of all the land within the town limits in large, separate, independent farms of the Lebanon variety.

Durham and Coventry represent the dilemma of Connecticut proprietors. Durham proprietors in 1707 planned a single albeit rather long highway 8 rods wide, upon which they placed all the home lots. The town prospered and other divisions of land followed quickly. (Fig. 26.)

The Coventry proprietors seem to have had sentiments similar to those held by the planners of Durham. A committee of four men who represented the legatees of Joshua, a Mohegan chief, first surveyed the property in 1708 but did not record their lot until 1714, when they felt that a settlement of the town should be made. The town that William Pitkin and the committee visualized had a single street, bounded by lots of moderate size running parallel to the south shore of Lake Wamgumbaug. It met at right angles a highway 20 rods wide which extended to the meetinghouse lot at the foot of the lake. From the other end of this lot a 10-rod highway ran southeast, parallel to the main street. This last street had lots laid off it on both sides; the millstream bounded those to the east, and the 20-rod highway those to the west. Lots were reserved adjacent to the meetinghouse site for the first minister, the parsonage, and the school. In 1708 the committee had planned a traditional communal village, and, had settlers immediately flocked to Coventry, it like Durham would have carried over seventeenth-century concepts into eighteenth-century Connecticut town-planning practice.[52]

But few persons came to settle in Coventry, and in 1715 a new lottery redivided all the town's land into large pieces, though still reserving the highways.[53] (Fig. 27.) Apparently the lot plan of 1715 attracted settlers; Josiah Conant, the surveyor, found in 1742 that the allotment of lands had dispersed settlement over a far wider area than had been intended in 1708 and that some seventy-six buildings stood on the seventy-eight lots drawn in the lottery of 1715.[54] Only in a few instances did more than one structure stand on each lot; as a result the town spread over a right triangle of land, the longest side of which measured 6⅓ miles.[55] (Fig. 28.) The town of South

---

pp. 38–42. The author regards such development of little importance and stresses the rectangular township outline as primary.

52. A committee of four men represented the legatees of the will of Joshua, a Mohegan chief. William Pitkin, Maj. Joseph Talcott, William Whiting, and Richard Lord composed the committee. MS map (no title), Connecticut Archives, Town Records, I.

53. Coventry Lots. MS map, Connecticut State Library, Connecticut Archives, Town and Lands, V, 45.

54. *Ibid.*

55. Coventry, 1742. MS map. Connecticut Archives, Town and Lands, VII, 162.

26. Durham in 1760

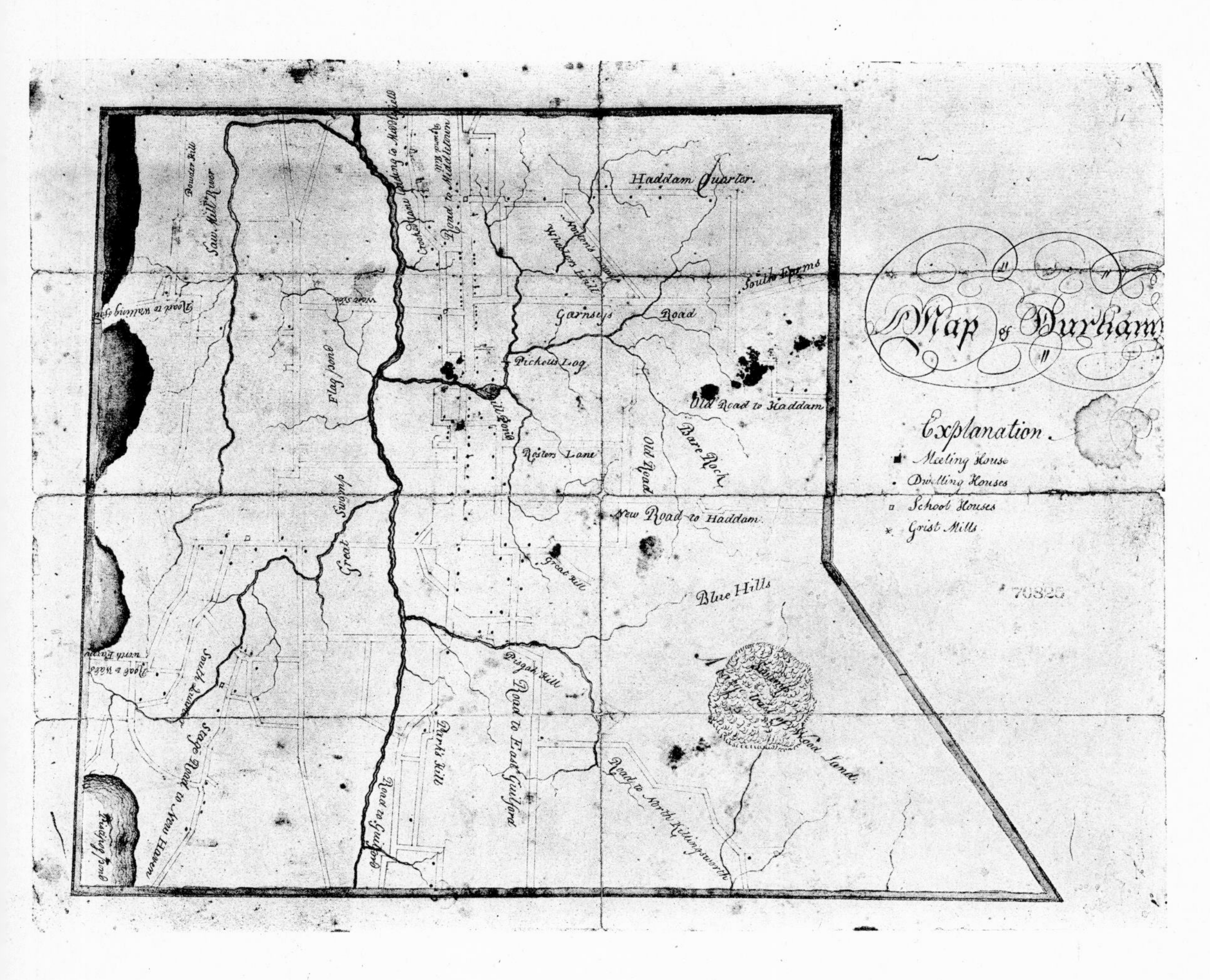

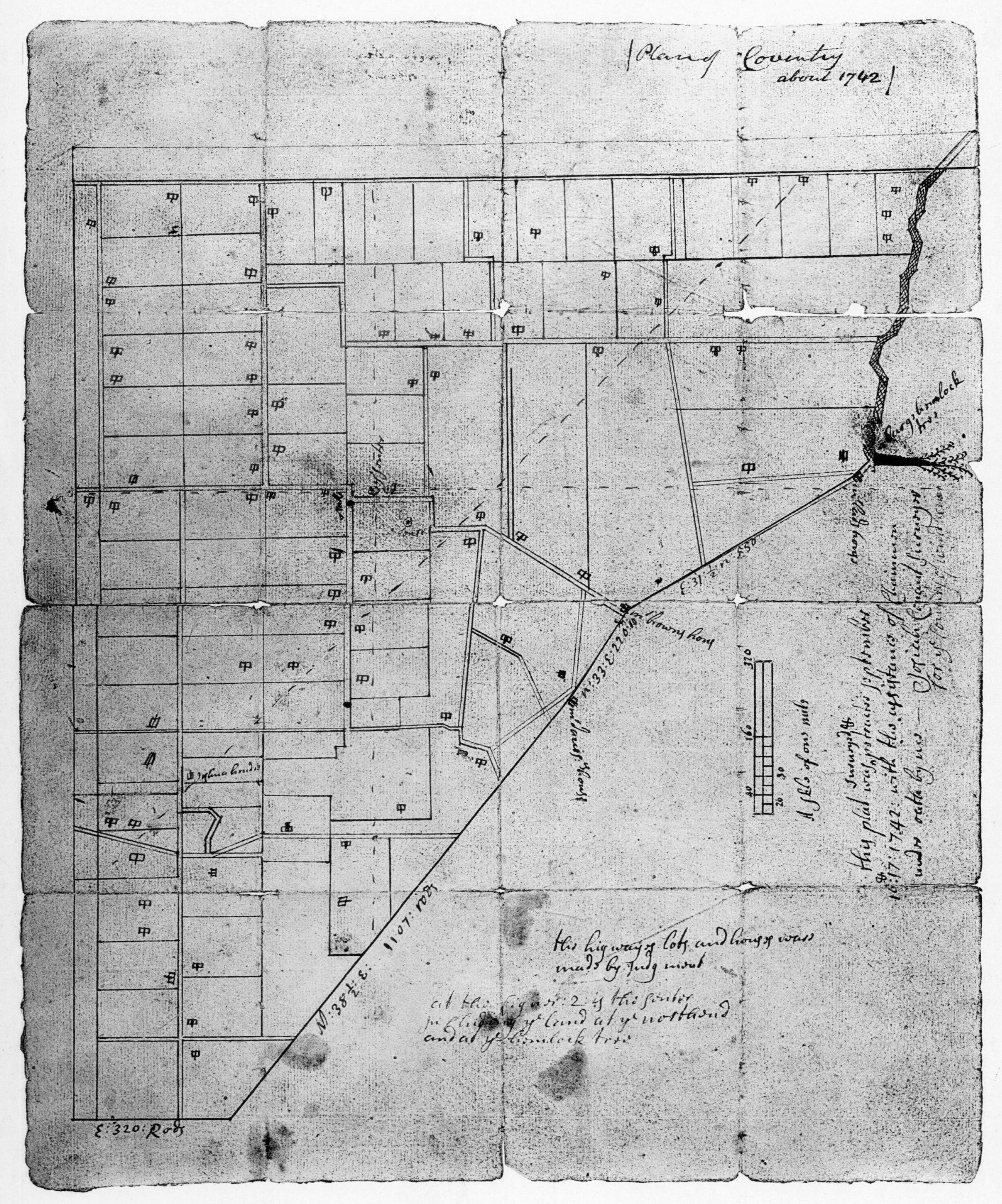

28. Coventry about 1742

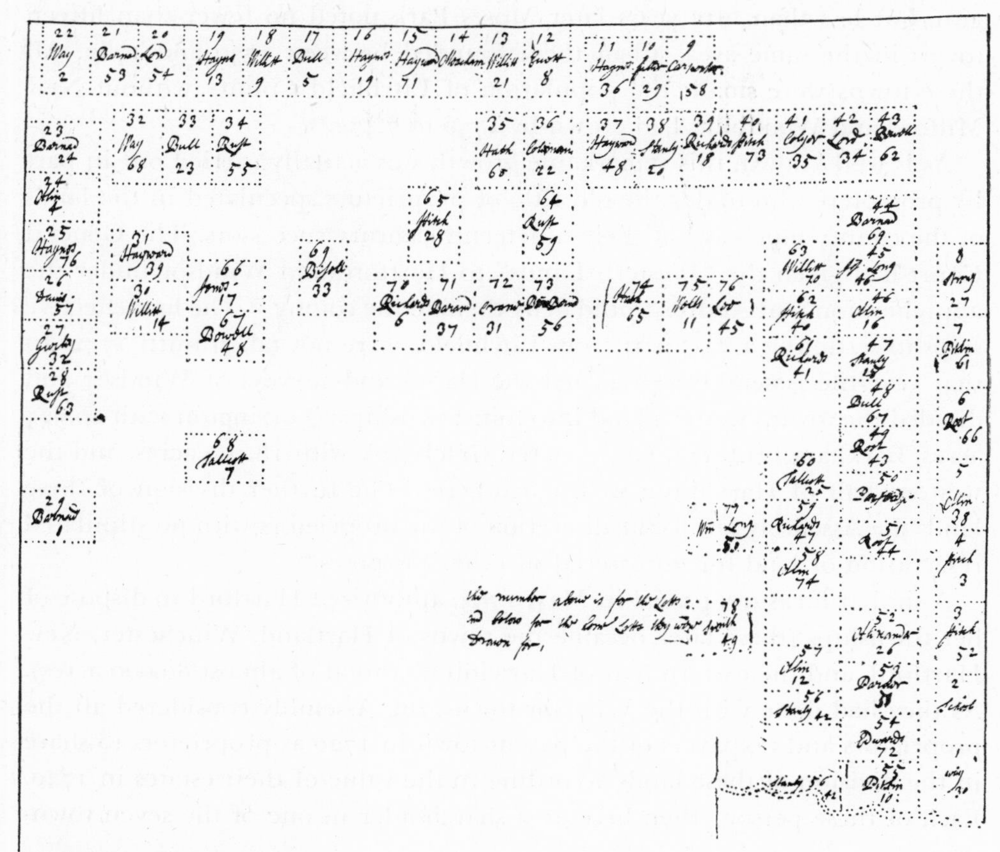

27. Coventry lots, 1715

Coventry today most effectively represents the intention of the earlier planners, while Coventry itself is an area of some 39 square miles with only slight, relatively recent concentrations of population at several town centers.[56]

On the whole, the settlement of Litchfield County is more significant in the history of town planning than the eastern part of the colony: a great many towns there had consistent and regular road plans; when they combined such plans with many of the traditions of the seventeenth century they created handsome and practical results. Hilly terrain and more easily cultivated lands available elsewhere in the colony had delayed settlement in the county.[57] In 1719 the first town north of Woodbury, Bantam (later Litchfield), was be-

56. Cf. O. W. Gray, *Atlas of Windham and Tolland County* (Hartford, 1869), pp. 28, 30, and United States Department of the Interior Geological Survey, *Coventry,* scale 1/31,860.

57. Almost the entire area has an elevation of over 500 feet. Rocky woodland was also a cause for delay in the exploitation of the area. Albert L. Olson, *Agricultural Economy and Population in Eighteenth-century Connecticut* (New Haven, Yale University Press, 1935), pp. 5–6. Connecticut Tercentenary Pamphlets, Vol. XL.

gun, but less than fifty years later Moses Park noted no fewer than fifteen towns in the same area, all of them founded between 1730 and 1760. All these towns were small; the population of Litchfield County without New Milford and Woodbury had grown by 1756 to 7,472.[58]

As is well known, this remarkable growth was actually carried out in part by promoters who under the old title of proprietors speculated in the lands of the county much as did their nineteenth-century successors. The General Court had given the "Western Lands" to Hartford and Windsor under the apprehension that Andros would deny them to the colony.[59] The first effective steps to settle the area, apart from Litchfield, were not taken until 1732. In that year the Assembly recognized the claims and surveys of Windsor and divided the town's western land into four townships: Torrington with 20,924 acres, Barkhamstead with 20,531 acres, Colebrook with 18,199 acres, and the western half of Harwinton with 9,650 acres. The further division of these lands the Assembly left to the discretion of the proprietors with no stipulated reservation of land for ministerial or other purposes.[60]

A similar measure, passed in May, 1753, authorized Hartford to dispose of her townships (these later became the towns of Hartland, Winchester, New Hartford, and the eastern half of Harwinton, a total of almost 80,000 acres). As they had done with the Windsor towns, the Assembly considered all the proprietors and taxpayers of the parent town in 1720 as proprietors to share in the division of these lands according to the value of their estates in 1720. Each of these persons then became a shareholder in one of the seven townships.[61]

The colony retained the remaining third of the county, the towns of Norfolk, Goshen, Canaan, Cornwall, and Kent (with the addition of Sharon and Salisbury after 1737), and offered them for sale in each of the five county seats. Sharon and Norfolk were auctioned in Hartford, Salisbury and Goshen in New Haven, Canaan in New London, Cornwall in Fairfield, and Kent in Windham. Each of the towns except Salisbury was divided into fifty-three rights, fifty of which were to sell at £56 apiece. Salisbury alone had twenty-

58. Moses Park, "Plan of the Colony of Connecticut" (1766), reproduced in D. Deming, *The Settlement of the Connecticut Towns* (New Haven, Yale University Press, 1935). Connecticut Tercentenary Pamphlets, Vol. VI. See also E. Thompson, *Maps of Connecticut before 1800,* pp. 34–35. *P.R. Col. Conn.,* X, 618. Litchfield County had almost no inhabitants in 1720; 11,827 in 1856; and 27,285 in 1774. *P.R. Col. Conn.,* X, 617–618; XIV, 490.

59. This land included all territory east of the Housatonic and west of the granted lands of Windsor and north of the granted lands of Fairfield. It is often forgotten that smaller grants were made at the same time to Kenilworth (probably Killingworth), Wethersfield, Middletown, and Farmington. *P.R. Col. Conn.,* III, 225.

60. *P.R. Col. Conn.,* VII, 388–390. A full and accurate record of lands dispersed was required.

61. *Ibid.,* pp. 445–449. Irving E. Manchester, *The History of Colebrook* (Winsted, Citizen Printing Company, 1935), p. 12.

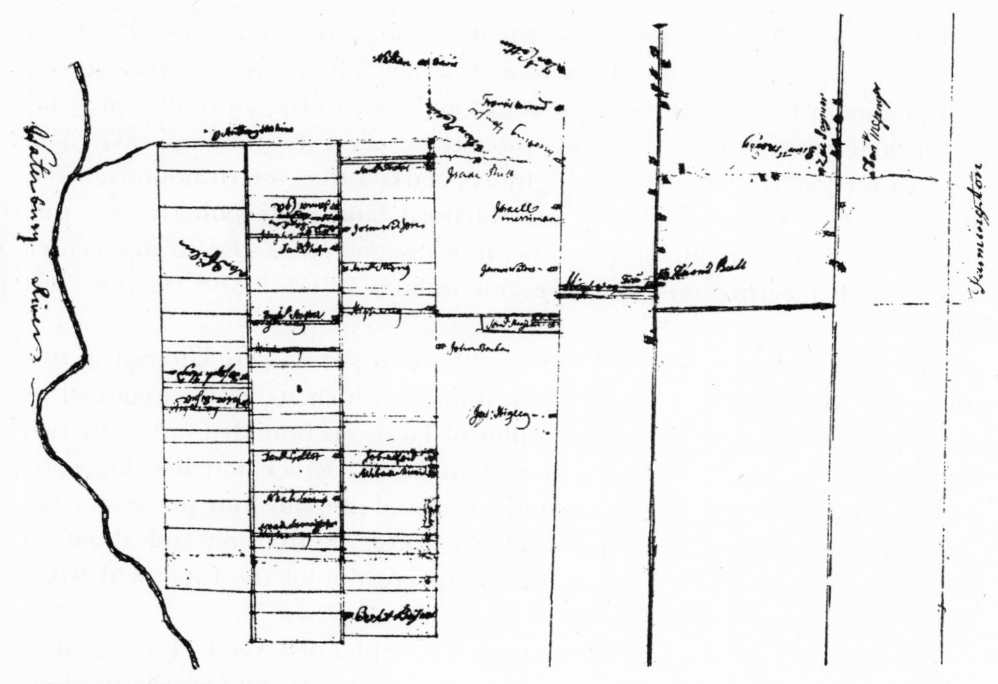

29. Survey of Harwinton in 1740

five rights only. In each town without exception three rights were reserved from sale for the first preacher, the parsonage, and the school.[62]

Because of the comparative tardy settlement upon these lands, the elaborate rules enacted by the Assembly to guide in their disposition, and, finally, the public nature of their disposal, it is easy to trace the developments of typical town plans. First settled of the western land towns was Harwinton, with a land history and town plan closely correlated. (Fig. 29.) Since Harwinton had been divided between Windsor and Hartford,[63] the proprietors held separate meetings in each of the two towns to allot their holdings. At Windsor some fifty-four persons or their heirs were qualified to participate in the divisions. Three meetings were held to complete the division of land; the first took place in Windsor in September, 1732, the second in December, 1733, and the third in 1738 after some twenty-four families had settled at Harwinton. The first two divisions were by far the most important, and within their limits most of the eighteenth-century inhabitants settled.[64] (Fig. 29.)

62. *P.R. Col. Conn.,* VIII, 134–136; VII, 458. The towns were at first numbered and in one case Township No. 1 incorrectly listed. Sharon and Salisbury were not on the first list.

63. *P.R. Col. Conn.,* VII, 390, 448.

64. Chipman, *History of Harwinton,* p. 104. Roger Newbury, "Harwinton 1st and 2nd Divisions, 1738 and 1740," MS map. Copy, Connecticut State Library. "Harwinton Houses, 1740," MS map, Connecticut Archives, Eccles., VII, 20.

The proprietors surveyed the town in a rough rectangle some 800 rods on its shortest (north) side. They took Litchfield Road as an east-west axis and planned three highways to the north and four to the south of that road. Occasional narrow east-west roads intersected these longer highways. The most easterly of the north-south highways marked the eastern bounds of the Windsor tract where it abutted on Hartford land. The point where this road crossed the Litchfield Road became designated as the town's center and the only meetinghouse site agreeable to both Windsor and Hartford settlers.[65]

Within this framework of roads some fifty-four shares were laid out in two successive rotations. Each share had a number which its holder retained in each of the two divisions, and each plot of land was bounded either by two highways or by the Waterbury (now Naugatuck) River and one highway. No land was reserved to the church or for school use, but four pieces of common land were retained on the southern tip of the division and about 80 acres of "undivided land" retained near the crossing of the Litchfield Road and the East Harwinton boundary.[66]

Although the fifty-four Windsor proprietors planned West Harwinton as a simple exercise in land allotment, their straight roads and orderly divisions proved of value. This western half of Harwinton has, since its beginning, contrasted sharply with the eastern half of the town in the rapidity of its settlement. The latter was laid out by forty Hartford proprietors with only two widely separated roads running north and south and only two cross highways in addition to the Litchfield Road. As a result settlement clung to these avenues and was slow to penetrate the interior. As late as 1859 some two thirds of the houses outside the center stood in the western part of the town.[67]

Surveyed early, West Harwinton was probably the best planned town in Litchfield County. Its proprietors provided an adequate and logical road system; the town adhered closely to its original property divisions, and its settlers maintained the roads as devised in 1732–33. Moreover, the immediate adoption of an arbitrary center for the town prevented endless and fruitless dispute within the Harwinton church society.

A sufficient number of town plans drawn by Windsor proprietors have survived or been reconstructed to indicate that Harwinton was by no means a unique venture. Indeed, the plans of Colebrook and Torrington bear a close resemblance to the Harwinton plan. At Colebrook the lots, laid out in eight

65. At the town's first meeting it was decided that "we agree thus that the Meeting House shall be set in the center line between the Proprietors of Hartford and Windsor" quoted by Chipman, *History of Harwinton*, p. 47.

66. Roger Newbury, "Harwinton," MS map. Copy, Connecticut State Library.

67. R. Clark, *Map of Litchfield County* (Philadelphia, 1859).

30. Eben North's plan of Colebrook, 1816

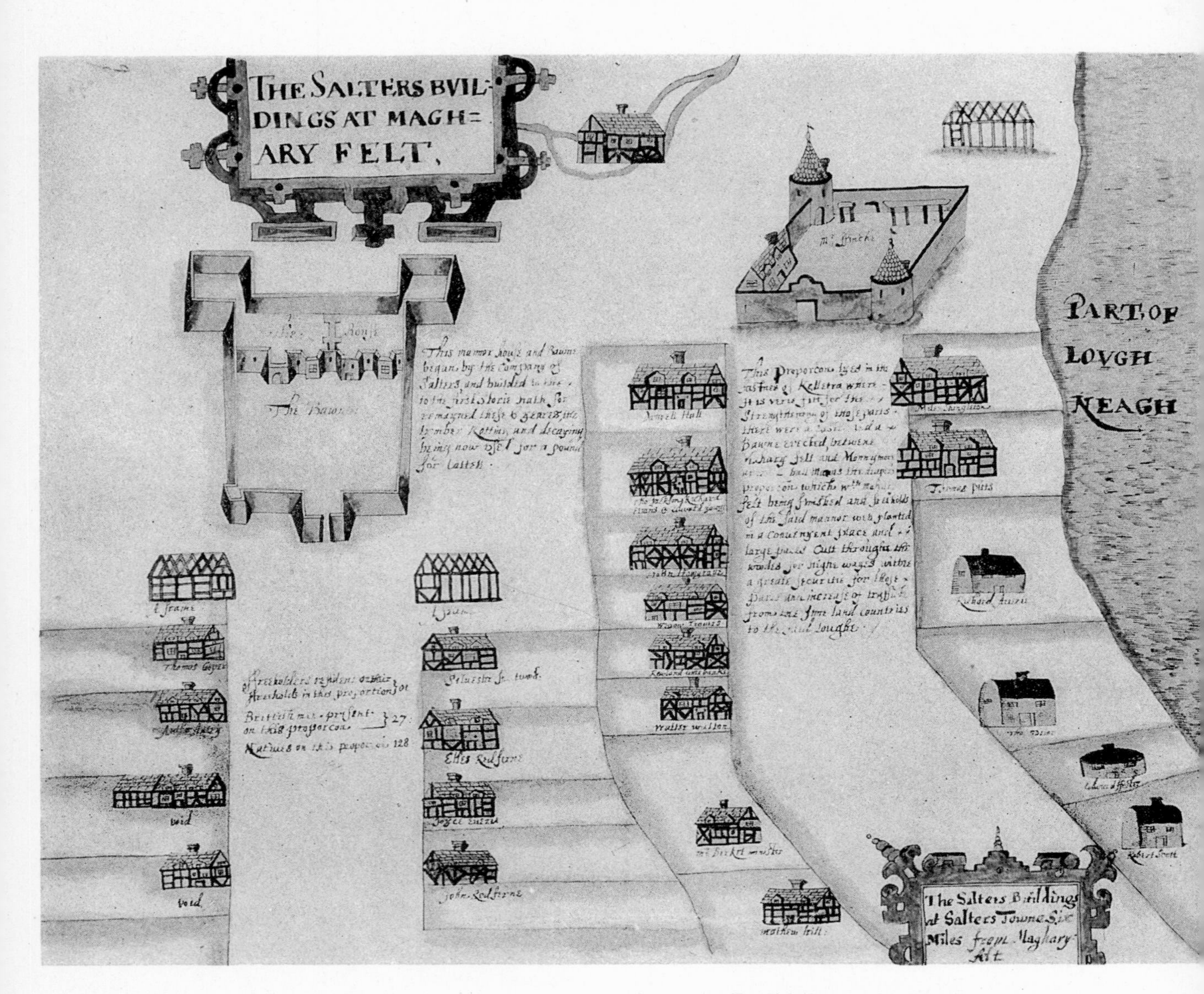

31. English houses in Ulster

tiers of 240-foot depth, just span the 4 miles between the Hartland and Norfolk boundaries. (Fig. 30.) Torrington was surveyed in tiers; each tier ran to a depth of ½ mile; so that the width of each lot in rods numerically equaled its area in acres. The 136 proprietors laid out twelve such tiers of lots running from east to west. The number of proprietors and their tax list in 1720 governed the property lines of the town. Chance determined the order in which they took up their allotments, as it had at Harwinton. They divided the land at Colebrook on a basis of 4¾ acres to the pound. A 10-rod highway separated each tier from its neighbor, and an occasional east-west highway 4 rods wide was laid out.[68] (Fig. 30.)

At Torrington the proprietors made specific provision for a meetinghouse and minister's lot. The Colebrook surveyor designated the land between lots Nos. 51 and 52 of the third tier as minister and parsonage lots, but the meetinghouse site was not selected until 1795 after a long and bitter controversy; and since the decision of the State Assembly at that time made the old parsonage lots of no value, they were sold. Because the original survey failed to provide a meetinghouse lot such as that at Harwinton, Colebrook had no center except the parade ground and parsonage lots for nearly fifty years.[69]

A further criticism often made of the towns laid down by the Hartford proprietors and those of Windsor was that generally they had no adequate provision to maintain and develop the town's highway system. The classification of all highway land as part of the proprietor's rights rather than as town or public land, aided in its sale and encroachment but not in its repair. Among all the Litchfield towns only Harwinton has more than a small portion of its original road system still in use.[70]

The towns laid out by the Hartford proprietors gave even greater consideration to the demands of the large property holders and less to necessities of settlement than the Windsor towns. In general their north-south highways were more widely separated than those of the Windsor towns, and often mountains prevented settlers traveling on the cross (west) highways that the proprietors had laid out. A local historian of Winchester attributed the slow rate of growth of that town in the nineteenth century in great part to an inadequate highway system. Certainly in Winchester no trace remained of

68. Eben North, "A Plan of Colebrook taken from the Original Survey" (1810–16), MS map, Connecticut State Library. Samuel Orcutt, *History of Torrington* (Albany, 1878), p. 10. Manchester, *History of Colebrook,* pp. 20 ff.

69. Orcutt, *History of Torrington,* p. 10. Manchester, *History of Colebrook,* pp. 59–67.

70. Most roads of the colonial period laid out by proprietors in Western Lands of Litchfield County run north and south and east and west. This can be readily checked by an examination of the United States Department of the Interior Geological Survey maps for Litchfield County.

over-all road planning in 1850, although colonial property lines were still distinct.[71]

The tiers of Winchester were six in number. The first five were each a mile wide, to which width provision for a 6-rod highway was added wherever it might best run. The last tier was to absorb the remaining land. Lots were to be laid out to each of the 106 proprietors at a rate of 3 acres per pound of their taxable estate in three successive divisions. Since the tiers were long and narrow and since each proprietor had some land in each of six tiers, only persons of large estates received single pieces of land wide enough to be farmed with profit. This method so subdivided the land of the small taxpayer that only 18 persons out of 106 proprietors had allotments in parcels of 100 acres or more.[72] Such conditions discouraged settlement by small landholders: they preferred to sell their rights in the new town to the remaining proprietors who, as large land speculators, then had to advertise for settlers.

Hartland, like Winchester, reflected its proprietors' interest exclusively. Between 1750 and 1782 eight tiers of plots were surveyed in four major divisions. The proprietors planned only a few scattered east-west highways and made no provision for north-south travel of any kind. Although they allotted land in the northeast corner of the township in small parcels, most of the communal centers are now in the southern half of the town and have grown independently of any plans made by the town's founders. Even on aerial photographs the traces of colonial roads and property divisions have virtually disappeared. Hartland proprietors laid out their town without regard for the people who would settle there, and as a result the town did not prosper.[73]

If Winchester and Hartland can be considered typical, it was not the custom of the Hartford proprietors to reserve land for schools or churches.[74] They allotted some 300 acres of Winchester land to the two resident clergymen of Hartford, but did not expect that they would settle in the new town. Indeed, the town did not for many years organize as an ecclesiastical society.

71. John Boyd, *Annals and Family Records of Winchester, Connecticut* (Hartford, 1873), pp. 18, 32. Clark, *Map of Litchfield County*. These cross highways are indicated by dotted lines, i.e., see above Lot 14 in the first tier. Eben North, "A Plan of Colebrook taken from the Original Survey," MS map, Connecticut State Library.

72. Boyd, *Annals . . . Winchester*, pp. 14–19.

73. One additional very small division was made in 1805. C. H. Tiffany, "Proprietors' Lots in the Town of Hartland," MS map. Copy, Connecticut State Library, 1912; United States Department of the Interior Geological Survey, *Granby* (1892, 1925), scale 1/62,500. Inadequate prior knowledge of the topography of the township or a deliberate concealment of such knowledge in order to sell the worst land first may also be indicated by the choice of settlement sites.

74. Tiffany, "Proprietors' Lots in the Town of Hartland," MS map.

Not until 1772 did the congregation install the first minister.[75] The Hartford towns in Litchfield County were essentially exploitative, planned not for the joint benefit of settler and proprietor but for the advantage of the proprietor alone. This handicap slowed their settlement and development.[76]

The Windsor and Hartford towns in Litchfield County had the last of the transitional plans which lay between the nucleated villages of the seventeenth century and the Assembly or colony towns of the eighteenth century. These transitional towns had represented the maximum possible advantage which the land could give to its proprietors. If the soil were rich and the proprietors had carefully tended their interests such schemes might prosper. Certainly their large home lots, their complete initial division, their refusal to condemn valuable land for roads and to reserve central acres for public or common purposes all encouraged speculation and quick sale. No doubt such unabashed concern for profit also discouraged many permanent settlers and heavily handicapped social life within the towns. In all probability the transitional towns deserved to be held suspect by the colonists.

The Assembly, it would appear, was well aware of the disadvantages of settlement on the land of the Windsor and Hartford proprietors and organized its third of Litchfield County far more in the interest of the actual settler. The basis for land ownership in the seven towns left to the colony's disposal was laid in 1733 when the legislature divided its land; east of the Housatonic River five townships were laid out, and on the land west of the river two townships were surveyed.[77]

Unlike the Hartford and Windsor settlements, the Assembly limited the number of shares in each town to fifty-three. Moreover, only fifty of these shares were to be sold: one share each was reserved for the use of the school, the first minister, and the support of the future ministry. No specific town plan was suggested nor were any details of sale given save that all "monies realized from the sale of these lands were to be divided among the already existing towns of the colony, for the use of the schools kept in said towns according to law." [78]

Four years later legislation made the terms of sale more specific and fixed the value of the shares in each township. Each town was to be sold in one of the existing county seats within the next year (1738) at a price ranging

75. Boyd, *Annals . . . Winchester,* pp. 19, 89.

76. United States Bureau of the Census, *Heads of Families,* p. 9.

77. Kent, Canaan, Cornwall, Goshen, Norfolk, to the east; Salisbury, Sharon, to the west of the Housatonic River. Sometime after 1743 the land west of the Housatonic and south of the Cornwall boundary was annexed to Kent.

78. *P.R. Col. Conn.,* VII, 457–458.

from £30 per right for Salisbury and Sharon to £60 per share for the Goshen and Canaan lands. The price per acre varied with the size of the township (some towns had more than 27,000 acres): at Cornwall a typical share purchased some 550 acres. Since Salisbury was divided into only twenty-five shares at £30 each, which included the three reserved rights, the price per acre in that town went even lower.[79]

Not only did the price of the land sink low in the colony's western townships, but the Assembly enacted further measures to hasten their settlement. Most important, it stipulated the qualifications of purchasers. Any persons wishing to buy a right might do so, but such purchasers were "obliged, within three years next, after their purchase, to build and finish a house of eighteen feet square and seven feet stud and to subdue and fence at least six acres of land in such town where he is a settler or hath fixed his agent." Failure to accomplish these tasks meant forfeiture of the purchaser's rights to land within the township. Moreover, the purchaser could continue to enjoy title to the property only if he built a house within two years and remained on his land "for the space of three successive years commencing after the two years aforesaid." A minimum of five years' occupancy was required for the final title. Since all purchases were bonded, any evasion of these stringent provisions was virtually impossible.[80] For its part, the Assembly attained at once a dual object: first of all it eliminated speculation of the kind familiar in Hartford and Windsor towns; in these colony towns, although some absenteeism was noted, conditions were never as bad as elsewhere in Litchfield County (it was not possible, as in some Hartford towns, for settlers to own only one third of the land, have none retained for their common benefit, and the remaining two thirds held for the proprietors who hoped to sell at a high profit); at the same time, the settlers on the land became its proprietors; ample provision was made for a church, and most of the conditions were stipulated which had created such communal towns as Branford and Guilford in the seventeenth century.[81]

The town plans which some of the seven colony towns evolved strikingly reflect their novel origin. None is more interesting in this respect than Cornwall. (Fig. 32.) Some thirty-eight persons bid at auction for the fifty rights. Of these thirty-eight persons, ten bought dual rights and one person held three shares.[82] Eight months after the public sale in September of 1738 at

79. *Ibid.*, VIII, 135–136. Edward C. Starr, *A History of Cornwall, Connecticut* (New Haven, Tuttle, Morehouse & Taylor, 1926), p. 35.

80. *P.R. Col. Conn.*, VIII, 135–137.

81. *Ibid.*, III, 203–204. Olson, *Agricultural Economy and Population in Eighteenth-century Connecticut*, pp. 24–25.

82. Theodore S. Gold, *Historical Records of the Town of Cornwall* (Hartford, 1877), pp. 10–11. Starr, *History of Cornwall*, p. 35.

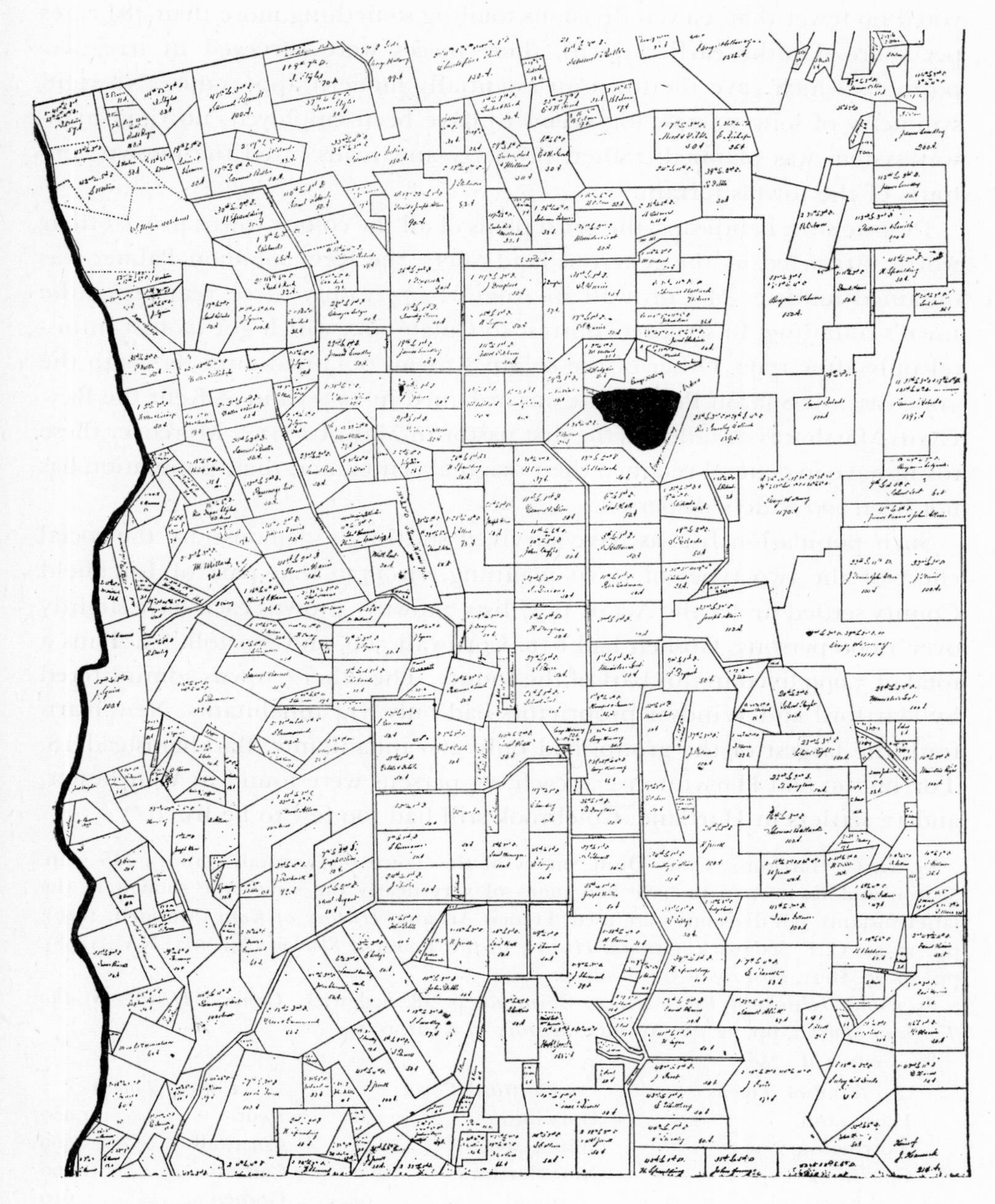

32. Reconstruction of Cornwall land grants

Fairfield the proprietors voted two divisions of 50 acres to each proprietor. These lands they laid off in approximately square pieces on either side of a north-south highway.[83] At the foot of this town street they surveyed the

83. Gold, *Historical Records . . . Cornwall,* p. 9.

minister's plot and those of the church and school. Thereafter the proprietors voted no fewer than eleven divisions totaling something more than 484 acres per share. Unlike earlier towns, these pieces were surveyed in irregular polygons which gave the town an essentially modern appearance. No rigid symmetry of long narrow lots seems to have been employed; no rigid highway system was planned; rather, property and roads fitted the known contours of the town's terrain.[84]

Despite such handicaps, the town plans of all the colony towns proved their worth. Attracted by the generous land offers, the Rev. Solomon Palmer was ordained minister of Cornwall in August, 1741, only three years after the town's founding, in striking contrast to Colebrook, which got its first minister only after 1790. Other of the colony's towns obtained ministers with the same ease. At Sharon Peter Pratt was ordained in 1740, and at Kent the Rev. Cyrus Marsh was installed as the first pastor in May of 1741.[85] Moreover these towns have in general retained their original center, and their population has not been too widely dispersed.

Such population lists as have survived startlingly demonstrate the social effect of the two types of town planning. In 1756 that part of Litchfield County settled under the Act of 1737 lists 7 towns: 4 towns each have slightly over 1,000 persons; Goshen had 610, Cornwall 500, and Norfolk 84. Thus a total of 5,099 lived in this part of the county. The other 7 towns administered by Hartford and Windsor proprietors had only 814 inhabitants. New Hartford, the largest of the group, had only 260 inhabitants, Barkhamstead 18, Torrington and Harwinton 250 each; 24 persons were found in Winchester, and 12 settlers in Hartland. Colebrook still had too few to be listed.[86]

84. G. C. Harrison, "Crazy Quilt Survey of the Town of Cornwall" (1894), MS map. Sharon and Kent seem to have had plans of very nearly the same type though in the latter instance ten divisions were used. Francis Atwater, *History of Kent* (Meriden, 1897), pp. 17–22. C. F. Sedgwick, *General History of the Town of Sharon* (Amenia, N.Y., 1898), pp. 26–27. Starr, *History of Cornwall,* p. 35.

85. Gold, *Historical Records . . . Cornwall,* p. 48. Sedgwick, *General History of the Town of Sharon,* pp. 32, 42. Atwater, *History of Kent,* p. 55.

86. *Census of 1756*

Windsor Towns		*Hartford Towns*		*Colony Towns*	
Harwinton	250	Harwinton	250	Kent	1,000
Torrington	250	Winchester	24	Cornwall	500
Colebrook	—	New Hartford	260	Canaan	1,100
Barkhamstead	18	Hartland	12	Goshen	610
				Norfolk	84
				Salisbury	1,100
				Sharon	1,198

The *total* population of Harwinton was 250 including both East and West Harwinton. No separate figures could be found.

Total 7 Proprietor Towns 814.

Total 7 Assembly Towns 5,592 plus 7 Negroes.

P.R. Col. Conn., X, 617–618.

Although the Windsor and Hartford towns grew rapidly from 1750 to 1784, their overall gain in population was not greater than that of the colony towns. At the last colonial census in 1774 the 7 colony towns had a total population of 10,378, the 7 Windsor and Hartford towns had only 4,070. Three colony towns each had a population of just short of 2,000 whites: Kent 1,922; Salisbury 1,936; and Sharon 1,986. The largest proprietor town was Harwinton with a population of 1,015, which slightly exceeded only 2 of the colony towns. All in all, settlers went to those towns with the fairest land systems and the best plans.[87]

The colony towns did manage to merge the public concern and corporate sense of the seventeenth century with the speculative zeal of the eighteenth. Like the transitional towns they had dispersed home lots and early complete allotments of land which would attract the ambitious settler, but from the first Connecticut towns they had copied the planned road system and reserved public lands which had proved so necessary for the social life of the colonists. At the same time that the speculator tended to be discouraged by the restrictions which threatened his title if he could not make a genuine, permanent settlement upon each parcel of his land, the agricultural colonist was attracted to settle and farm his land, assured of an enlightened public policy.

Land division in Connecticut was essentially practical and embodied few aesthetic considerations. Nonetheless, the original plans of Coventry and Harwinton had the same scrupulous regard for equal property rights, direct routes, and square divisions as the seating plan of a meetinghouse, but, although the demands of time and the needs of economic geography have wrought havoc with the roads of colonial townships and their property divisions, the proprietors' surveys remain to tell what might have been had Connecticut soil been more fertile and her wilderness kinder.

87. *Census of 1774*

Windsor Towns		*Hartford Towns*		*Colony Towns*	
Harwinton	1,015	Harwinton	1,015	Kent	1,922
Torrington	843	Winchester	327	Cornwall	957
Colebrook	150	New Hartford	985	Canaan	1,573
Barkhamstead	250	Hartland	500	Goshen	1,098
				Norfolk	966
				Salisbury	1,936
				Sharon	1,986

Total 7 Proprietor Towns 4,070 white, 33 Negroes.

Total 7 Assembly Towns 10,438 white, 239 Negroes.

Harwinton's total population listed twice as no division is possible between East and West Harwinton.

P.R. Col. Conn., XIV, 483–492.

IV. The Country Builder

The colonial townscape gave the appearance of unity not because it was designed by a single architect but because the way in which the colonists built their homes and meetinghouses grew out of their experience in the land division and rural life of seventeenth-century England. Fortunately for them this experience proved sufficient to survive the wilderness, and within the property lines they had sketched the settlers were soon cutting and hewing timbers to erect their buildings.

As he turned from the long straight lines of his land division to the task of building a home, rural customs still guided the colonist. In the matter of actual construction he felt bound by the body of traditional practices which were part of the common knowledge of seventeenth-century Englishmen. One reason for the wide distribution of such knowledge was the novelty of the professional architect in 1630. The term had first appeared in 1563 on the title page of *The First & Chief Groundes of Architecture* which described its author, John Shute, as "paynter and archytect." Since little is known about Shute and no buildings have been authoritatively attributed to him, it is small wonder he felt it necessary to tell his readers that "that whiche is of the grekes called Architectonica, and of the latines Architectura I think not altogether unfite nor unaptlie by me termed in Englishe, the arte and trade to rayse up and make edifices and buildings." [1]

For his successors English society turned to men with virtues far more concrete than the knowledge of "Musix, Geometry and Philosophy" which Shute extolled as the prerequisites of the "Perfect Architecte." What was needed was a man who could make a visual image of a house which might easily be changed or altered before building began. One class of English

1. *Dictionary of National Biography*. Martin S. Briggs, *The Architect in History* (Oxford, Clarendon Press, 1927), pp. 2–4, 240–243, 255–256. John Shute, *The First & Chief Groundes of Architecture* (London, 1563; republished Country Life, Ltd., 1912), Preface.

society had such skills, and it is to that class that John Thorpe, the first English Renaissance architect, belongs. His life span is uncertain but he worked between 1570 and 1618 as surveyor and architect. Like Robert Smythson, his contemporary, he left many measured drawings of which only a few were his own design, the remainder, like the sketches of the Sole of Kirk which he and John Norden, the author of *The Surveyors Dialogue,* drew in 1616, were simply accurate surveys or measured drawings of houses already in existence.

In the untutored countryside of Stuart England intelligent surveyors like Norden and Thorpe often found themselves required to sketch a new wing for a manor house in order to retain its owner's favor. The "upright" and "plots" which these surveyors designed cannot now be distinguished from the measured drawings of houses then standing which the surveyors only recorded. Fantasy, design, and reproduction mingled indiscriminately within the handsome red and gold borders of the estate survey; gilt dividers encompass the same traditional scale near one corner of both field maps and mansion façades.

In 1618 the first popular description of the use of scales, ruler, and dividers as well as of theodolite and plane table appeared in Norden's *Surveyors Dialogue,* published in London. Earlier editions of the same work had mentioned these subjects but the 1618 dialogue between the surveyor and his questioner first clarified the art of measured drawings.[2]

Norden did not, however, state in so many words how a science of land measurement might be applied to architecture. This was reserved for Vincent Wing, who in *Geodates Practices or the Art of Surveying* (London, 1664) advertised his work as "very usefull for Surveyors Architects and Engineers." The volume did not belie its title page; the whole of Book Seven describes the measurement of building surfaces and volumes by the application of geometric principles. Wing explored the detail of his problem and even made the complex calculations necessary to find the surface area of chimney stacks.

In one important aspect the *Geodates Practices* differed from architects' and builders' plan books of the eighteenth and nineteenth century: the elevations and plans chosen for illustration seem abstract and unrealistic, like sketches in a geometry exercise book. By 1668 Stephen Primatt had remedied the impracticality of such architectural works. His *City and Country Purchaser and Builder* devoted only some ten pages at the end of the volume to land measurement and virtually all the remaining text to the value of land, the prices of artisans' work, and detailed house plans of both city houses and country seats. Even as late as 1678 Joseph Moxon recognized

2. John Norden, *Surueyors Dialogue,* pp. 126–136, 148. His scale is illustrated.

the closeness of the two professions of surveyor and architect when he described the necessity for accurate plans, elevations, and detail drawings and then wrote: "The drawing of Draughts is most commonly the work of a Surveyor." [3]

The long life of John Thorpe embodied in its course the changes which came over the building profession in the late sixteenth and early seventeenth centuries. Descendant of two generations of masons, he was born about 1563. At the age of nineteen he went to London and remained there as one of the clerks in the Queen's Works until 1601. By 1604 he had an independent practice as a surveyor for the government. About 1612 he adopted a coat of arms and began to enjoy his wealth and prestige. In his middle age he probably turned from surveying to the building and leasing of his own tenements; and he finally died, almost forgotten, in his late nineties. Although buildings by his hand were of little or no importance, he is the first-known Englishman to bring to domestic architecture both the skill of the mason and the vision of the surveyor, a blend which has seldom since been lost.[4]

The drawings of such men as Thorpe and Smythson indicate quite clearly the precise point at which the most advanced architects had arrived at the time of migration to America. Obviously if floor plans were such a novelty in the design of great houses, the humble cottage builder could not have read them, much less drawn them. He carried to his site not the ingenious plans of a contemporary but the ancient proportions of a long tradition.[5]

---

3. "It is usual and also very convenient for any person before he begins to Erect a Building to have Designs or Draughts drawn upon Paper or Vellum . . . in which . . . the ground plot or Ichonography of each floor or story is delineated and represented and also the fashion and form of each front . . . are to be shown in draught or designs of the Uprights or Orthographyer." Joseph Moxon, *Mechanick Exercises,* p. 252. That the making of such a plot was the business of the surveyor is indicated by Moxon, *ibid.,* p. 253.

4. John Summerson, "John Thorpe and the Thorpes of Kingscliffe," *Architectural Review,* CVI (November, 1949), 291–300, gives an exhaustive account of Thorpe. The classification of the Thorpe drawings into those which were done as surveys of existing structures and those which are plans for the building of new houses is a principal problem facing the student working with this material. John A. Gotch, *Early Renaissance Architecture in England* (London, B. T. Batsford, 1914), chap. xi. The conclusions reached by Gotch in relation to the Thorpe drawings are generally accepted. The Smithson (Smythson) collection of ninety-nine sheets has even more detailed drawings, including large-scale interior elevations, details of carpentry work, and so forth. Briggs, *The Architect in History,* pp. 244–249. G. Fordham, "Some Surveys and Maps of the Elizabethan Period," *Geographical Journal,* LXXI (1928), 59.

5. How rapidly this situation changed may be apprehended from reading Joseph Moxon, who described the duties of a carpenter in laying out his "ground plot." "With this rod (the ten-foot rod) they measure the length and breadth of the *ground plot* into feet and if there be odd inches they measure them with the *two-foot rule.* Their measure they note down upon a piece of paper and having considered the situation of the sites, east, west,

The scale by which Englishmen both in the colonies and in England made their measurements had little relation to abstract conceptions of space applied by Thorpe. Many generations had certainly known the foot as their basic unit of measure, and it had been specifically defined on a number of occasions. English long measure began with the "grain of barley." "Three barley-corns round and dry make an inch" was set as a standard in 1324.

Moreover, the inch was the twelfth part of a foot. The antiquity of the inch did not, however, insure the accuracy of English measurement, and a standard of measure in the modern sense could not be said to exist in England until after 1758 when laws were drawn up to enforce accurate and fair standards.[6]

This is not to say that the Winchester bushel or royal yardstick did not exist before 1758. On the contrary, the Winchester bushel had been the official standard from 1496, and from its dimensions builders could deduce a standard inch since its size was fixed at 8 inches deep and 18½ inches wide; it was round in shape with a plain bottom and 2,150.42 cubic inches in volume.[7] Divergence in the application of units of measure had arisen not through a lack of a royal standard but by virtue of the fact that Parliament made no provision until after 1758 to oversee the various standards deposited in towns and boroughs throughout England. Without supervision these local standards had become inaccurate and could no longer nicely check measurement within their vicinity. As a result minor alterations of the inch were to be found in every English county.[8] Such local variations in all probability account for most of the fractional parts found in modern measured drawings of seventeenth-century buildings both in England and in Connecticut.

These fractional measurements do not obscure the existence of two fundamental ratios of proportions which governed most minor building in

---

north, and south they draw on paper their several sites accordingly by a small scale, either elected or else made for that purpose." Moxon, *Mechanick Exercises,* p. 126.

6. House of Commons, *Report from the Committee . . . to Enquire into the Original Standards of Weights and Measures* (London, 1759), pp. 14–15. An earlier, somewhat longer report was issued in 1758. Patrick Kelly, *Metrology; or an Exposition of Weights and Measures* (London, 1816), pp. 59–60, 86. Hubert Hall and Frieda J. Nicholas, "Select Tracts and Table Books Relating to English Weights and Measures, 1100–1742," Camden Society, *Miscellany,* XV (London, Camden Society, 1929), 28. House of Commons, *First Report of the Commissioners,* 1819 (London, 1823), p. 9.

7. Joseph Moxon, *Mathematicks Made Easie: or, a Mathematical Dictionary* (London, 1692), pp. 182–183. P. Kelly, *Metrology,* pp. 36–37, 72–73, 89; and *Universal Cambist* (London, 1811), I, 260–261. Whether the present custom of maintaining a separate yardstick was instituted before 1758 is uncertain. *New English Dictionary.* House of Commons, *Report from the Committee,* 1758, pp. 14–17. *First Report of the Commissioners,* 1819, p. 10.

8. House of Commons, *Report from the Committee,* 1758, pp. 54–62. Slight variations from the strict inch as we know it today were found even in printed works.

the seventeenth century. The first was based upon the English "bay," a unit of about 16 feet with which almost all cruck, or "bent-tree," construction was laid out.[9] In this method of building pairs of bent trees or crucks met at the roof peak, framing the side walls and roof in one piece, and each additional pair of crucks formed a new bay. By such means buildings were often extended along the axis of their ridgepole to a length of several bays.[10]

Neither structural considerations nor domestic utility fixed the 16-foot dimensions of the bay between crucks. The widespread use of a single dimension originated in two agricultural customs. Sixteen feet barely housed two team of oxen (8 feet for each pair). Sidney O. Addy found numerous examples of the 16-foot bay in barns and buildings, part of whose space sheltered animals, and concluded that these buildings set a style which made construction by bays a natural tradition.[11] Moreover, 16 feet, or four standing stalls, was also the width needed for a four-ox plow team to stand abreast in a field and from which the 16½-foot perch and the modern rod derived as units of land measurement.[12] John Norden's description of the units of measurement used by his surveyor in 1618 stresses the importance of 16½ feet: "160 perches to one acre, 80 perches to half an acre, 40 perches to one roode which is ¼ of an acre, ten daies worke to a roode, foure perches to a daies worke, 16 foot and a half to a perche." [13] Despite the value of the sixteen-foot measure in country building and land survey, it was little known in urban London.

Within the narrow confines of the city an inflexible rule of proportions that developed from divisors and multiples of sixteen would have been impractical. In order to utilize each foot of valuable property Stephen Primatt in 1668 had recommended party walls and illustrated his text with house plans that closely followed the outline of the available property.[14] Joseph Moxon, whose excellent *Mechanick Exercises* describes most construction methods of the seventeenth century, speaks of the tools of a Londoner when he writes, "Carpenters use a *ten-foot rod* for expedition, which is a Rod about an inch square, and ten foot long; being divided into ten equal parts, each part containing one foot, and is divided into 24 equal parts, and their subdivisions." [15] For shorter dimensions carpenters used neither the modern

9. Sidney O. Addy, *Evolution of the English House* (London, Macmillan Company, 1898), pp. 70–74.

10. Charles F. Innocent, *The Development of English Building Construction* (Cambridge, University Press, 1916), p. 17, Figs. 16, 21, 27.

11. Addy, *Evolution of the English House,* pp. 65–68.

12. *Ibid.,* pp. 68–69.

13. John Norden, *Surueyors Dialogue,* pp. 148–149.

14. Stephen Primatt, *The City and Country Purchaser and Builder* (London, 1667), pp. 106, 122.

15. Moxon, *Mechanick Exercises,* p. 126.

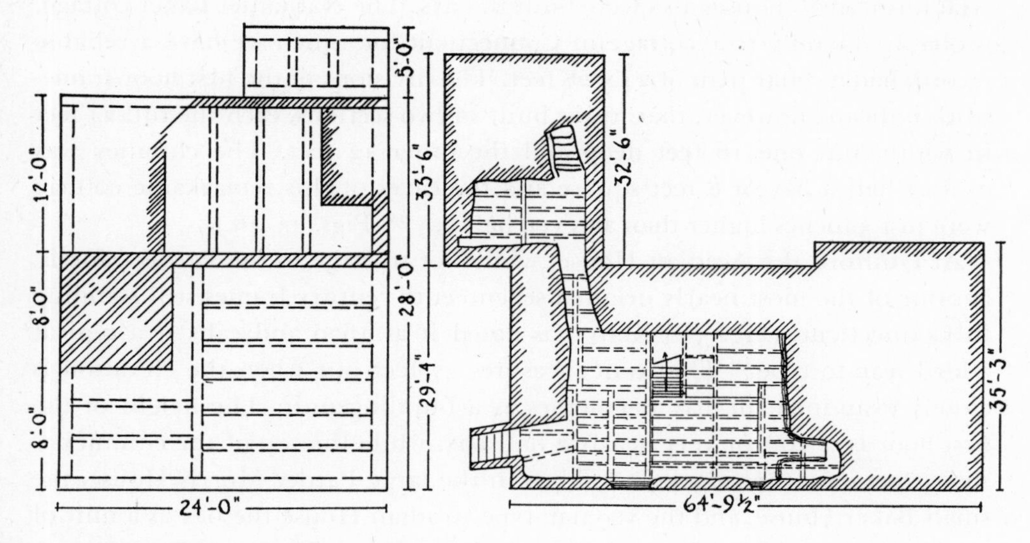

33. Ground floor of Nathaniel Baker Cottage and cellar of Pardee-Morris House

yardstick nor the one-foot rule, but a two-foot measure, which was perhaps more familiar to the rude countryman as one eighth of a bay and easier for him to use during his apprenticeship in the city.[16]

When the Englishman came to Connecticut he did not forget the traditional proportions of his countryside. An examination of the measured drawings of some ten houses generally acknowledged (though not documented) to be seventeenth-century structures indicates in all but two instances the use of the bay and in almost every case many dimensions divisible evenly or nearly evenly by eight, a half bay.[17] For example, the Pardee-Morris House foundation is 64′ 9½″ x 35′ 3″ (or about 4 bays x 2 bays). The west section is 33′ 6″ on one side, 32′ 1″ on the other. The distance between the great stone chimneys is 48′ 6″ or 3 bays; the first floor is 7′ 11″ high, and, various multiples of eight are repeated throughout the building.[18] (Fig. 33.)

Although the Pardee-Morris House is one of the colony's largest in its

16. *Ibid.*, p. 103. Inches "are marked upon the flat and smooth sides of the *Rule*, and numbered . . . so that every inch is divided into eight equal parts; and these inches are numbered from one end of the *Rule* to the other; which commonly is in all 24 Inches: which is a Two-Foot *Rule*." The two-foot folding rule is of course still commonly used by carpenters today.

17. Two exceptions are the Painter House in West Haven and the Buttery Mill, Silvermine. All the dimensions of the former run large except one 8 x 12 foot bedroom (½ x ¾ bay). The Mill is by its location possibly later than the seventeenth century. Historic American Buildings Survey, *Connecticut*, Nos. 62, 63, hereafter referred to as H.A.B.S.

18. H.A.B.S., *Connecticut*, No. 27.

final form, small houses also were built in bays. The Nathaniel Baker cottage, probably the only true cottage in Connecticut for which we have a reliable record, had a cellar plan of 24 x 28 feet. The divisions of the first floor framework indicate, however, that it was built in two sections, each the full 24 feet in width, but one 16 feet deep and the other 12 feet. The chimney was exactly half a bay or 8 feet square and the eaves of this remarkable cottage were just 3 inches higher than an even half bay.[19] (Figs. 33, 48.)

At Guilford the Acadian House, while not so large as the Pardee-Morris, has one of the most nearly original seventeenth-century frames still standing in Connecticut. (Fig. 53.) Kelly has dated it as 1670 and calls it a typical added lean-to type.[20] The front measures 37 feet but when the elevation is closely examined the bay re-emerges as a building unit. The height of the first floor is 7′ 10″, or very nearly a half bay, while the top of the chimney is just 4 feet over the ridgepole.[21] Thus in the large Pardee-Morris House, the small Baker House, and the yeoman-type Acadian House the bay as a unit of measurement was clearly used, though the point of departure for measurement varied in each case.[22] (Figs. 33, 48, 53.)

Only the masonry of the chimney seems to have been largely independent of measurement by bays. Probably laid after the foundation walls but before the house frame was assembled, the colonial chimney was a new development of an old architectural form. Masonry construction seldom appeared in minor English building until the end of the sixteenth century when the elaborate chimney, as will be seen, became a symbol of considerable wealth.[23] Occupying at its base perhaps 20 per cent of the basement and the first floor, the chimney tapered to a square about 4 feet to a side at the roofline. In Connecticut it was laid almost always of field stone at the base and brick from the second-story level to its top, a practice which preserved externally, at least, the appearance of the English brick chimney.[24]

Unlike the chimney, the masonry of the house foundation, either as a low wall or as a cellar, actually bore the weight of the house timbers.[25] Built

19. H.A.B.S., *Connecticut,* No. 41.

20. J. Frederick Kelly, *Early Domestic Architecture of Connecticut,* pp. 9–10.

21. H.A.B.S., *Connecticut,* No. 5.

22. For other seventeenth-century examples, see Comfort Starr House, Guilford; Col. Stephen Ford House, Milford; and the Painter House, West Haven. H.A.B.S., *Connecticut,* No. 14, pp. 62, 82.

23. See Chapter V. Authorities seem agreed on this point. Martin S. Briggs, *A Short History of the Building Crafts* (Oxford, Clarendon Press, 1925), pp. 95 ff. Innocent, *Development of English Building Construction,* pp. 33, 119. Even the stone chimney was an innovation for most houses at the end of the sixteenth century. Addy, *Evolution of the English House,* pp. 112–115.

24. Kelly, *Domestic Architecture,* pp. 72–80.

25. Moxon indicates that cellars were known but were by no means the rule at the end of the seventeenth century. Moxon, *Mechanick Exercises,* p. 254.

generally of field stone, the walls were laid either dry or with oyster-shell mortar.[26] Their purpose was clearly not to provide a cellar in the modern sense, although upon occasion this was necessary in order to lay a large foundation for the chimney stack. Rather, these foundations gave a dead level base for the construction of a framed house. Collapse might occur only if a foundation wall gave way and the frame had to carry the weight of the house cantilevered over space. The frame was so interlocked that it almost never failed in a sideways direction. Thus one finds that the foundation walls of houses on a hill took full advantage of the slope but leveled at the height of the first floor plates. Moreover, most foundation walls stood some inches higher in the seventeenth and eighteenth centuries than they now do, as witnessed by the drawings of Barber.[27] (Fig. 51b.) Time and the earthworm have built the soil of their sites up to give them a ground-hugging look which their builders never intended. They were satisfied if their foundations were level, immune to hard frosts, and carried the house timbers well above the damp ground.[28]

When he had laid his footing the seventeenth-century builder began his house frame. Unlike his grandfather he did not have to search for bent trees to support the ridgepole. Scarcity of timber, low height, the difficulty of protecting walls from weather and of adding to them had hastened the decline of cruck architecture. In its place Tudor Englishmen had introduced post-and-truss construction, which saved oak and filled the needs of large or small houses.[29]

Between the years 1550 and 1660 the cost of timber had gradually become the controlling factor in all wood building, large or small. The price of English oak in the early seventeenth century was midway between the very low prices of the sixteenth century and the prohibitive prices of the late seventeenth and early eighteenth centuries. The value of a load of timber had risen from 16*s.* 6¾*d.* in 1592 to 17*s.* 3½*d.* by 1633. The highest average price recorded was 21*s.* 2*d.* in the ten years between 1603 and 1612. On the other hand, by 1692 the price of a load had risen to 39*s.* 2*d.* and cut plank rose even more sharply between 1583 and 1702 from 11*s.* 2¼*d.* to 40*s.* per hundred feet. How very rapid this rise was may be gauged from the fact that bricks rose

26. Kelly, *Domestic Architecture,* p. 70.

27. J. Barber, *Connecticut Historical Collections,* pp. 215, 237 *passim.* Almost all his cuts illustrate this point.

28. Moxon's advice on foundation walls, though designed for the bricklayer, is interesting. Moxon, *Mechanick Exercises,* pp. 254 ff. It was the decline of cruck and the rise of post-and-truss construction that made the foundation so important. Crucks were carried on individual stone piers. Innocent, *Development of Building Construction,* Figs. 16, 19, 20, shows such piers.

29. Innocent, *Development of Building Construction,* pp. 35, 62–63, 76. Addy, *Evolution of the English House,* pp. 17 ff.

only from 12*s.* 6¾*d.* to 19*s.* 33*d.* per thousand during that same period.[30]

In 1633 the rise in timber prices caused misgiving, but it had not yet made oak too valuable for domestic construction. Robert Reyce described Suffolk in 1618 and indicated that a new sort of "compacting, uniting, coupling, framing and building with almost half the timber that was wont to be used and far stronger" had been devised.[31] Englishmen hoped that by the importation of continental woods English oak might be saved for the frames of houses and ships. Henry Best, writing in 1641, gave his approval to fir deal boards from Norway as siding for barns. He pointed out that the light weight of such cured wood lowered the cost of transportation and that sixty green oak boards had almost broken a wain in coming only 5 miles.[32] Prices in 1630 had forced the economical use of oak and the abandonment of crucks but had not gone so high as to make the householder build brick or stone walls.

Post-and-truss frames met the needs of the times. A four-room house two stories high, perhaps 2½ bays long and 1 bay wide, took only thirty pieces of large-size oak (roughly 12 x 15 inches in cross section). For the roof and incidental braces smaller pieces were used even by the best workmen.[33]

Moreover, such frames had great strength. Shiplike, they not only carried the whole weight of the building but were also mortised and tenoned together so that they withstood any horizontal thrust of the elements. Assembled so as to resist maximum stress at the ridgepole, which it was felt carried the roof, they had reserves of strength unknown in modern wood architecture.[34] Colonial frames carried the side walls, they were not themselves walls. Even today hurricane winds can do little damage to these sturdy land galleons.[35]

These ideas have little to do with present-day balloon carpentry. In the latter the roof weighs a small portion of its seventeenth-century thatch predecessor; its outward thrust is well understood and distributed along the whole length of the building. Moreover, no attempt is made in the frame of the lower stories to withstand any but a vertical thrust. Timbers are nailed

30. James E. T. Rogers, *History of Agriculture and Prices in England,* VI, 544–546.

31. Robert Reyce, *Suffolk in the Seventeenth Century* [MS title: "The Breviary of Suffolk . . . 1618"] (London, J. Murray, 1902), p. 51.

32. Henry Best, *Rural Economy in Yorkshire in 1641,* Surtees Society, Publications, XXXIII, 111–112. The fact that Henry Best always compares seasoned fir to green oak indicates that seasoned oak was scarce and that it was often used green.

33. A breakdown of the uses of these pieces leaves 22 horizontal pieces, including girts, summer beams, and sills, and 8 vertical posts—with a lean-to 38 pieces. Norman M. Isham and Albert F. Brown, *Early Connecticut Houses* (Providence, Preston and Rounds Company, 1900), p. 214. Moxon, *Mechanick Exercises,* pp. 138–139.

34. Innocent, *Development of English Building Construction,* p. 31.

35. Addy notes the close relationship between the vocabularies of medieval shipbuilding and architecture. Addy, *Evolution of the English House,* pp. 27–29.

34. Cutting and hewing timbers

so that their deepest dimension runs parallel to the direction of vertical thrust. At any other angle the timbers are weak and even pliable. Many small 2 x 2 and 2 x 4-inch members collectively support the load which the widely spaced 12 x 15-inch posts and horizontal timbers of the seventeenth century supported.[36]

There is no evidence that the seventeenth-century house frame was changed in any of its essentials by English colonists. In Ulster as in Connecticut once the foundation was laid the builder began the work of cutting and hewing the timbers for the lower story. (Fig. 31.) In seventeenth-century England the rapid growth of the leather industry and its need for bark in tanning had forced the cutting of timber in the spring when the bark might easily be stripped from the trunks.[37] (Fig. 34.) Once cut, English oak was seldom seasoned since seasoning was unsure and very slow.[38] Instead, the joists,

36. Giedion regards the balloon frame as a relatively abrupt departure in building techniques. Sigfried Giedion, *Space, Time and Architecture* (Cambridge, Harvard University Press, 1946), pp. 269–272. Posts, however, had been thinning and had been put closer together throughout the nineteenth century.

37. Gervase Markham, *Cheape and Good Husbandry* (London, 1631), p. 154. This practice lowered the quality of the timber. George Sturt, *The Wheelwright's Shop* (Cambridge, University Press, 1923), p. 28.

38. For excellent contemporary discussions of seasoning, see William Salmon, *The London and Country Builder's Vade Mecum* (London, 1745), frontispiece, and *The Builder's Guide* (London, 1736), frontispiece and p. 47. Seasoning of English oak was too slow and

plates, and posts were hewn from the oak logs on the spot and hauled to the building site by a timber cart which might be drawn by men for a short distance or fitted with shafts and pulled by a team on longer trips.[39] In Connecticut construction with green timber sometimes had disastrous results, and Isham believes that Connecticut timber was seasoned when time permitted.[40]

Contrary to what one might expect, Connecticut timbers in general ran a little smaller than those considered suitable in England. The size of English and Connecticut timbers governed their place in the house frame. Thus ground sills, the equivalent of the English ground plates, were in Connecticut generally about 8 inches square regardless of their length. Moxon indicates that in England the better sort of house should have plates as large as 10 x 6 inches.[41] For Connecticut posts 9 x 8 inches or the standard 8 x 8-inch posts seem to have been the general rule.[42] The ideal English post 13 x 12 inches mentioned by Moxon was considerably bigger than its American contemporary.[43] Horizontal girts and summer beams were deeper in England in order that they might resist the outward thrust of the thatch roof. In Connecticut girts ran as large as 9 x 12 inches and summer beams 1 foot deep in each direction were often found. The summers described by Moxon are slightly larger than Connecticut timbers in one dimension but not in cross section. He indicated that girders (girts) or summers 10 to 15 feet long should measure 11 x 8 inches but if 18 to 21 feet long, 14 x 10 inches.[44] In general Connecticut timbers seem to have been a little smaller in cross section than English timbers of the period, but in both areas they became larger in the upper stories of the building.[45]

---

unsure a process to be much used. Innocent, *Development of English Building Construction,* p. 101. Moxon describes seasoning of boards only. *Mechanick Exercises,* p. 149. *Dictionary of the Architectural Publication Society* agrees. One divergent opinion is to be found. Sir Balthazar Gerbier, *Counsel and Advice to All Builders* (London, 1684), p. 43, insists on seasoning but does not mention oak specifically.

39. Moxon, *Mechanick Exercises,* Plate IX, shows a seventeenth-century timber cart. For a modern cart virtually unchanged in design, see Walter Rose, *The Village Carpenter* (Cambridge, University Press, 1937), p. 80.

40. Isham and Brown, *Early Connecticut Houses,* pp. 201–202. *Records of the Colony and Plantation of New Haven* (1638–84), ed. by Charles J. Hoadly (Hartford, 1857), I, pp. 37–38, 54–56. Eight inches square was the largest post mentioned.

41. Moxon, *Mechanick Exercises,* pp. 138–139.

42. This refers to the dimension of the post at the first floor level. Isham and Brown, *Early Connecticut Houses,* pp. 212–219. *P.R. Col. New Haven,* I, pp. 37–38, 54–56. Some larger posts are mentioned in Kelly, *Domestic Architecture,* p. 31.

43. Moxon, *Mechanick Exercises,* p. 138.

44. *Ibid.* Isham and Brown, *Early Connecticut Houses,* pp. 219, 228. Kelly, *Domestic Architecture,* pp. 36–37. Innocent, *Development of English Building Construction,* p. 76.

45. The slightly lighter frame in Connecticut may have been adopted because shingles were used which made a lighter roof than thatch or slate.

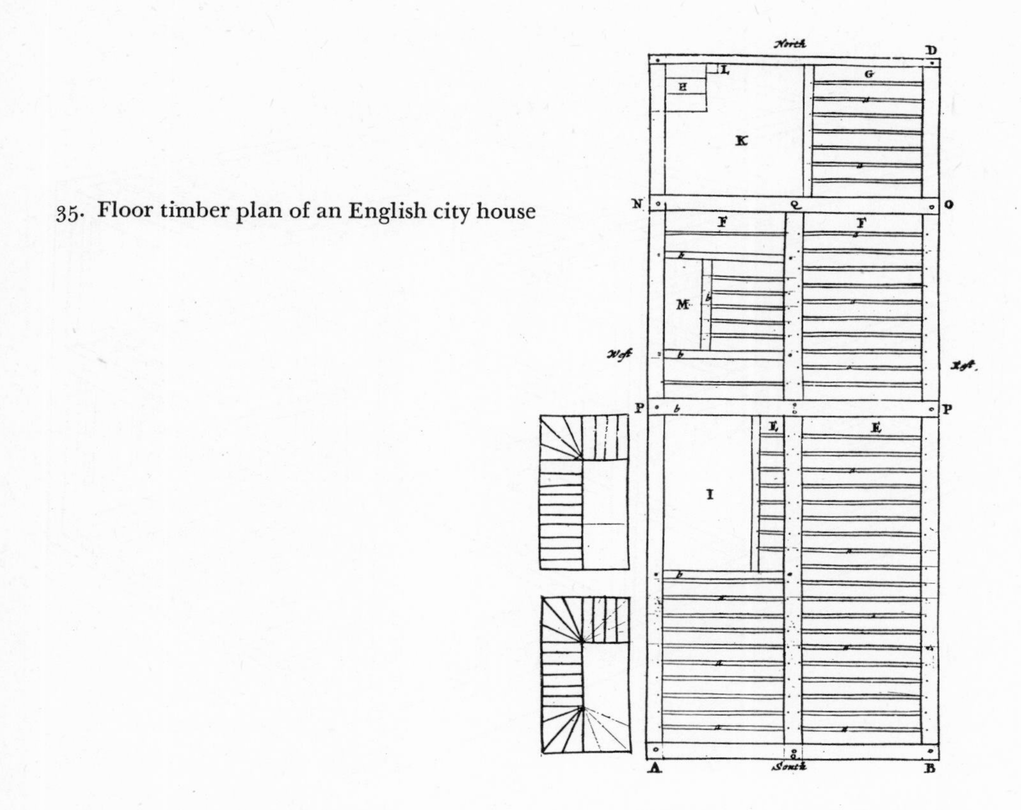

35. Floor timber plan of an English city house

Both English and Connecticut house frames, which grew sturdier as one climbed up until the foot square summers of the second story were reached, reflected the concept that the task of the frame was to carry the weight of the roof and ridgepole, not just to resist their outward thrust. Mortise-and-tenon joints alone prevented the collapse of the immense weight of oak.

This general (and correct) feeling that the roof thrust became greater at the top of the frame also manifests itself in the way in which the frame was erected. Here Connecticut settlers closely followed English precedent. The ground plates or sills were laid loosely on the foundation until the girders, which were large crossbeams lying parallel to the chimney or entrance way, were let into the plates.[46] Next the joists, which were about 10 feet long, 3 inches thick, and 6 to 8 inches deep, were let into the plates and the floor frame was complete. All the frame members of the floor were then pinned together and made firm. (Fig. 35.)

To erect a second floor the carpenter first let the vertical posts into the ground sills or plates and supported them temporarily with boards to hold

46. Moxon clearly indicates that summer beams were used for the first floor frame in England but such was not the case in Connecticut. Moxon, *Mechanick Exercises,* pp. 132–133. Kelly, *Domestic Architecture,* pp. 65–68.

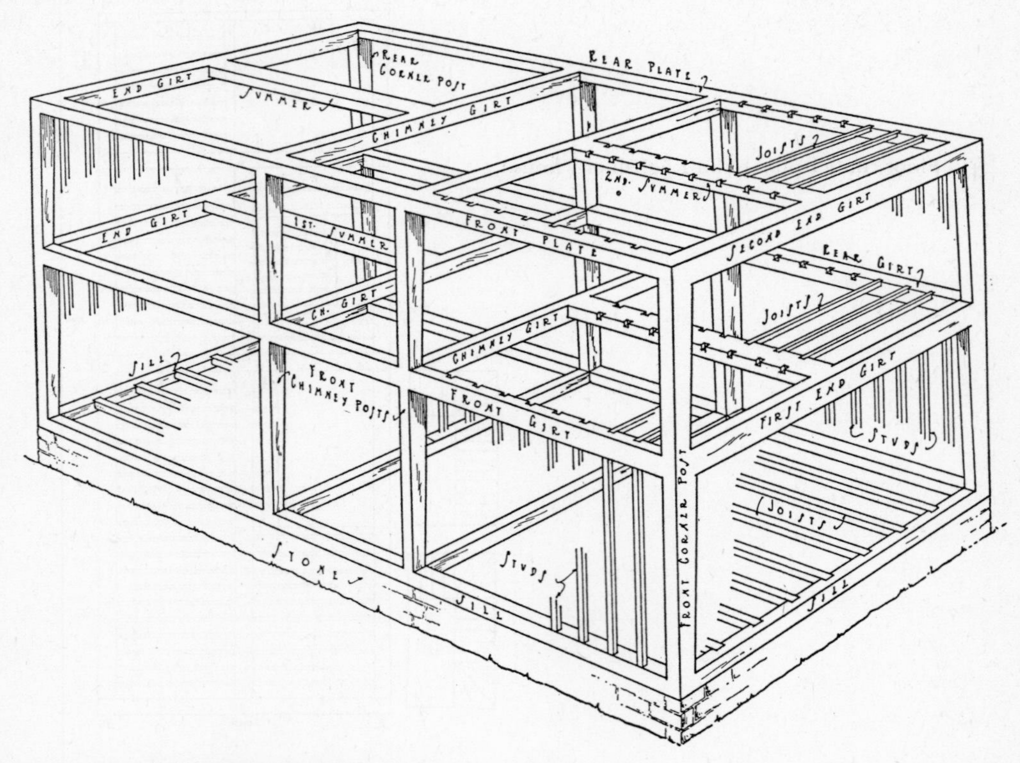

36. Typical Connecticut house frame

them erect. The posts were raised opposite to the direction of their growth, butt upward. This served the builders' purpose, since it was believed that the life of the timber was prolonged if erected in a direction opposite to the sap flow. Probably more important was the fact that the broad butt of the tree gave a wider surface for the heavy top floor plates and a stronger joint to withstand the outward thrust of the roof.[47] Moreover, the second floor in Connecticut always had the summer beam, a long central stick of great strength, which provided the principal binder of the whole frame. (Fig. 36.)

The second floor, after having been fitted on the ground, was raised piecemeal to fit the principal posts and there fastened by round oaken pins driven in auger holes which had been lined up with a hookpin. Quarters and braces were then fitted vertically between the two floors and these carried the wall filling. This procedure was repeated for each floor of the house until the attic floor was framed. Finally rafters were let into the raising piece or uppermost horizontal timber which ran parallel to the frame's longest axis.[48] These rafters

47. Innocent, *English Building Construction,* p. 75. Isham and Brown, *Early Connecticut Houses,* Plates I–IV.

48. Moxon, *Mechanick Exercises,* p. 141, plate p. 145. See also Kelly, *Domestic Architecture,* pp. 21 ff.; Isham and Brown, *Early Connecticut Houses,* pp. 210 ff.

met in the ridge piece and carried the roof. (Fig. 37.) Structurally the house was complete. All that now remained was to make its strong frame weather-tight and to lay the floor boarding. (Fig. 31.)

In the filling of the wide interstices of the frame the seventeenth century showed a slow trend away from tradition. In England before 1600 most house wall construction came from contemporary agricultural practice. Daub thrown upon sticks set closely and sprung into the timbers of the frame was the oldest method of wall building. The wattle, as the framework for the clay daub was called, closely resembled the woven hurdles so familiar in illuminated manuscripts and still to be found in isolated English country districts. In both field and house walls stiff vertical sticks were closely interwoven with flexible green thorn branches and the whole daubed over.[49] Henry Best illustrates how close the two processes were when he describes the roofing of a mud field wall for which his thatcher took roofing thatch from an old house and mortar of "dirte mire." The straw and mortar were laid in alternate layers with the thatch projecting over the wall's edge to give it protection from rain. The final step was to cover the top thatch with mortar to hold it firm.[50]

The seventeenth century saw the beginning of the separation of architectural and farming practices. By 1630 brick was often used and sometimes covered with plaster.[51] Hand-riven laths often replaced the traditional thorns and sticks. The plaster which was applied by the dauber had a wide variety of roughing and in some cases displayed carving in relief. The wall filling became chiefly a matter of what the land itself offered in each county. East Norfolk, eastern Suffolk, Essex, Middlesex, and North Kent combined clay with timber construction. Hampshire, Surrey, Sussex, and South Kent used clay, flint, and chalk with post-and-truss frames. Yorkshire, Lincolnshire, Cheshire, Stafford, Shropshire, Worcester, and Hereford used sandstone and timber.[52]

None of these wall fillings could withstand dampness for a long period of time. Constant repair work was necessary or the walls had to be protected from the rain. A wide variety of devices secured this end.[53] The most elaborate was the overhang, an upper story which projected out over the lower walls of a house and thereby deflected rain from them. Because it gave additional

49. Innocent, *Development of English Building Construction,* p. 129.

50. Best, *Rural Economy in Yorkshire,* pp. 146–147.

51. Royal Commission on the Ancient and Historical Monuments and Constructions of England, *An Inventory of Middlesex, the Historical Monuments in, . . .* Plate XXX. Hereafter referred to as Roy. Com. Hist. Mon. (with county name).

52. Sidney R. Jones, *The Village Homes of England* (London, "The Studio," Ltd., 1912), p. 5. Harry Batsford and Charles Fry, *The English Cottage* (London, B. T. Batsford, Ltd., 1939), p. 81.

53. Innocent, *Development of English Building Construction,* p. 136.

space in the upper story it had been found very useful in crowded London.[54] With the general increase in demand for two-story yeoman houses in country districts at the end of the sixteenth century the overhang became a symbol of its owner's London contacts and also served the function of protecting the interstices of the frame.

Such projecting stories, though almost impossible in masonry construction, were easily framed in wood. If an overhang or jetty were to be built the carpenter simply laid upon his frame at the second-story level heavier joists and a summer beam, both a little longer than the room directly below. Then on their ends which projected perhaps 24 inches over the lower story he laid a wall plate and into this set the vertical posts for the next story.[55]

In London the overhang was generally found on the gable end facing the street.[56] When it became a rural fashion, the overhang still extended over the entrance but now the main doorway was on the long side of the building and gable-end projections were narrower or omitted altogether.[57]

Naturally the countrymen who settled Connecticut imported the rural overhang. Framed overhangs extending along the whole front of the house parallel to the ridgepole were well known, but were rarely used on the gable end of Connecticut houses.[58]

This does not mean however that Connecticut houses were built without any projecting gables. The hewn overhang was widely used until the late eighteenth century. These overhangs—far more modest than the framed jetties—were made by hewing a corner post so that its butt end, placed uppermost, was nearly vertical on the inside but projected over the outside wall some few inches. In this way it carried the horizontal timbers of the upper story a short distance out over the wall surface of the first story and created a narrow overhang.[59]

This hewn overhang was clearly a colonial simplification of the elaborate

54. W. Hollar, "London from Bankside," engraving.

55. Descriptions of the overhang or jetty's frame are common for both English and American architecture. Isham and Brown, *Early Connecticut Houses,* pp. 231–243. Kelly, *Domestic Architecture,* chap. v; A. H. Powell, "Country Building and Handicraft in Ancient Cottages and Farmhouses," *Studio Yearbook of Decorative Art* (London, 1920), pp. 40–41. There is need for a serious analysis of the later English frame building. Such works as Claude J. W. Messent's *Old Cottages and Farm-houses of Norfolk* (Norwich, H. W. Hunt, 1928) and Basil Oliver's *The Cottages of England* (London, B. T. Batsford, Ltd., 1929) dovetail and repeat earlier studies.

56. Hollar, "London from Bankside," engraving.

57. Roy. Com. Hist. Mon., *Herefordshire,* Plates XXXI, XXVI (Wigmore No. 8), *Essex,* IV, 52.

58. See Edwin Whitefield, *The Homes of Our Forefathers* (Boston, 1882). Whitman and Porter houses in Farmington. Kelly, *Domestic Architecture,* p. 62.

59. Kelly, *Domestic Architecture,* p. 26. Isham and Brown, *Early Connecticut Houses,* pp. 237–238.

spur or corner post which Reginald Blomfield found in Sussex and Kent timber work. The spur, like the hewn corner post, carried the upper story out over the lower on a curved support rather than a simple horizontal timber. Since Kent and Sussex both sent many settlers to Connecticut it is safe to assume that the hewn overhang is not a unique American device but a development from local English building traditions.[60]

The jetty was by no means the only architectural practice which the colonists imported to protect their wall surfaces from the weather. Even more familiar to Americans is the use of horizontal boarding. Until the growing iron and shipping industries destroyed England's forests, boards often covered the walls of all types of minor buildings. Diaries and builder's dictionaries illustrate how completely and rapidly boarding disappeared from the architectural vernacular. In 1641, as we have seen, Henry Best had indicated his approval of imported fir boards, a commonplace necessity of a Yorkshire farmer for "bordeninge." [61] Joseph Moxon, writing some fifty years later, included only a definition of "weather boarding" and did not explain in his text the technique to be used in applying these boards.[62] In 1733 the terms "weatherboard" and "clapboard" were still current but such wall covers appeared only occasionally on the "walls of some barns, stables, and other outhouses." [63] Apparently the decline of post-and-truss building and the introduction of brick and stone for house construction had rendered boarding unnecessary. English building prices give an index of the abandonment of board-wall techniques. The cost of boarding, which had risen so rapidly in the seventeenth century, compared favorably with tile and slate per square (100 square feet) in 1736, indicating that despite the depletion of the timber supply a declining demand had kept the cost of boarding commensurate with that of other materials.[64]

But in 1630, at the beginning of the Great Migration, minor timber-framed buildings were often boarded in whole or in part.[65] The geographical center of the still-existing clapboarded structures has been found in Essex.

60. Isham and Brown, *Early Connecticut Houses,* pp. 236–237. Reginald Blomfield, *A History of Renaissance Architecture in England, 1500–1800* (London, G. Bell & Sons, 1897), II, 234. Similar construction was to be found in Surrey. W. Galsworthy Davie and W. Curtis Greene, *Old Cottages and Farm-houses in Surrey* (London, B. T. Batsford, Ltd., 1908).

61. Best, *Rural Economy in Yorkshire,* pp. 110–112, 125–126.

62. Moxon, *Mechanick Exercises,* pp. 139, 160, 163.

63. Richard Neve, *City and Country Purchaser's and Builder's Dictionary* (London, 1736), Walls IX, Weatherboarding.

64. *Ibid.,* Tyles #3, Weatherboarding.

65. Martin S. Briggs, *The Homes of the Pilgrim Fathers in England and America, 1620–1685* (London, Oxford University Press, 1932), pp. 5, 56. Briggs traveled through the counties from which the colonists are known to have come.

In that county, farms, cottages, mills, and a few fair-sized houses present the rhythmic façade of overlapping boards familiar to every New Englander.[66] Perhaps the even tenor of Essex as an agricultural county and the absence of mining and of enclosure (until the nineteenth century in Epping and Hainault forests) have helped to preserve in this one county a practice which had been much more widespread in 1630.[67]

Within the county clapboard construction seems unevenly distributed. In the southeastern portion Orsett, Stifford, Tillingham, Wickford, Horndon, Vange all have typical timber barns or houses covered with boards.[68] Toward the southwest, while clapboards are not rare, they are not the most common sort of building.[69] In northern Essex only a diligent search revealed some wood-covered buildings.[70] Individual inclinations and local supplies of boarding produced a variety of outside house walls.

Boarding was not, however, confined to domestic buildings and was often used on outbuildings and mills. Expense still limited it to the large farm standing independent of the village and to farm buildings of wealthy estates.[71] An excellent example of the latter was to be found at Ingatestone Hall. The barn itself showed all the typical New England characteristics including the main door at the center of the longest side and shingle roof pitched at about 45°.[72] Barns almost invariably seem to have used horizontal board walls, and since the rise of enclosures increased the need for such animal shelters many were built at the end of the sixteenth and the beginning of the seventeenth centuries.[73]

Water mills of the seventeenth century, if made of wood, had post-and-truss frames and clapboards. The great length and area of their walls precluded the use of open framework, since overhanging eaves and projecting stories gave insufficient protection from the erosion of the weather.[74]

66. Briggs's historical method was to submit the locality in question to a minute search for boarded buildings without exact regard for other features of construction or relative dates. The variety of buildings used to illustrate this point is clearly seen. *Ibid.*, Figs. 16–63.

67. *The Victoria History of the Counties of England, Essex* (London, A. Constable & Co., 1907), II, 313, 323.

68. Roy. Com. Hist. Mon., *Essex*, IV, plate facing p. xl.

69. *Ibid.*, II, 48, 96–97, 110, 144.

70. Briggs, *Homes of the Pilgrim Fathers*, p. 5.

71. *Ibid.*, p. 57 n. 1, Stanesgate Abbey Farm at Steeple.

72. Roy. Com. Hist. Mon., *Essex*, II, 144.

73. Horndon-on-the-Hill, Linsteads Farm Barn Monument No. 12; Vange, Merricks Barn early seventeenth-century, Monument No. 3; Wickford, Shot Farm Barn Monument No. 6, late sixteenth century. Roy. Com. Hist. Mon., *Essex*, IV, 76, 163, 172. Simply a few examples illustrated on p. xl; see also *Herefordshire*, II, Plate XXXIII.

74. Briggs, *Homes of the Pilgrim Fathers*, pp. 109, 111, Figs. 50, 51, 52. Boarding was of course standard English practice for windmills of all kinds. *Ibid.*, p. 115.

In Connecticut the boarding, which had been known but was never universal in England, became an enduring symbol of the New England village and village life. While authorities agree that not all seventeenth-century Connecticut houses were boarded when built, no half-timber work is still standing, and boarding was known in America during the early years of English settlement in Connecticut.[75]

Connecticut clapboard was not a strictly derivative form but showed considerable independence of design. It was first of all riven from quartered oak with a frow. To do this the workman set his log on end, split it into quarters, and then split each of the quarters into many clapboards. The boards as finished seem to have been invariably 4 to 6 feet in length, 4 to 8 inches wide, and about ⅜ to ½ inch thick on the outside edge, which tapered to a "featheredge." [76] If examined carefully they cannot be confused with weatherboards which were rarely found in the colony but used extensively in England. Weatherboards were usually longer than clapboards. Since they were sawn they had an even thickness for their whole breadth. Moreover, they were often 12 inches broad while the widest clapboards were 8 inches.[77]

Clapboards were nailed directly to vertical studs set between the large posts of the house frame. Considerable artistry was used upon occasion. Since the boards were usually 4 to 6 inches wide an overlap of 1 inch would leave 3 to 5 inches of clapboard showing on the wall exterior. This overlap was sometimes varied precisely so that at the sills or ground level the clapboards had an exposure of only 1⅞ inches while just below the cornice they had an exposure of 3½ inches. Although existing examples of such care are late, they are an indication that American craftsmen had not forgotten the subtle British gradation of tile courses on Cotswold roofs and in their material preserved a high sense of artistry and skill.[78]

The substitution of clapboards for weatherboarding in seventeenth-century Connecticut was probably economic in origin, however artistically the form may have been elaborated. Clapboards had the same width and thickness as the barrel staves which were exported to the West Indies early

75. Sidney Fiske Kimball, *Domestic Architecture of the American Colonies and the Early Republic* (New York, Charles Scribner's Sons, 1922), pp. 11–12. Kelly, *Early Domestic Architecture*, pp. 3–4. Isham and Brown, *Early Connecticut Houses*, pp. 247–248.

76. This probably was the source of the "hewn planks" which Kimball felt was a house of vertical hewn logs. Kimball, *Domestic Architecture*, p. 6. Kelly, *Domestic Architecture*, pp. 82–85. *P.R. Col. New Haven*, V. It should not be assumed featheredge boards were unknown in England. Weatherboards so shaped were found upon occasion. R. Neve, *City and Country Purchaser's and Builder's Dictionary*, "Featheredge."

77. Kelly, *Domestic Architecture*, pp. 83–84. Isham and Brown, *Early Connecticut Houses*, p. 244.

78. Kelly, *Domestic Architecture*. Harold J. Massingham, *Country Relics* (Cambridge, University Press, 1939), pp. 26–27.

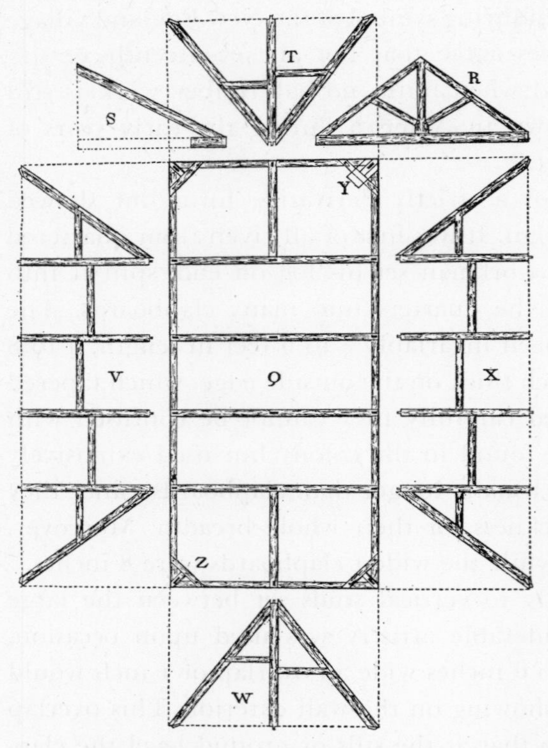

37. Attic plates and roof pieces as fitted on the ground

in the seventeenth century and intermittently became a part of the trade with the West Indies in the eighteenth century. Moreover, the splitting of clapboards required no saw pit or sawmill, and yet a reasonably flat surface could be obtained if the splitting was done with skill. Tools, especially saws, were rare in the seventeenth century, and so the simplicity of quartering oak must have appealed to the early Connecticut settler.[79]

With the side walls sheathed, the frame secured, and his chimney laid the builder of the seventeenth-century house needed only the roof frame and cover to finish the exterior of his house.[80] In his roof frame he felt guided by a strict tradition that was only very slowly changed. Virtually all seventeenth-century roofs were simple peaked roofs, with axis lying parallel to the longest axis and the main façade of the house.[81]

The erection of Connecticut roofs for almost a century after the colony's founding showed one important variation from the timber roof sketched by

79. Isham and Brown, *Early Connecticut Houses,* pp. 270–272, gives a fine discussion of available tools. See also p. 246.

80. The roof might of course be covered before the clapboards were nailed to the studs.

81. Additional gables were known but the hip and gambrel are late introductions.

Moxon in the late seventeenth century. The roof members were fitted on the ground and then raised to the ceiling plates of the top floor into which they were let by a variety of joints; yet the roof framing, however similar its outline was to English construction, did develop a system of rafters rarely found in English building.[82] (Fig. 37.)

The reason for this was not hard to find. In Connecticut the central chimney, if carried directly through the center of the house, precluded the use of any system of supports which incorporated a single ridgepole. Since the ridgepole was thought to carry the weight of the roof and since it could no longer run through the chimney as a single beam, a system of common rafters without any ridgepole was devised. A tie beam fastened these rafters together below the peak of the roof. When purlins were used they were split on each side of the stack if necessary.[83]

The system of principal rafters used in Branford and Guilford is clearly a continuation of Sussex framing. In both towns, principal rafters were used to carry a short ridgepole and horizontal purlins. The Harrison-Linsley House in Branford, for example, has two 8-foot bays on either side of a 9-foot chimney opening. The chimney emerges just behind the ridgepole. An exactly similar roof frame, even to the chimney position, was taken as typical of Sussex construction by Alfred Powell,[84] and it may well be that a careful study of English post-and-truss construction would reveal the use of common rafters in one of the southern counties. Tie beams were well known in England and it would have been a simple step to eliminate the ridgepole.[85]

The disappearance of the ridgepole, however minor a variant from English practice, marked the difference between framing practice in England and the colony. The ridgepole and the belief that it carried the weight of the roof grew out of the custom of using thatch. At the beginning of the seventeenth century the roof of the average English cottage or farm building expressed more clearly than any other part of the village its primary concern with agriculture.[86] Thatch roofs were a part of the village economy, and so long as many of the lands were laid out in food crops the roofs were thatched. Only when increased wealth demanded a more permanent and ostentatious covering and it was no longer profitable to use the straw of wheat, rye, and other grains did the thatch roof go out of use.

82. The best contemporary plan of roof timbers showing many variations of roof types as if combined on a single roof is shown in Francis Price, *British Carpentry* (London, 1735), Plate F. See also Francis Price, *The British Carpenter* (London, 1735), Plates F, G.

83. Kelly, *Domestic Architecture,* Figs. 49–55.

84. Cf. *ibid.,* Fig. 58 and *Studio Yearbook of Decorative Art* (1920), p. 40.

85. Innocent, *English Building Construction,* pp. 79–80.

86. *Ibid.,* pp. 188–190, states its first competitor. H. Batsford and C. Fry, *The English Cottage,* p. 65.

Thatching began in the farmyard where the straw, reeds, or wild grass were left to lie. In summer the stalks kept wet but in winter snow and rain dampened them. The thatcher started at the eaves and laid his thatch progressively thicker as he went up the roof. He worked in strips ladder wide that ran from the eaves to the ridge. The ridge was crowned by a band of horizontal straw. Thus laid the straw was secured to the rafters, ridgepole, and purlins by interlacing a rope and bands of plaited straw.[87] The ridgepole served to hold the topmost thatch and to keep the whole from sliding down over the eaves. The time of year chosen for thatching was governed by the crops; late spring or late September was thought best as they were not too cold and came between harvests.[88] When finished the farmer had a roof made of otherwise almost useless straw that might last as long as a hundred years.[89]

By 1630 English roofs had begun to feel the effects of enclosure and the new economy. Cottagers sometimes used tiles and larger farms substituted slate for thatch. Closer to the towns thatch had almost disappeared even on ancient cottages.[90] Shingles were known but the high cost of wood precluded their use.[91] In country where open fields still predominated thatch flourished, but where enclosed pastures had been introduced thatch was scarce since unused straw was less common. Thatch declined in value as a roof covering as the amount of straw grass on individual holdings fell off and more costly roofs became fashionable.[92]

Thatch was by no means unknown in Connecticut. Early statutes sometimes mentioned thatching, thatchers, and a fair price for their work.[93] After 1640 the danger from fire was recognized and in some towns specific ordnances were drawn up that governed the use of thatch roofs.[94] Why the danger from

87. A variety of other more primitive methods were known. Innocent, *English Building Construction,* pp. 196 ff.

88. G. Markham, *A Farewell to Husbandry,* p. 156.

89. This description is taken from Best, *Rural Economy in Yorkshire,* pp. 138–140, 145–148.

90. David Loggan, *Cantabrigia Illustrata* (London, 1690, and Cambridge, Macmillan & Bowes, 1905), Plates XVI, XVIII, XXI. Batsford and Fry, *English Cottage,* p. 65.

91. Innocent, *Development of English Building Construction,* pp. 184–185.

92. Haulm or straw was used for fuel in champion or open-field country. Presumably it was too rare and valuable to be used as such on enclosed land.

> "In champion country a pleasure they take
> To mow up their haulm for to brew and bake
> And also it stands them instead of their thack
> While being well inned they cannot well lack."

The haulm is the straw of wheat or rye. T. Tausser, *Five Hundred Points of Good Husbandry* (first printed 1573; reprinted London, 1812), pp. 84–85.

93. *P.R. Col. New Haven,* I, 37.

94. *Ibid.,* I, 212. Fire hooks were provided by the town to pull thatch off the roof and the owner of such houses had to sweep his chimneys and provide a ladder.

fire should have been greater in Connecticut than in England is not clear. Perhaps it was because the cold of the New England climate forced the settlers to keep larger fires burning than were necessary in England. Probably more important, no truly suitable thatching grass was found in Connecticut after the river meadowland had been grazed and mown for fodder. Certainly Connecticut was never "champion country," and so it is little wonder that a roofing practice intimately associated with open-field farming soon died out.

Soon after the colony's foundation shingle roofs became a universal covering for most buildings; barns, meetinghouses, homes, and inns all used the wood shingle. Shingle roofs have been often replaced, and the best guide to the size of the seventeenth-century shingles is the list of New Haven prices of 1640 which describes shingles ¾ of an inch thick, 6 to 8 inches broad, and 2½ or 3 feet long. So far as I know no such shingles are still found on roofs, but their dimensions are identical with those found occasionally on walls of houses near Greenwich. Once more it was the hewn or riven rather than the sawed oak shingle which roofed the early houses.[95]

Sometimes the builders did not nail their shingles to horizontal boarding but pegged them to closely spaced small-section timber sticks. In this way they preserved the ancient tradition of English slate work though there is no evidence that they followed the more subtle slate craftsman and varied the length of shingle exposed according to its position on the roof proper. The brief archaic survival of pegging emphasized the colonial concept of shingles not as an independent material but as a cheap and fairly durable facsimile of English slate.[96]

Each part of the colonial house from its foundation to the shingled roof was shaped with specific tools designed in each case to perform a small number of exact tasks in the hands of craftsmen. Since frontier life presented no new conditions in relation to house construction, except in the value of labor, the tools used by the colonial craftsman remained European in design and often in manufacture. In Connecticut as formerly in England the settler had oak and pine but in greater abundance. He understood logging techniques since he had always found his trees in English forest parks, as indeed Englishmen do today. Quarries were impracticable for many years, but field stone was plentiful and a modified mortar of shells could substitute for English mortar.

As we have seen, the first operation in the construction of the framed

95. Kelly, *Domestic Architecture,* p. 85. W.P.A. Bldg. Survey, *Greenwich.*

96. Harold J. Massingham, *Country Relics,* p. 27. J. F. Kelly, *Domestic Architecture,* p. 49. Thomas J. Wertenbaker, *The First Americans, 1607–1690* (New York, Macmillan Company, 1929), p. 286, quotes a description of houses "covered with shingell for Tyle." Innocent, *English Building Construction,* pp. 183–185.

house was cutting and hewing logs to shape. Either in the forest or at the house site each piece of the frame had to be fitted to its companion before being raised into position.

The primary tool of the house carpenter in this operation was the ax which, until the mid-eighteenth century, remained little changed from English design. In essentials it was like the modern ax except that the bit or cutting edge greatly outweighed the poll or dull end and was some 3 to 5 inches long. Double-bitted axes were not used until the nineteenth century. A straight handle was universally fitted to the long-bladed carpenter's ax.[97] (Figs. 34, 38a.)

The house builder squared his timbers after they had been cut and roughly hewed to shape with his adz. The adz was double bladed and had the cutting edge of its blade turned at right angles to the shaft. (Fig. 38b.) To use it the workman stood over his log with his legs spread well apart and, swinging the adz in pick fashion, guided it so that it chipped the log a little in front of him and produced the characteristic rippled hewn appearance of the structural timbers of most colonial houses in Connecticut.[98]

To move his heavy timbers after shaping them the workman used a "crow" or crowbar with sharply pointed claws (Fig. 38l) to bite into the log which was then lifted on a timber cart or "drug" and pulled by two men wherever needed. A simple block and tackle usually sufficed to lift his timbers, but the seventeenth-century carpenter was familiar with many engineering systems designed to give mechanical advantage.[99]

A few other tools seem to have had specific application to the problems of the framed house and either are no longer used or are used for very different purposes. Most impressive of the lost seventeenth-century tools is the "commander": "A very great wooden Mallet with a handle about three feet long to use in both the Hands . . . to knock on the corners of framed work, to set them in their position." [100] (Fig. 38k.) Most ingenious was the hook-pin, the "office" of which "is to pin the Frame of a Floor, or Frame of a Roof together whilst it is framing." Driven into the pin holes of mortise-and-tenon joints, it was easily removed by knocking on the bottom of its specially shaped

97. H. C. Mercer, "Ancient Carpenters' Tools," *Old-Time New England,* XV (April, 1925), 164–169. Moxon, *Mechanick Exercises,* pp. 118–119.

98. "It [the adz] is most used for the taking off the irregularities on the framed work of a floor, when it is framed and pined together, and laid on its place for . . . the edge of the axe being parallel to its Hande . . . cannot come at their regularities to take them off, but the adz having its edge athwart the handle will." Moxon describes other functions of the adz as well. Moxon, *Mechanick Exercises,* pp. 119–120.

99. *Ibid.,* pp. 125–126, 159. The "crab" and its "appurtenances . . . *snatch blocks* and *levers.*" The "crab" is the equivalent of the modern windlass, "snatch blocks" are pulleys and pulley systems.

100. *Ibid.,* p. 125.

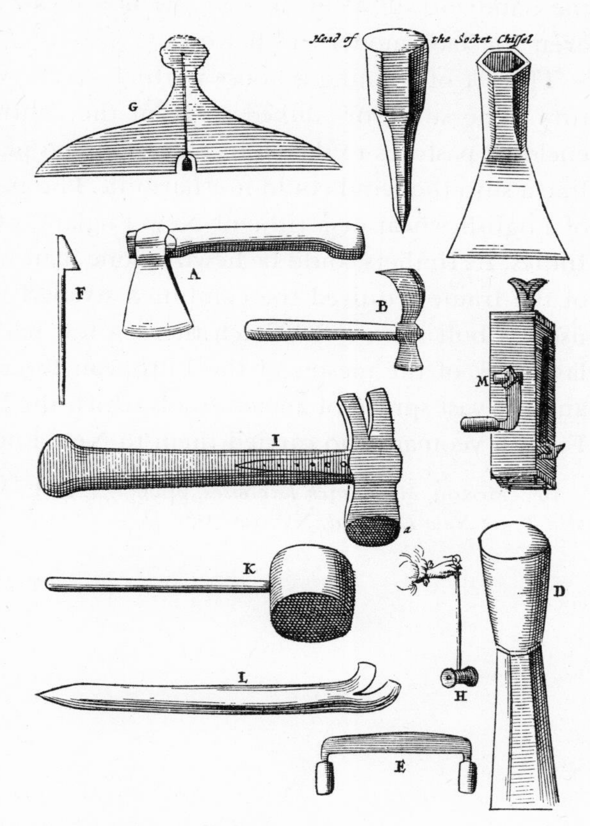

38. Seventeenth-century house-framing tools

head.[101] (Fig. 38f.) Such special tools however were the exception; the great majority of the carpenters' tools are familiar to modern builders.

Saws, planes, and chisels were all known but rare until the eighteenth century. Saws varied greatly in shape from the ancient frame or bow saw to small hand saws. The pit saw was used both by carpenters and joiners to saw in a vertical plane and a few small specialized saws were known.[102] Most elementary of the planes was the drawknife. It consisted of a sharp-edged single blade to which two handles were attached, and the work was smoothed by drawing the blade toward one's body. (Fig. 38e.) Planes as we know them today were carried in wooden frames and sometimes had blades ground unevenly so that that they would cut moldings directly into the wood. Great variety was possible with the hand-ground seventeenth- and eighteenth-century planes, and

101. *Ibid.*, p. 123.

102. *Ibid.*, pp. 99–103. Moxon lists the uses of the pit saw, whip saw, bow saw, tennant saw, and compasse saw. H. C. Mercer, "Ancient Carpenter Tools," *Old-Time New England*, XV, 180–197.

the handwork done at or near the house can always be distinguished from even the best modern mill work.[103]

The art of framing a house partook of every skill of the seventeenth century. The surveyor walked in from the controversial hedges of the newly enclosed pastures to sketch its elevation and plan its floors. Since it was built like a ship the wind could not harm it. The roof was covered with the straw of English wheat or a tithe of New England's cargoes destined for the West Indies. Its timbers could be hewn by one man working alone; only the raising of the frame required the combined strength of many men. Iron was little used: a bolt here, a doorlatch there, a few nails. The framed house was the last work of the master of the European forests. Its traditional proportions and the vast spread of ancient tools which the builder used long survived the English yeoman who carried them to New England.

103. Moxon, *Mechanick Exercises,* pp. 65–74. H. C. Mercer, "Ancient Carpenter Tools," *Old-Time New England,* XV, 126–137.

v. Wilderness Homes

The naked post-and-truss frames of Connecticut were scarcely more traditional than the floors and chimney pieces of the houses they supported. In the colony a house type peculiar to some classes of Stuart society in England became by virtue of its primacy in the wilderness the starting point for all domestic architecture. Architectural style, like the religious and political convictions of the first planters, was pressed into a far narrower mold than that which shaped the minor arts. Silver and furniture were often replenished by the latest European taste, but the Connecticut house scorned foreign fashion in its plan and elevation; instead it elaborated for more than a century what would have seemed an archaic idiom even to Restoration Englishmen.

Today the streets of England and New England look little alike. Some decades ago a Boston banking house published views of English, Irish, and Scotch towns and their New England namesakes but found, perhaps to its dignified surprise, virtually no resemblance.[1] Especially in the colonial period the paths of the colony and mother country were so divergent that the architecture which faithfully served the colonist was for his relatives at home expensive, impractical, and even sometimes dangerous.

The divergence of New England architecture from that of Europe has been explained for the past fifty years by the hypothesis of a unique and singular development of a colonial style in the American wilderness.[2] Starting from humble beginnings this house style has been supposed to have grown by

1. State Street Trust Company, *Towns of New England and Old England . . .* (New York, State Street Trust Company, 1920–21).

2. The application of a crude Darwinism is more familiar in political history but was so strongly emphasized in Connecticut studies it came to dominate most colonial architectural history. Cf. Norman M. Isham and Albert F. Brown, *Early Connecticut Houses* and J. Frederick Kelly, *Early Domestic Architecture of Connecticut,* with Michael Kraus, *A History of American History* (New York, Farrar & Rinehart, 1937), p. 337.

accretion and additions from a single-room, end-chimney house [3] into a two-room plan with central chimney, and finally incorporated the lean-to—device of expediency—into its floor plan.[4]

The theory is pretty if one assumption be made—that the early seventeenth-century settler knew only one type of English house which he reproduced as his logical answer to wilderness conditions. Upon this assumption Isham, Kelly, and their followers forged an architectural evolutionary chain without missing links on the forest frontier.[5] (Fig. 47.)

But on second thought this assumption seems unjustified.[6] Every English village sported a variety of homes, each suited to the station of its owner. (Fig. 9.) Indeed it would be most extraordinary if the houses of a stratified society did not in some measure reflect the classes of that society. A multitude of architectural variations, each more or less specialized for a particular class of English society, had appeared by 1630. Actually all house types found in seventeenth-century Connecticut were to be found in seventeenth-century English villages. Not only colonial methods of construction but plans and elevations as well imitated English models. In 1640 the colonist's architectural heritage was large and complex; far from adding to that heritage colonial conditions tended to simplify architectural design so that before 1700 many styles known in 1640 had become forgotten curiosities.

Port authorities recorded the variety of the passengers bound for New England, and the surveyor's quill has done the same service for the architectural experience of those passengers. Traveling from one end of England to the other the surveyor saw village after village caught in the torments of enclosure. The boundary lines he drew, the green water color he brushed on his parchment, separated pastures from arable fields; similarly the house

3. Isham found a sequence of elaboration from the simple to the more complex house, but he very carefully indicated that though small single-room end-chimney houses existed they were not necessarily the earliest homes. Isham and Brown, *Early Connecticut Houses,* p. 6.

4. The earliest and most recent statements of this theory are to be found in Isham and Brown, *Early Connecticut Houses,* pp. 6–11; and J. F. Kelly, *Architectural Guide for Connecticut* (New Haven, Yale University Press, 1935), p. 8. Kelly, *Domestic Architecture,* p. 97, Fig. 102.

5. That some colonial houses passed through successive additions is indisputable. The Harrison-Linsley House in Branford still has the original outside clapboards on the inside wall of its added lean-to. That such remodelings provided the only basis for style development is still to be demonstrated.

6. The possibility that the evolutionary theory is too simple an explanation is suggested by the reluctance of authorities to designate a date for any particular house. Working with documentary evidence only, Fiske Kimball assigns the Ebenezer Grant House (1757–58) in East Windsor as the earliest Connecticut house whose building date is documented positively. Sidney Fiske Kimball, *Domestic Architecture of the American Colonies and of the Early Republic,* p. 266.

sketches he made fixed the rents of tenants or the valuation of freeholds. His experiences as seen through his maps reveal an English architecture of great diversity, not only between counties but also within individual villages. To posit that the English villager was unaware of house types which he passed or entered in the pursuit of his daily affairs is like suggesting that a Restoration Puritan, because he affected sober clothing, had never seen a silk skirt or low bodice.

The English village sketched by the surveyor reflected all the social conflicts of its time. The simplest form of human shelter in general use was the "cot" or cottage. Evolved for the poorest tenant and the small copyholder who tended the hedges and flocks of the large landholders, these cots were primitive affairs.[7] Cots with one room, roughly a bay square, a single door, a shuttered, glassless window, and a single chimney appeared again and again in manorial surveys. Their humble pretensions are further underscored by their rudely hewn frames, exposed wall filling, and thatched roofs.[8] (Fig. 39.)

Except in rare instances time and their owners have dealt harshly with the single-cell cottages.[9] The husbandmen found them impractical since they provided no room for animals, and their hearths could not accommodate the many tasks of a prosperous farm kitchen.[10] Other owners impatiently tore them down or built elaborate additions around their humble frames. The one-room cottage has been almost useless for the past century because it could shelter only the poorest rural labor without land, a large household, or animals. Two nearly unique examples, both timber framed but one filled with wattle and daub and the other with bricks, can be seen in Elstead, Surrey. The Royal Commission on the Ancient and Historical Monuments, and Constructions of England could discover only a few genuine cottages. In Herefordshire a pair of minute seventeenth-century dwellings still stand, one at Letton and one at Norton Canon, both having heavily thatched roofs on post-and-truss frames.[11] Before World War II, Essex, whose monuments have been the most carefully recorded of any English county, had only a few

7. *A New English Dictionary on Historical Principles.*

8. Sidney O. Addy, *Evolution of the English House,* pp. 66–69.

9. Much of the decline of the cottage took place during and after the Napoleonic wars in a period of terrible rural depression. For examples, see Francis Stevens, *Domestic Architecture; a Series of Views of Cottages and Farm-houses in England and Wales* (London, 1815), Plates II, IV, X, XVI, XVII, XX, XXIII, XXVIII, XXIX, XL, XLIII, XLVIII, and comment on Stevens in H. Batsford and C. Fry, *English Cottage,* pp. 105–106.

10. Addy, *Evolution of the English House,* pp. 71, 77.

11. Royal Commission on the Ancient and Historical Monuments, *An Inventory of the Historical Monuments in . . . Herefordshire* (London, H.M. Stationery Office, 1931–34), III, Plate XXXIII. Numbers in my text refer to monument numbers, e.g., Letton Monument No. 4, Norton Canon No. 2.

clear-cut examples, at Stifford, Great Hallingsburg, and Canvey Island.[12] (Fig. 40.)

On the other hand, contemporary surveys list many such cottages in the seventeenth century, and on maps they were often the most numerous sort of building. An Elizabethan plan of Tynemouth Castle shows the town at the foot of the castle hill as a group of small, single-story dwellings each with one door and a few windows.[13] A late sixteenth-century map of the grounds of the Augustine Steward in what is now St. Leonard of Shoreditch Parish, London, pictures eight or ten such tenant houses.[14] These drawings should not be considered mere conventions; a similar survey of the Christ Hospital estate clearly distinguishes between one such cottage and several other house types. Ashbourne, chosen by Gomme as a typical seventeenth-century town, had many similar simple structures on its main street. Indeed in the seventeenth century there seemed to be no geographical limit to the building of such cottages. Examples appeared not only in the south of England but at Laxton in Yorkshire and Lucker in Northumberland. Although it is probable that these northern cottages were not framed but made of stone, their plan and elevation seem to have closely resembled the small cots of southern England.[15] Here, as in the south, surveys, not existing buildings, supply the most information about the simplest type of building with which the earliest Connecticut settlers were acquainted.

The husbandman "who followeth in the next place"[16] felt dissatisfied with the cheerless tenant cottage. His needs had become so diverse that he could not simply add another chamber. He needed a hall and a parlor, at least two chambers for sleeping, many fireplaces, and a smoke chamber to cure his meats. Stairs, a big chimney, and perhaps a lean-to all had to be fitted in.

Neither the rude cot nor the sophisticated manor house suited his needs, but somewhere in the village hierarchy between the two stood the sixteenth-century copyhold house, a one-and-a-half story house with two rooms on the ground level—one for animals, the other for all domestic purposes. This

12. Roy. Com. Hist. Mon., *Essex,* II, 97; IV, xl.

13. Northumberland County History Committee, *A History of Northumberland* (London, 1893), VIII, 148. Hereafter referred to as *History of Northumberland.*

14. London County Council, *Survey of London* (London, Eyre & Spottiswoode, 1922), VIII, Plate II.

15. *Ibid.,* X, Plate LXXVIII. George L. Gomme, *The Village Community* (London, 1890), p. 44. *History of Northumberland,* I, 234. Charles S. Orwin, *The Open Fields.* Also see Charles R. Smith, *Antiquities of Richborough, Reculver and Lymne,* p. 192, and "Plan of the Manor of Wadsworth and Parish of Newington, Surrey," London Topographical Society, Publications, Vol. LXV (1932).

16. Robert Reyce, *Suffolk in the Eighteenth Century* [MS title: "The Breviary of Suffolk"], p. 57.

39. Typical survey sketches of cottages

40. Cottage at Stifford, Essex

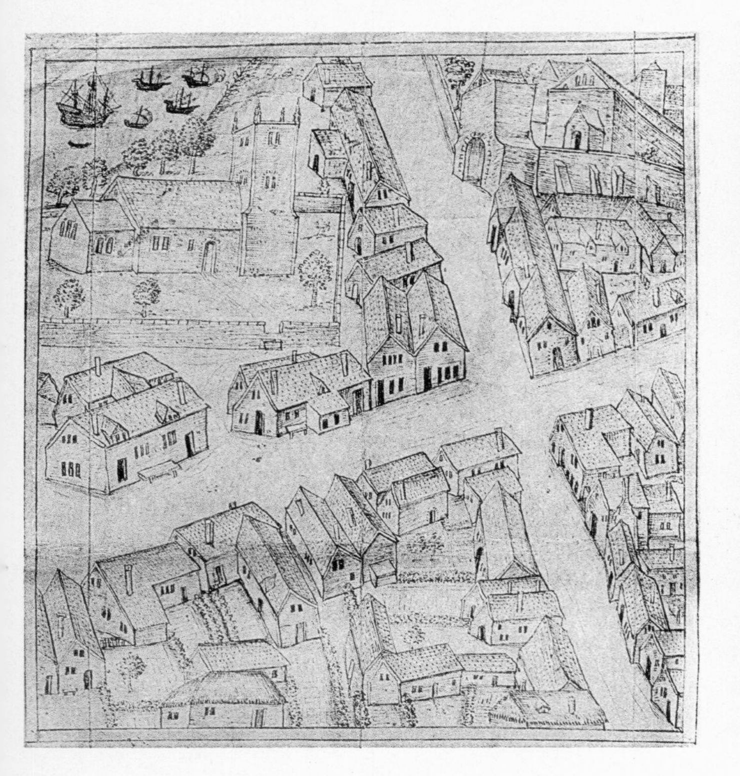

41. Paignton in Devon about 1567

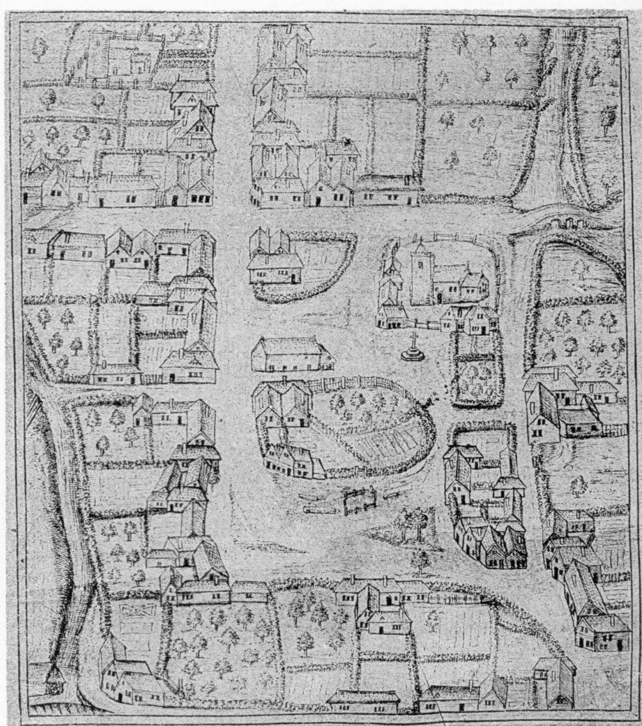

42. Wilton about 1570

house the husbandman of the seventeenth century enlarged into a well-balanced structure by using the two rooms on the ground floor for his family and building a separate barn.

Such small houses dotted the lands and lanes of the seventeenth-century husbandman wherever the stiff hedges of enclosure or the better hulls of the mariner brought a little prosperity. Many still stand almost unchanged today; others beautifully caught by the surveyor's art exist only in drawings. The villages of Paington and Wilton on the Pembroke lands, which were recorded with scrupulous care for the first earl (Figs. 41, 42), had many different sorts of structure but the one-and-a-half story house that predominated strongly suggests the New England Cape Cod house. In Essex a score of such houses still look out on village greens. Countless other examples line the lanes of villages from East Anglia west to Devon and north to the Northumberland border.[17]

Common as they seem to have been, neither the one-room tenant cottage nor the small husbandman's house became the typical English enclosure house. Most new village building in seventeenth-century England served the prosperous yeoman. Beginning in 1550 and lasting for almost a century, the economic prosperity of enclosure and the development of new building techniques had coincided to create the golden age of English domestic architecture.[18] This third style of house was destined to become in time not only the architectural symbol of the English yeoman but the criterion of New England architectural taste.

The yeoman by 1630 had worked no less a transformation of his dwelling than he had of his fields. First of all, as often as convenient he moved his house outside the village proper, nearer his largest pastures. Thus isolated, he found he had need of space to house his teams, his grain, and his farm implements, the use and shelter of which he had formerly shared with his neighbors, so he built a larger barn or even a separate farmyard.

The walls and roof of the yeoman house gave more than mere shelter. Each room and each floor had a specific purpose and came to be designed for that purpose. In the ground plan of such a farmhouse at Hawlands in Surrey the chimney and fireplaces were in the center of the house, the parlor and living room on one side, the kitchen on the other. Additional space furnished by the lean-to served as a buttery or storeroom.[19] (Fig. 54.)

The upper story, which often incorporated an overhang, was divided into

17. Hubert Hall, *Society in the Elizabethan Age* (London, 1887), Plate I. *Survey of the Lands of William, First Earl of Pembroke,* ed. by Charles R. Straton (Oxford, Roxburghe Club, 1909), I, 182; II, 388.

18. H. Batsford, *English Cottage,* pp. 3–4.

19. Ralph Nevill, *Old Cottages and Domestic Architecture in South-West Surrey* (Guilford, 1889), pp. 13, 58.

two large chambers reached by a modest stair well and two narrow chambers crowded under the sharply sloped lean-to roof. In order to gain space, steady the whip of floor joists, and at the same time protect the lower walls, this second story often projected 20 or 24 inches over the first-floor walls. Such overhangs, which were carried on diagonal dragon beams at each corner, had in addition certain social implications which, as we shall see, the country yeoman was most anxious to secure.[20]

Not all yeoman houses had so consistent and practical a design. Often sentiment or a lean purse imposed conditions that only an enlarged cottage could fulfill. Such designs lengthened the too narrow rectangular cot into a building of some pretension, with a high thatched roof, haphazard chimney arrangement, two full stories, attic dormers, and broad eaves. Although far larger than the true cot the shallow depth, great length, and steep roofs of such houses often cause them to be mistaken for cottages, so well do they fit the English landscape. In parts of Hereford and Huntingdonshire and some other counties these seventeenth-century buildings set a style for domestic construction which has characterized many rural villages until the present century.[21]

In southern England the well-to-do yeoman built a more original elevation. Unlike the rectangular house his did not extend a large cottage but had a consistent and logical plan oriented about the central chimney. From this chimney and its assorted ovens and hearths came the famous meats and drinks of the yeoman's table. Beef, mutton, veal, pork, capons, hens, wild fowl, and fish were all prepared over its open fire and in its ample ovens. In the kitchen the yeoman's wife brewed his beer, ale, and mead, and baked his bread and pies. To preserve meat, smoking in the chimney smoke chamber was preferred to salting. It is little wonder that the central chimney stack became the most ornate and decorative feature of the yeoman's house; it stood as the sign of his prosperous fields and well-kept farms, and at its hearth count could be taken of the profits of enclosure.

On the exterior a fluted chimney was not the only mark of the yeoman's prosperity. Into the main façade of his house he introduced order, and for haphazard growth and numerous additions he substituted a degree of balance and proportion. Regular five-window fenestration and a central door became the rule in the early years of the seventeenth century. At Little Horkeseley, Feering, Earls Colne, Stanford Rivers, and Terling, carpenters

20. Hugh Braun, *The Story of the English House* (New York, C. Scribner's Sons, 1940; London, B. T. Batsford, Ltd., 1940), p. 46.

21. Additions to houses of this class were very common. Mildred Campbell, *The English Yeoman*, p. 228. Roy. Com. Hist. Mon., *Huntingdonshire,* Plates XLVII, CXXX; *Herefordshire,* I, Plate XXII (especially Blakmere Church House Farm).

tried self-consciously to introduce Essex villagers to London sophistication by building overhangs. To fill the frames local materials were used, and often boards were laid overlapping the less weatherproof fillings. Such boarded houses recall to American visitors their own New England village commons.[22] (Fig. 50.)

Since his pastures often lay at some distance from the village the post-enclosure yeoman took some pains to build not on the green but near the largest of his holdings. Thus for the first time houses other than the manor were found at some distance from the town green and village church. (Fig. 50.) Many of these dwellings continue to serve modern farmers. The Sparrow farm, a rather better yeoman's house of the seventeenth century, still stands today more than 1 mile from the Terling village church, and the Egart farm in the same village is well over ½ mile southwest of the center. The West Hyde House, whose white clapboards and elevation suggest Connecticut, is 1¼ miles from Tillingham churchyard and stands on what in the sixteenth century would have been a suitable site for a manor house.[23] (Fig. 50.)

Seventeenth-century surveyors, concerned as they were with the problem of enclosure, took special care to note the homes of the new landholders on their pictorial township maps. Even in poor reproductions of these surveys the houses of this new class emerge clear and distinct. For example, Thomas Marshall found, in the course of his survey of the Sussex lands of the barony of Buckhurst, that John Kent's farm, called Dales Gnewnhams, had one small house bordering the Crowborough common, and that the tendency was for new houses to become isolated from the village throughout the barony.[24]

In more detailed surveys the isolated farmhouse was often realistically portrayed. Near Lucker in Northumberland the surveyor found Mr. Edward Conien's house at some distance from the village and clearly distinguished from it by its large size, dormer windows, and twin chimneys. All the 230 acres of Conien's estate, with the exception of a farm in Lucker, adjoined his house. Newstead Manor in 1620 gave evidence of an earlier enclosure than

22. Campbell, *English Yeoman,* pp. 243–251. Louis C. Rosenberg, *Cottages, Farmhouses and Other Minor Buildings in England* (New York, Architectural Book Publishing Company, 1923), p. 42. Most of the buildings listed as cottages are far too large and almost every house can be assumed to have belonged to a yeoman or very wealthy farmer. Roy. Com. Hist. Mon., *Essex,* I, Introduction, xxvii; II, 129; III, 178, 188. The West Hyde farmhouse at Tillingham is an almost perfect New England house. *Ibid.,* IV, Introduction, xl.

23. *Ibid.,* II, 230; IV, 160.

24. Thomas S. Dorset, *The Buckhurst Terrier, 1597–1598,* Sussex Record Society, Publications, Vol. XXXIX, Plates V, XII, XIII, XVI. It is felt that the houses are symbolic only in this survey. The fact that the reproduction is not photographic makes it impossible to check this hypothesis. It is important to note that the relative importance of buildings is stressed. *Ibid.,* p. 85.

neighboring Lucker, and its survey showed two such post-enclosure houses—one erected on a former common. A similar house which, though its plot was small, belonged to a rising landholder stood south of Tughall Manor Hall in 1620. The new, large yeoman house appeared important to the seventeenth-century surveyor, and if he was a careful workman, he recorded its elevation accurately and much as it appears today.[25]

Indeed so careful are some of these surveys that we need make no hypothesis as to the antiquity of building features found in seventeenth-century English houses that are still standing. Certainly the lean-to familiar to New Englanders appears again and again. One large house at Wilton had a lean-to which joined the roof over the main house smoothly enough to have been built at the same time as the main part of the house.[26] (Fig. 42.) A common English device, the lean-to grew up as a result of the limitations of post-and-truss building when the need for more space forced an addition and it appeared that the wall might buckle if the heavy thatch roof spanned more than one room. Since lean-tos carried the thrust to a new outer wall, they added little to the stresses and strains of the main frame and so made welcome additions to yeoman houses.[27] (Fig. 54.)

The most impressive of all English country dwellings were of course the manor houses. (Fig. 10.) Because they have often been well preserved, there has grown up around them a body of literature likely to give the unwary the impression that these buildings typified the English countryside and represent "English domestic architecture." [28] Actually, of course, manor houses were rare and greatly outnumbered by lesser dwellings. They influenced New England only indirectly since few lords of the manor came to America. But the manor house, however unattainable, embodied in the seventeenth century England's finest rural architecture and as such exercised some influence over smaller farmhouse building.[29] The chief distinguishing feature of the manor house, the central hall, had been converted in the seventeenth century to a two- or three-story block. On each end of this block and at right angles to it a narrower gable-roofed wing was attached which gave the floor plan an H shape. The whole house almost invariably had two stories of timber con-

25. *History of Northumberland,* I, 234, 243, 256, 342.

26. *Pembroke Survey,* ed. by C. R. Straton, I, 182.

27. Braun, *Story of the English House,* p. 89.

28. This preoccupation with the large house is characteristic of Thomas Garner. Arthur Stratton, *The Domestic Architecture of England during the Tudor Period* (London, B. T. Batsford, Ltd., 1929), I, 8, 211. Cf. Roy. Com. Hist. Mon., *Essex,* IV, Introduction, pp. xxx, xxxvi.

29. Braun, *Story of the English House,* p. 44. See examples in Roy. Com. Hist. Mon., *Essex,* IV, Plates facing p. xxxv show several houses which, though they are not manor houses, are built in the manor-house style.

struction but was seldom boarded.[30] Occasionally its owner had completed only one wing, but the basic plan of a two-storied, timber-framed house with one or two projecting eaves or gables might be found throughout southern England.

Since the lord of the manor generally commissioned land surveys, seventeenth-century surveyors delineated the manor house with disproportionate scale and accuracy.[31] These drawings show it isolated from the village, often the center of a large park, three stories high with gables, a balanced plan, and at least two chimneys. Surrounded by forests and enclosed pastures, the seventeenth-century manor house overlooked both the village of tenant cottages and the remote farmhouses of prosperous yeomen. Still untouched by Italian classicism, it showed the workmanship of local builders and combined their efforts into a single impressive monument.[32] (Fig. 9.)

Increased specialization of domestic architecture had its effect upon the farms and other outbuildings of the rural community. Abandonment of open fields and the spread of enclosure led to a demand for shelter for growing flocks of sheep and cattle. Thus a seventeenth-century village had many more barns than its predecessors could boast. Formerly the long tithe barns stored much of the grain; after 1600 the individual farmer felt he needed his own shelter for hay, grain, and cattle. As early as 1563 more than half the cottages and tenements of the manor of Nunburnholme in Yorkshire had barns within their individual crofts.[33] By 1611 on the manor of Sheffield many prosperous husbandmen had barns and in addition separate "beast houses." [34] Wealthy noblemen built stables which even in the nineteenth century were unsurpassed for size and elaborateness.[35]

Barns varied greatly in size but almost invariably had timber frames and

30. Roy. Com. Hist. Mon., *Essex,* IV, 4, Introduction, xxxv.

31. The only exception I have found is the drawing of Buckhurst House in Sussex and even in this case there seems some possibility that the drawing may be accurate. *The Buckhurst Terrier, 1597–1598,* Sussex Record Society, Publications, XXXIX, p. 85, Plate XV.

32. For other contemporary drawings of manors, see William P. Baildon, *Baildon and the Baildons* (London, privately printed, 1912–26), I, 539. Pearl Finch, *History of Burley-on-the-Hill* (London, J. Bale, Sons & Danielsson, Ltd., 1901), p. 7. Charles C. Brookes, *A History of Steeple Aston and Middle Aston* (Shipston-on-Stow, King's Stone Press, 1929), p. 171. J. Shawcross, *A History of Dagenham* (London, Skeffington & Son, 1904), p. 189. For the house of the period, see Arthur S. Turberville, *A History of Welbeck Abbey* (London, Faber & Faber, 1938–39), p. 58. For Essex see *Essex Record Office Catalogue of Maps 1566–1855,* ed. by G. Emmison (Chelmsford, Essex County Council, 1947). Hereafter cited as *Essex Rec. Off. Cat.*

33. Marmaduke C. F. Morris, *Nunburnholme; Its History and Antiquities* (London, H. Frowde, 1907), pp. 235–242.

34. Addy, *Evolution of the English House,* pp. 207–210.

35. Turberville, *A History of Welbeck Abbey,* p. 58. This is incidentally the best contemporary representation of a seventeenth-century house I know.

clapboarding. Unlike houses they have retained clapboards until the present day in almost every instance.[36] On the long side a high, wide door gave access in what became the New England manner to the farm wain or cart and it was here that grain was threshed at harvest time.[37] During the seventeenth century thatch was generally used for roofing but this material has since been in part replaced.[38] The barn was almost without exception free standing and few walled farmyards were built before the eighteenth century.[39] The basic agricultural unit carried from enclosed counties to America consisted of the house and separate barn.[40] (Figs. 9, 56.)

The spacious rectangular barn with high doors on its longest side by no means prevailed throughout England. Where enclosure spread slowly, or the land was poor, the village cottages stood in a single row, devoid of outbuildings of any sort.[41] Gervase Markham as late as 1660 described the storage of grain upon ricks as very common and gave elaborate instructions for their construction.[42] But the idea he envisioned was that the grain might be threshed on the barn floor as rapidly as possible and then put into garners so tightly built that they would keep out moisture.[43] Storage space in 1630 remained at a premium, and many husbandmen did not yet have enough to serve their needs. Some perforce used abandoned cottages or other deserted buildings which had once been religious edifices. Oxford, as seen by David Loggan, well illustrated the contrast between the effective boarded barn and the row of cottages which Trinity College had converted into farm buildings.[44]

Not the least of the influences affecting the design of yeoman and manor houses was familiarity with city architecture in London. The constantly widening importance of the city's wool and shipping interests forced more and more countrymen to make occasional journeys to London. Upon their

36. This statement is based on descriptions of such monuments in Roy. Com. Hist. Mon., *Middlesex, Essex,* etc., and the survey of Boxted 1586, *Essex Rec. Off. Cat.*

37. Gervase Markham, *Farewell to Husbandry,* pp. 142–143.

38. Roy. Com. Hist. Mon., *Essex,* IV, Introduction, xli.

39. I have been unable to find any such yards except in manor houses in seventeenth-century surveys. Great Britain, Board of Agriculture, *General View of the Agriculture of the County of Essex* (London, R. Phillips, 1807), p. 44. M. S. Briggs, *Homes of the Pilgrim Fathers,* Fig. 41.

40. The development of the barn coincided with the rise of animal husbandry and the difficulties attendant upon an excess of animals to graze the exhausted common land. Walter Blith, *The English Improver Improved* (London, 1652), p. 7, dedication. Gervase Markham, *Cheape and Good Husbandry. See* survey of Stock (1575) and Ingatestone (1600), *Essex Rec. Off. Cat.*

41. *Northumberland County History,* II, 424.

42. Gervase Markham, *The Inrichment of the Weald of Kent* (London, 1660), pp. 69 f.

43. Markham, *Farewell to Husbandry,* pp. 86, 107, 143.

44. David Loggan, *Oxonia Illustrata,* Plates XXI, XXVII, XXVIII.

return they tried in their village homes to imitate, though modestly, the towering overhangs and projecting upper stories of London before the Great Fire.[45] When Wenceslaus Hollar, the royalist Bohemian protégé of the Earl of Arundel, saw London the houses already stood as much as five stories high, and their many projecting floors nearly met across the narrow streets below. The almost universal building materials, until after 1660, were wood frames with varied fillers and tile or shingle roofs.[46] (Fig. 6.)

Indeed so great had been the growth of housing and so sharply had the value of land near the bridge risen that London houses had not as a rule developed symmetrical plans or given much indication of the influence of classical concepts but instead took advantage of every available inch of space; as a result, the precise rectangle and square of country plans were almost unknown. City builders gave first consideration to the utilization of the street and built houses with narrow gable ends facing upon it. Shops or kitchens generally stood on the ground floor, apartments and work rooms above.[47]

Street façades were very narrow, often as little as 9 to 13 feet in width, although occasionally a house might have as much as a 65-foot frontage. Stairs were always located in the rear of the ground floor, which in most cases ran at least 12 or 15 feet back from the street before the first partition. Then a long series of rooms, shops, warehouse, and kitchen perhaps led to the yard and property adjoining at the rear. Walls met at any angle which the property lines dictated, although in general an effort was made to frame right-angle junctions, if space would not be sacrificed.[48] Thus high property values and crowded conditions kept London from following the lead of continental countries until after the Great Fire had leveled much of the city and made

45. The overhang as a constructional device was well-known and may have been employed to protect lower stories from the rain. Its application to the rectangular yeoman's house after 1600 is anachronistic, however, and on open farms offered little protection. Here it was employed to emulate the sophistication of London. See Roy. Com. Hist. Mon., *Essex,* IV, 52. Great Sir Hughes is essentially a London shop front 1¾ miles from the center of the village of Great Baddow in Essex.

46. Wenceslaus Hollar, "London from Bankside," engraving, 1647. Arthur M. Hind, *Wenceslaus Hollar and His Views of London and Windsor in the Seventeenth Century* (London, John Lane, 1922), Plate XVIII. Franz Sprinzels, *Hollar Handzeichnungen* (Vienna, Verlag dr. Rolf Passer, 1938), Plate LII.

47. John Goslying, "A Plot of the Building upon the Ground of Sir Nicholas Bacon" (1670), London Topographical Society, Publications, Vol. LVIII. Fetter Lane and Nevill's Court were largely preserved from the Great Fire. Walter G. Bell, *The Great Fire of London in 1666* (London, John Lane, 1920), pp. 165–166.

48. This description based on "Survey of All Lands and Tenements Belonging to the Worshipful Company of Clothworkers of London made by Ralphe Treswell the Elder in the Month of July A D 1612 . . . ," London Topographical Society, Publications, Vols. LXXII–LXXV.

possible a fresh start.[49] Because of this limitation, London architecture before the Great Fire did not fit the needs of less crowded districts, and style-conscious colonial builders of the seventeenth-century had to remain content with the degree of fashion set by metropolitan ornament and interior details. (Fig. 6.)

Social conditions as much as nautical miles separated the Ulster settler from the London city dweller. In Ulster unsettled land and a small population produced the antithesis of crowded London. Ulster building styles followed those of rural England. At the bottom of the scale lay the cottages of the poorest inhabitants, the Irish tenants. As sketched by Phillips between 1600 and 1629 they had low rounded walls topped by thatch roofs apparently much like the modern Irish cottage.[50] Their small size clearly indicates the inferior social position of their tenants. (Fig. 31.)

When the Scotch and English settlers turned to the construction of their own homes, they did not use any Irish prototype but took as their model the familiar yeoman farmhouse of England. Thus at Agivey, on the Mercers' lands at Movangher, or in the Vintner's village, the predominant house type was a two-story structure of post-and-truss construction, probably roofed with slate or tile.[51]

Settlers on deforested land preserved the general outline of the framed yeoman house, although they built in stone and often let attic dormer windows into the slate roofs. Whether of timber or stone, these houses which so closely resembled the detached English farmhouse were in Ulster built closely together on the village street in accord with the Plantation Articles.[52] (Figs. 8, 14, 31.)

An Englishman visiting Ulster might be struck by the familiarity of the cottages and settlers' homes, but he would certainly be surprised at the absence of any manor house. An entirely new sort of building, the Irish bawn, filled the place of the manor house.[53] These bawns as developed by the London companies were stone houses built into one side of a large walled courtyard with one or more sides of the house thus forming a part of the walls of the enclosure. Set a little apart from the village, they housed the adminis-

49. For immediate post-fire construction, see Bell, *The Great Fire of London in 1666,* pp. 98, 112, 128, 166, 264, 272, 281, 294, 308.

50. *Phillips MSS,* pp. 113, 124, 133, 152. These are the most detailed of the plats. Arthur H. Johnson, *History of the Worshipful Company of Drapers of London,* IV, 540.

51. *Phillips MSS,* pp. 12, 92, 152.

52. *Ibid.,* pp. 28, 145.

53. " 'Bawn' is an Irish term meaning a stone or wooden enclosure in which cattle and other valuable property were collected at night to protect them from wolves or from the raids of neighbouring chieftains." Constantia E. Maxwell, *Country and Town in Ireland under the Georges* (London, George G. Harrap & Co., Ltd., 1940), p. 67.

trative officials of the London companies in time of peace, and the entire English population in time of strife. As a result their design varied from a close approximation to a small English manor house with attached wall, like that of the Merchant Taylors or the Mercers, to the enormous building of the Skinners at Dungiven which had been elaborated from their experience with a previous house and bawn at Crossault.[54] The earlier bawns seem to have been small, strong houses with attached walls, the principal purpose of which was defense. The later ones more closely resembled guild buildings in London and reflected the increasing profit and pacification of the administration of Ulster lands.[55] (Figs. 8, 14, 31.) This tendency in design is the only indication of direct London influence and should not be overrated. Elsewhere the architectural style of Ulster was one taken from rural England and modified only to fit the new conditions of Irish unrest and settlement. (Fig. 57.)

Unfortunately, information is less specific for Jamestown and other American settlements before 1630. Excavations and the few sketches which remain show that two sorts of dwellings were built. One type was an independent free-standing house of one-and-a-half stories, the familiar yeoman or farmhouse style. These had two rooms 17 x 18 feet, with a central and two end chimneys.[56]

The other type strongly suggested urban origins. Forman believes that existing foundations closely followed London practice and therefore based his reconstruction on Moxon.[57] Excavation had uncovered a row of three cellars, each with central chimney, 20-foot street frontage, and party walls. Close as this connection would appear to be, plans drawn by Moxon do not present a satisfactory comparison (he was not born until 1627, and the earliest edition of *Mechanick Exercises* was published in parts from 1677 to 1680). Moreover, as might be suspected since this work appeared more than a decade after the Great Fire, the elevation of the house floor plan which Forman compares to Jamestown is a three-storied brick townhouse with a hip roof not unlike William Penn's house at Philadelphia and totally dissimilar to anything built in Virginia before 1690.[58] Such regularity certainly did not typify London streets in 1612 when the clothworkers surveyed their holdings, and it is very doubtful that contemporary London practice provided the design of these Jamestown houses.[59]

In other English ventures overseas the construction of adjoining buildings

54. *Phillips MSS*, pp. 101, 124, 160.

55. See "Plan of the Clothworkers' Hall, 1612," London Topographical Society, Publications, Vol. LXXII.

56. Henry C. Forman, *Jamestown and Saint Mary's*, pp. 117–119.

57. *Ibid.*, pp. 104, 107.

58. Joseph Moxon, *Mechanick Exercises*, Plates IV, V.

59. London Topographical Society, Publications, Vols. LXXI, LXXIV.

with common walls became a practice early in the seventeenth century, suggesting that it was colonial conditions rather than London experience which led to its adoption. Both Derry (Fig. 7) and Coleraine plans clearly show the houses adjoining, and Lord Carew's report specifies that forty-three tenements had been built at Coleraine by August, 1611. Most of these measured 12 x 18 feet, were a story and a half high, and were surmounted by an attic dormer. Each had a chimney and occasionally "three of these tenements are described as forming one house." Other larger tenements of two-and-one-half stories, 72 x 26 feet, were also built a little later.[60] Thus before 1611 the custom of close units in fortified posts existed in both Ulster and Virginia.

The influence of other continental English colonies in America upon Connecticut architecture is difficult to gauge. Few if any buildings still standing in Massachusetts predate the Connecticut colony. The paucity of early pictorial material adds to the difficulty of specifying the architectural relationship between Connecticut and Massachusetts in the seventeenth century. Since the earliest strictly documented date for a Massachusetts house is 1651, the pre-1630 influence of the Bay colony upon Connecticut must be purely conjectural.[61]

The dating of early houses is doubly difficult in the architectural chronology of Connecticut. One writer has gone so far as to state that no house is documented before the Ebenezer Grant homestead of 1757 in East Windsor.[62] While such a position is extreme, it reflects the astonishing lack of documentation that characterized private buildings in New England prior to 1800. Only eighteen Connecticut and New Haven towns were founded before 1650; there were forty-two by 1700, of which twenty-eight were large enough to pay taxes to the colony. Even allowing for decay and fire the first three generations of settlers built only between 2,100 and 2,500 homes; it is little wonder that a mere twenty existing houses can be attributed to the seventeenth century. Of these many have only a small section built before 1700, which is now well concealed by a later and more ample structure.[63]

Most features of English rural architecture suited conditions in Connecticut and were incorporated into the colony's townscape. Meanwhile English society, changed by the Civil War and the Restoration, turned after the Great Fire of London to brick architecture and a fresh interpretation of classical design. This early divergence laid the foundation for a theory of independent colonial architectural development.

60. Theodore W. Moody, *Londonderry Plantation,* p. 103, Plate IV.

61. Pickering House, Salem, Massachusetts. Kimball, *Domestic Architecture of the American Colonies,* p. 265.

62. *Ibid.,* p. 266.

63. F.W.P. "Blds. Census," Farmington, No. 36, William Lewis House, now the Elm Tree Inn. Yale MSS Copy.

43. House at North Guilford

44. The Norton House

45. The husbandman house as painted by George Durrie

46. Wilcox House, Killingworth

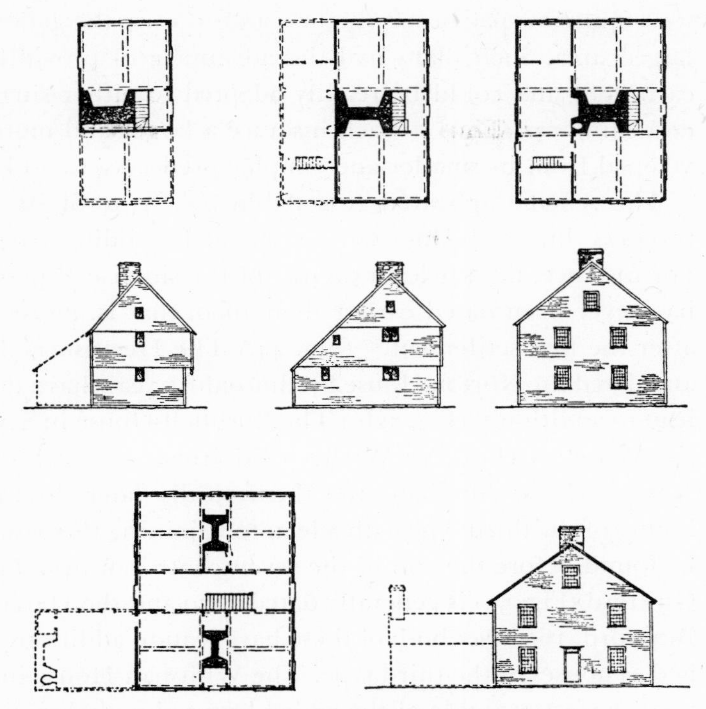

47. The evolutionary theory of colonial house design

Continuing and extending the evolutionary concept of history so popular in the early twentieth century when Norman Isham first advanced his correlation of Connecticut house types, J. Frederick Kelly, through the detail and skill of his structural illustrations and his intimate acquaintance with the houses he described, colored all succeeding interpretations of New England architecture. (Fig. 47.) Kelly's theory identified the simplest, most elementary architectural construction with the earliest. Thus he chose the one-room Norton House in Guilford with side chimney as the classic example of the single-cell house from which all others grew. (Fig. 44.) On Hempstead Court in New London he found the second stage—the addition of a second room on the open side of the chimney to the Hempstead House built in 1643.[64] (Fig. 51b.)

Such two-room, central-chimney houses, he believed, were modified further in the third stage by a long lean-to which carried the eaves close to the ground, gave an extra room along the whole length of the longest side on the ground floor, and opened a cramped little chamber at the second-story level. The fourth step assigned the lean-to across the rear to the time of original construction. The final stage was so to deepen the house as to make the second

64. Kelly, *Domestic Architecture,* pp. 1 ff. The added lean-to was often made to appear integral. *Ibid.,* pp. 12–17.

story quite as spacious as the first and to raise the gable roof to span this enlarged area. Such plans had the advantage of providing four chambers on each floor and could be readily adapted to either single central or double-end chimneys. Thus in each instance a larger and more elaborate house developed from its smaller and simpler predecessor.[65] (Fig. 47.)

The scheme appeared reasonable by virtue of its appeal to a sense of progress, but it did not fit the assigned building dates of existing houses. For instance, the earliest example of the single-cell plan, the Norton House, has never been dated earlier than 1690, that is, more than two generations after the first settlement.[66] (Fig. 44.) The Hempstead House of 1643 which antedated the Norton House by almost fifty years has a double-room plan with lean-to addition.[67] (Fig. 52b.) The Bushnell House in Saybrook (1678–79) and the Williams House in Wethersfield (1680) are both contemporaries of the Norton House but have the theoretically later double-room plan.[68] Even houses of the third type with a lean-to adjoining the basic two-room house can be found before the end of the seventeenth century. The Acadian House in Guilford (Fig. 53) is generally dated 1670 and the Harrison-Linsley House in Branford, 1690; yet both of these have lean-to additions and rightly are classified as houses of the third type. The Whitman House in Farmington is an almost perfect example of the added lean-to house, but Kelly himself asserts it was built about 1660.[69] (Fig. 55a.)

The Norton House is not the only late seventeenth-century single-cell house. In 1922 Snyder found a strikingly similar North Guilford house (Fig. 43), and the asymmetrical plan of the Graves House in Madison (Fig. 51a) indicates that structure was originally a single-cell design to which additions were later made. But Kelly dated the house 1675, and other authorities think even this date too early.[70] Since Isham's and Kelly's theory was based on existing remains of seventeenth-century Connecticut architecture, it is difficult to see how so confusing a pattern of house types could have produced so regular a theory of architectural development. To all appearances, simple and complex houses were built at much the same time.

The evidence presented by early Connecticut architecture is contradictory

65. *Ibid.*, pp. 8–11.

66. *Ibid.*, p. 7. The house is first mentioned in the land records of 1762. An excellent description of it is to be found in Bertha C. Trowbridge and Charles M. Andrews, *Old Houses of Connecticut* (New Haven, Yale University Press, 1923), p. 11.

67. The dating of the Hempstead House is still controversial. See F.W.P. "Blds. Census," New London, No. 21.

68. F.W.P. "Blds. Census," Wethersfield, No. 76. Kelly, *Domestic Architecture*, p. 8.

69. F.W.P. "Blds. Census," Farmington, No. 54; Branford, No. 13. H.A.B.S., *Connecticut*, Acadian House. Kelly, *Domestic Architecture*, pp. 9–11. Trowbridge and Andrews, *Old Houses*, pp. x–xi.

70. Kelly, *Domestic Architecture*, p. 12.

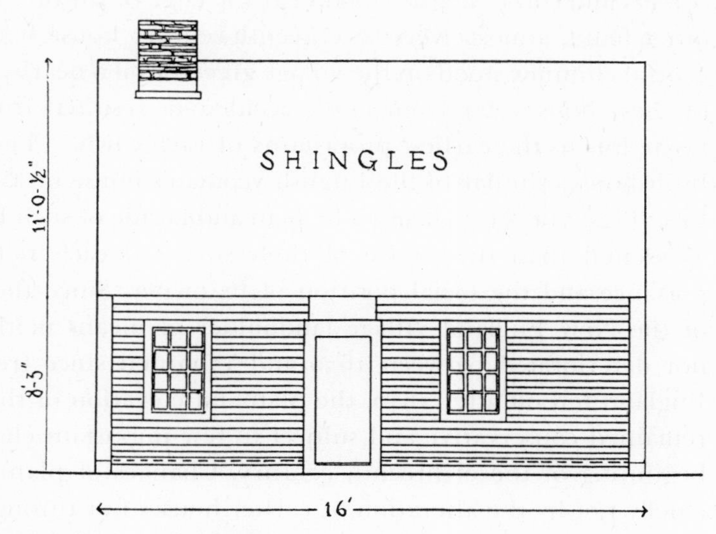

48. Front elevation of Nathaniel Baker Cottage

only in terms of a concept of progress from a single origin. Otherwise, the chronological evidence of the various remaining monuments presents no difficulty but falls rather into much the same pattern as the homes of the city of London's settlers in Ulster.

Clearly no strict chronology based on plan can be inferred. Houses of all three early types survived from 1660 until the end of the century, and no single type can be said to dominate any one of these periods. If the contradictions in dating certain houses as, for example, the Hempstead House, are carefully considered, any conclusions regarding the chronology of seventeenth-century domestic architecture in Connecticut based on plans alone seems impossible.[71]

Actually the difficulty is simply resolved if it is assumed that instead of a single starting point for English colonial architecture there were several. In other words, one must abandon the assumption that all types of colonial dwellings developed from a single model and substitute in its place the notion that the English colonists were familiar with many house types and each settler chose that which suited his particular class and station in life.[72] (Fig. 56.)

Thus the Norton House and others like it, though built late in the seventeenth century, were the homes not of proprietors but of comparatively late-

71. The Hempstead House has been dated between 1643 and 1678 by various works. See Edwin Whitefield, *Homes of Our Forefathers,* Plate XVI. Trowbridge and Andrews, *Old Houses,* p. 19. F.W.P. "Blds. Census," New London, No. 21.

72. Certainly this would seem to be the case. See above, Chapter I.

comers and consequently stood near the edge of town.[73] (Figs. 43, 44.) On the other hand, almost every seventeenth-century house with two stories and a central chimney stood on the village green or on a nearby street. The position of these houses, far from being accidental, resulted from the allotment of home lots to the earliest proprietors of each town.[74] These proprietors then built houses similar to the English yeoman's house on their respective home lots. (Figs. 51a, 53, 55a, 58.) The plan and façade of such houses were no more accidental than the choice of their site, and each reflected both the importance and the social position of its owner. Since the economic position of the New England village landholder of means neither improved much nor deteriorated between 1650 and 1700 and since fresh migrations from England fell off after 1640, the plan and elevation of the proprietor's house remained conservative and subject to few important changes until after the beginning of the eighteenth century. Changes of plan and elevation came chiefly not by the alteration of earlier houses but through the adoption of a completely new house type of equal antiquity which better suited the changed social position of its owner. Thus houses of the lean-to type, just as well known to the Connecticut settler as they had been to the English yeoman, were built throughout the seventeenth century and into the eighteenth. Such houses became the symbol of the town proprietors and the wealthier late-comers of the village and were abandoned only after the eighteenth-century immigration. All types of the Connecticut house plan as it developed before 1700 were known in England in 1630. The evidence indicates that this knowledge was used and not forgotten in the New England plantation. If so, then the existence in Connecticut of a 1660 lean-to house and a 1690 house of the one-room sort is not a contradiction but a result of the survival of the social degree and economic status of its colonial owner. (Fig. 56.)

The conservatism of Connecticut design contrasted markedly with the work done in such Restoration colonies as Pennsylvania, where architecture took as a point of departure the London that was built on the ruins of the Great Fire and developed without direct reference to the earlier period. Midway between these two extremes stand such colonies as New York and Massachusetts, founded early but with a population often increased by migrations. In these colonies domestic architecture followed European styles more closely and each fresh wave of migration that surged through Boston

73. Trowbridge and Andrews, *Old Houses,* pp. 11–18. Kelly, "The Norton House, Guilford, Conn.," *Old-Time New England,* XIV (January, 1924), 122–130.

74. A spectacular illustration is Norwich. The area occupied by home sites tripled from 1705 to 1795. Mary E. Perkins, *Old Houses of the Ancient Town of Norwich* (Norwich, 1895), pp. 104, 168.

49. Bishop House, Guilford

50. Seventeenth-century yeoman house in Essex

51a. George Graves House, Madison

51b. The Hempstead House, New London, 1836

and New York produced changes of style quite foreign to the nine-window, central-chimney house of Connecticut.[75]

Style changes in Connecticut came, like Yankee humor, in small things and subtle details. Once a visitor has stepped from the tiny entrance way of a seventeenth-century house into its kitchen or hall he can sense the period in which the interior was finished. If he chances to visit the Hempstead kitchen first (Fig. 59) he will find a dark room with thick walls heavily plastered between the now nearly black oak timbers of the frame. The chimney summer beam, he will notice, was framed hastily while still green, so that as it seasoned it dipped over the fireplace opening. Wide floor-boards, almost uncarved posts, a stone fireplace, and beams simply hewn out of the oak give the room a primitive or rustic aspect. The pattern of plaster and post runs around the room haphazardly. The room gives a sense of shelter and strength, its fireplace warms it well, but its visual effect is naïve and unfinished.

Later builders took obvious steps to enhance the sophistication of their keeping rooms, and parlors, paint, paneling, and paper all had a share; even if they left the frame unhidden, they introduced a new quality into their interior design which suited their William and Mary furniture better than did the provincialism of the Hempstead House. In 1670 Joseph Clay, a Guilford settler, framed and fitted a handsome two-room house for his bride near the junction of Pent Road and Back Lane. Here as in the Hempstead House the kitchen is a rectangle, the frame and plaster make a similar black and white pattern, the boards of the floor are wide in both houses; but two generations separate the workmanship of the two rooms. Securely founded

75. Kimball, *Domestic Architecture,* p. 48. Moxon, *Mechanick Exercises,* Plate V.

52. Huts of oystermen at Milford, about 1836

on a solid rock ledge, the Acadian House (as Clay's home came to be called) has all its timbers running plumb and true; horizontal beams are evenly spaced, smoothed, and carefully carved with a lamb's tongue; each corner post has a well-cut cap at the ceiling level; the fireplace itself appears symmetrical and the flues draw well. The haphazard quality is removed and with the possible exception of the windows the room seems intelligently planned.

Although the retention of open timber and plasterwork and exposed members became rare after 1700, where it was done the final elaboration is indeed handsome. On a rocky ledge near Leete's Island there is a lean, weathered house built about 1730 for Deacon Pelatiah Leete. In its orderly rooms seventeenth-century design is given a final twist. Here the posts, beams, floors, and window frames all have a studied, polished air. They are smoothed and well cut, the rhythm of their relation to other parts of the room has been carefully determined; no consideration whatever of time hurried the task in hand. Without introducing new elements the colonists could go no further.[76]

Most of the features which Connecticut artisans elaborated into a colonial style were taken from the English yeoman's house in the first instance and then modified more or less to fit colonial conditions. In both countries the house was built about the central chimney stack but for somewhat different reasons. In England the chimney and the large hearth symbolized the growth of enclosure and the ample meat that the new pastures provided for the fortunate few. In Connecticut the chimney was less elaborate but still of an

76. These elements were introduced and in due course elaborated and polished like the exposed frame. Paneling, corner cupboard, boxed beams, paint, and eventually wallpaper all were used.

imposing mass suggesting rather the warmth of the New England kitchen and the comfort of a home in the wilderness.[77]

The first houses appear to have had casement windows, of which less than half a dozen remain. These had small, narrow, wooden frames, diamond or square panes, and followed English practice. The sash window had completely replaced the casement window long before the end of the colonial period. Window placement seems to have been done on functional lines except along the entrance façade. There the five or nine windows were spaced symmetrically between the vertical posts to give the central door a visual emphasis totally lacking in the haphazard arrangement of windows on the gable ends. (Figs. 53, 55a, 58.) In Connecticut the studied proportion of the front façade became sure and more elaborate than anything found in the English yeoman's house before the end of the seventeenth century; fashionable tastes, foreign, even baroque scrolls and pediments were grafted to the main composition, but underneath the skilled tracks of the molding planes the simple traditions of the yeoman house continued to form the basic architectural pattern.[78]

The close resemblance between the yeoman house in England and the proprietor's house in Connecticut should not obscure the existence of other types of colonial houses in which the settlers clung to different English precedents. Though rare, the most impressive were the Connecticut bawns. The Henry Whitfield stone house in Guilford and the Gardiner House in Saybrook were excellent examples of the defensive fortified Ulster house which was, as we have seen, at the heart of the bawn required by law of all the city's plantations in northern Ireland. The Whitfield House (Fig. 60) as restored has the massive stone work and the asymmetry which were typical of so many of the English "strong houses" in Ireland. Its location—somewhat removed from the village green—the labor involved in its construction, and perhaps

77. Campbell, *English Yeoman,* pp. 231, 236, 247. Not only do the chimneys dominate existing monuments but they also are the most prominent feature of such contemporary sketches by colonial surveyors and artists as the Wadsworth "Plan of the City of New Haven Taken in 1748," MS map, Yale University Library. Most interiors throughout the century are completely dominated by the fireplace wall and the hearth itself. Kelly, *Domestic Architecture,* pp. 73–80. The importance of the hearth and chimney in America was recognized twenty years ago by Thomas J. Wertenbaker, *The First Americans,* pp. ix, xiv, 288. The carefully preserved rooms in the gallery of Fine Arts at Yale University illustrate the importance of the fireplace and the use of paneling to emphasize it.

78. As examples of Connecticut Valley façades, see *White Pine Series,* II (June, 1916), No. 3, 3–14. Despite the lack of skill of the artist the Wadsworth drawings of New Haven show the typical elevation to be that of a two-story building with central door and chimney, five or nine windows, and often an overhanging second story. Whitefield's drawings confirm the fact that such houses were located on the sites of greatest antiquity, and the earliest buildings documented by the Historic American Buildings Survey are of this type. See MS map, New Haven, 1748; Whitefield, *Homes of Our Forefathers,* n.p.; Kelly, *Domestic Architecture,* p. 97.

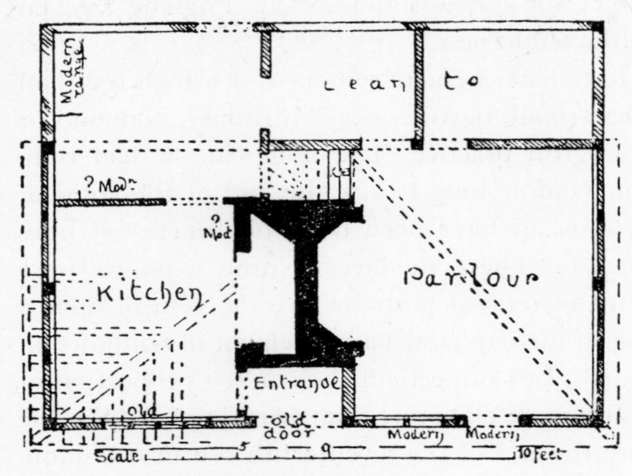

54. Plan of a yeoman house in Surrey

even the small window restored across the southwest corner become intelligible when viewed from the point of view of defense.[79]

At Saybrook, if Winthrop's plan is to be believed, Lion Gardiner designed a strong house that approximated some of the most elaborate London Company buildings in Ulster. Sixty feet to the side, it enclosed a courtyard 30 feet square. Along one side of the courtyard lay the pantry, kitchen, and hall flanked by the servants' quarters and facing the "dayre" and larder. While some questions remain as to how much of this area was completed and how much roofed but open, Winthrop's floor plan closely resembles the disposition of rooms in Clothworkers' Hall in London or the administrative buildings of the Ironmongers in Ulster.[80] (Figs. 56, 57.)

79. J. Frederick Kelly, *Henry Whitfield House, 1639,* Plates 6, 10, 11, 20, 34, 36. The best survey of Guilford was made in the early nineteenth century. Photostat of MS in New Haven County Historical Society.

80. On the fifth leaf from the back of the Winthrop Journal the drawings appear. The notations upon them seem to be in the hand of John Winthrop, Jr., and follow quite closely, but with a different ink and pen, letters in his hand written to his father in April, 1631. The notations are clearly not done in the crabbed, distinctive hand of the author of the journal, John Winthrop the elder. The surveying skill of the drawings seems comparable to the technique employed by the younger Winthrop when he mapped his father's estate in 1637, and the pen and ink of the latter plot come very close indeed to that used on the final leaves of the journal. The content of the drawing shows that John Winthrop, Jr., knew of livery company practice in Ulster and may represent the way he hoped Saybrook would look. MS in Massachusetts Historical Society. *Winthrop Papers* (Boston, Massachusetts Historical Society, 1931), II, 178, 193, 276–277; IV, 416. Another drawing on the sixth leaf has been tentatively associated with a commission which Isaac Johnson suggested for the younger Winthrop in December, 1629, to survey the fort at Landguard near Harwich but the sketch must have fallen far short of Johnson's expectations in its accuracy. *Ibid.*, and *Victoria History of the Counties of England, Essex,* II, 292–294. W. B. Goodwin, *Old Saybrook* (Hartford, 1944), pp. 7–9. Many of Goodwin's assertions appear

53. The Acadian House, Guilford

55a. The Whitman House, Farmington

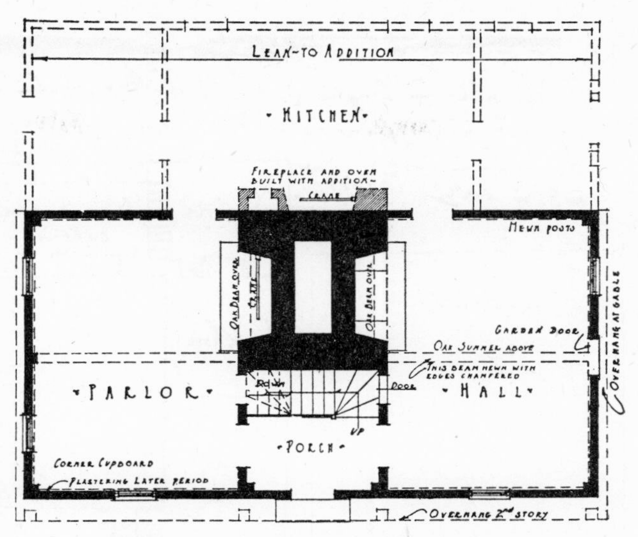

55b. Plan of the Whitman House in Farmington

It was no mere coincidence that Saybrook and Guilford had the two Connecticut buildings that most closely resembled the Ulster bawns. Lord Saye and Sele had extensive holdings in Armagh, and George Fenwick, Saybrook's founder, sailed from England with his lifelong friend, Henry Whitfield, the leader of Guilford and builder of the Old Stone House. Moreover, Fenwick, a patentee of the Warwick deed to Saybrook, paid part of the expense of Whitfield's voyage to New Haven and gave him permission to settle within the Warwick Patent.[81]

Defensive and administrative structures were not the only large-scale buildings erected. The leaders of the New Haven colony and Connecticut built several homes during the first generation of settlement that closely resembled the English manor houses to which they were accustomed. Even discounting the often repeated criticism of New Haven ostentation, the inventory and will of Theophilus Eaton describes in no uncertain terms a house that was not inferior either in size or in design to many English manor houses of the day; a house which had at least ten rooms laid out in two full stories carried about a U-plan.[82] A different but no less impressive type, which had a projecting porch chamber over the central door like the large Virginia house, was known in Hartford. The Thomas Hooker House, if Barber is to be believed, had such a chamber which gave it an appearance quite distinct from that of

---

based on material external to the drawings themselves. "Survey of All the Tenements belonging to the Worshipful Company of the Clothworkers, 1612," London Topographical Society, Publications, Vol. LXXII.

81. C. M. Andrews, *Colonial Period of American History,* II, 161.

82. G. D. Seymour, *Memorials of Theophilus Eaton* (New Haven, privately printed by Tuttle, Morehouse & Taylor, 1938), pp. 21, 33–41.

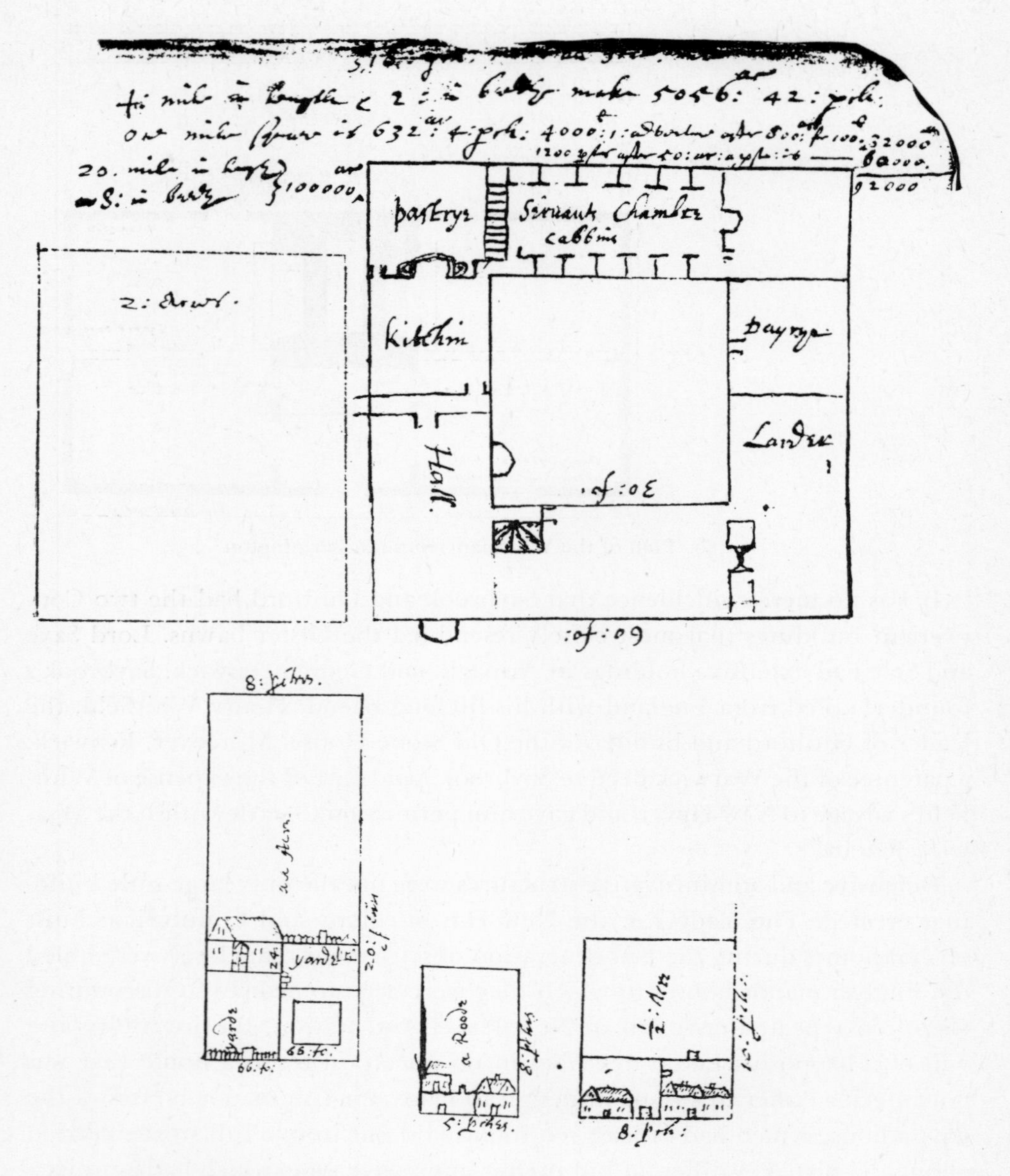

56. Sketch of bawn and home lots, Winthrop Diary

even the largest building developed from the yeoman house of England.[83] The relative equality of wealth, the shortage of hard money, the high price of labor, all made such large houses mere curiosities after the ideals of the first generation had been buried. Only a few lingered to the nineteenth century; all are gone today.

83. John Barber, *Connecticut Historical Collections,* p. 43.

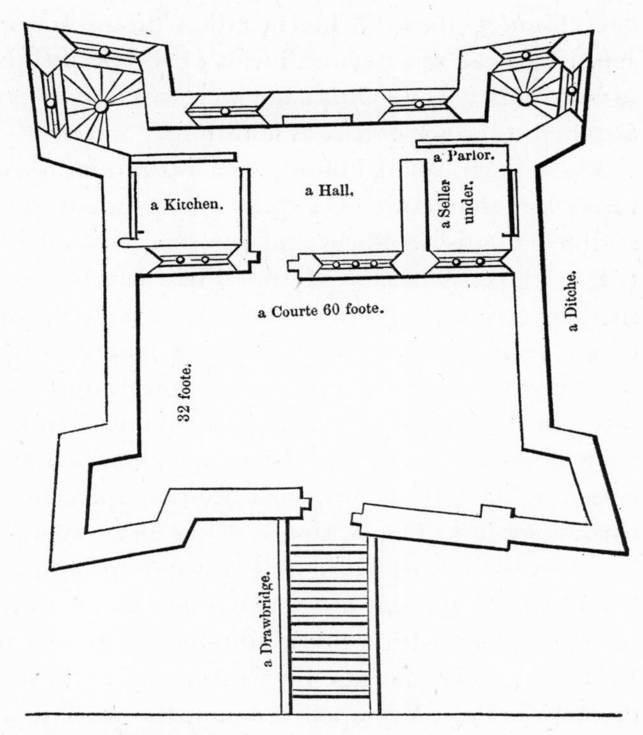

57. The Ironmongers' Irish bawn, about 1615

Next in the hierarchy of colonial architecture after the few large manor houses and the many yeoman-proprietor houses stood a class of building which did not fit in what has been hitherto regarded as the main stream of Connecticut's architecture. (Figs. 45, 46.) Something less than a yeoman house and something more than a cottage, these one-and-a-half story homes seem in English surveys to have belonged to husbandmen of the better sort, in colonial Connecticut to planters of moderate means. They were characterized by steep roofs and had either a single central or two gable-end chimneys (in any case far smaller than the fine stacks of the yeoman house), low ceilings, and modest fenestration which was sometimes symmetrical on the front façade. Though on occasion the gable ends of these small houses were made of stone they more often had wood construction, but even in wood their silhouette recalls the small brick houses of seventeenth-century Virginia and Maryland.[84]

The cottages of the poorest planters have suffered no less than the ostentatious homes of the colony's leaders. Single-room structures a bay square, with

84. Kelly, *Domestic Architecture,* Plate XXVI, Bradley House. Henry C. Forman, *Early Manor and Plantation Houses of Maryland* (Easton, privately printed for the author, 1934), pp. 58, 59, 64.

end chimney, they did not fit either the prosperity of the early nineteenth century or the sentimental ideals of recent antiquarians, and soon fell into disuse. (Figs. 48, 52.) Only a few were saved from extinction because they were attached to larger houses as additions.[85]

These early small houses were no miniature of their larger contemporaries but the result of a quite independent development that closely resembled English cottages and the smallest houses of the Ulster settlement. (Fig. 48.) Yet neither Kelly nor Fiske Kimball gave much attention to this smallest class of building. Occupied in large measure with the development of the yeoman-proprietor house they ignored the problems raised by more modest structures.[86] Moreover these lower, single-story buildings are not only rare but located on sites somewhat removed from the center of the village. Such homesites were allotted to newcomers only after the more desirable sites near the village green had been occupied by the town's proprietors and earliest settlers. The existence of the newcomers' houses on outlying home lots does not mean that houses of the proprietor type were not also built on similar plots. Indeed, every newcomer seems to have wished to replace his modest cottage with a house suitable either to a proprietor or a yeoman as soon as he could increase his wealth and attain social standing equal to that of early settlers. Yet upon occasion the earliest small cottage was retained as an L-addition to the main structure erected during the eighteenth century; rarely were small cottages to be found near the meetinghouses of early towns.

At its inception Connecticut had a rich variety of architecture. Traces remain of virtually every sort of building the colonists had known in England and Ulster, but the social and economic isolation of the colony began to enforce homogeneity and the seventeenth-century promise of diversity was not kept. The Whitfield House at Guilford remained the colony's only important stone house; the Eaton House at New Haven had fallen into decay less than a century after it was erected; John Barber's quaint early nineteenth-century sketches of Connecticut villages recorded only one true cot or cottage then used by Milford oystermen. (Fig. 52.)

One style neither too large nor too small came to represent the architectural ideal of the Connecticut colonist. In views, maps, and present-day remains the clapboard lean-to house, directly descended from the yeoman post-enclosure farmhouse of eastern England, crowded out all other styles

85. Several examples of such additions still remain, probably the most famous are the Cowles House, the Chaffee House (Windsor), and the Return Jonathan Meigs House (Middletown). Trowbridge and Andrews, *Old Houses,* pp. 60, 370. Kelly, *Domestic Architecture,* pp. 20, 72. All of these examples, while preserving the small plan of the true cottage, have late-type roofs and, though on ancient sites, are altered.

86. Kelly draws no plans of any such houses and illustrates only a few possible examples of this class. Kelly, *Domestic Architecture,* chap. ii, Plates IV, VII, XXXI.

58. North Guilford house

59. Interior of the Hempstead House, New London

60. Whitfield House in Guilford

61. St. Bavo Church in Haarlem, about 1630

62. Salomon de Brosse's design for the Second Temple of Charenton (1623–24)

and laid the foundation for later architectural development in the colony.[87] Architectural uniformity recalled the high per capita land wealth of the colony, its equitable land division, its absence of great trade, its homogeneous population—all conditions which led to stable society and aversion to architectural novelty.

87. A large almost square house type of two and one-half or three stories was built in small quantities for merchants and shipowners from 1790 until after the War of 1812. Though very handsome with Palladian windows and four end-chimneys, the design seems to have had little effect on building generally. Kelly, *Domestic Architecture,* Plate XXI, pp. 17–19.

VI. Public Buildings

No factor better illustrates the character of the colonial town in Connecticut than the poverty of its public architecture. The colonist, unmindful of His Majesty's government in England, averse to ostentation in his religion, and satisfied with home education, had no real need for public buildings. Because the colony remained corporate the Crown felt no obligation to initiate large-scale building. Only the passage of time and the slow multiplication of the colony's population could provide the need for genuine public architecture; the seventeenth century in Connecticut was an age of modest meetinghouses and comfortable homes.

Perhaps this very absence of monumental architecture contrived to focus the town's attention on its first meetinghouse to a degree that few of its larger and more handsome successors enjoyed. In most towns it occupied the central site, and its early erection was a matter of pride. Within its walls not only Sunday worship but also much town business was conducted. That architecturally the meetinghouse remained humble is the accident of its European heritage at the time of the colony's birth and Connecticut's subsequent isolation. Religious architecture in New England can best be understood as an offshoot of the European Plain Style which in England, Holland, Germany, and Huguenot France answered the militant challenge of Catholic architecture. In the first half of the seventeenth century radical Protestants everywhere in Christendom tried to dam up the sinful swirling waters of the baroque with the cool severity of their new designs. Without liturgy, ornament, or monumental scale, in the simplest of interiors they managed to present a clear reasoned solution for their house of prayer.

The full story of that style remains to be told; yet its outline is clear.[1]

1. I have presented a fuller account of the international Plain Style which post-Reformation Protestants initiated and have tried to explain the neglect with which it has been treated in "The Origin of the Plain Style," *Journal of the Society of Architectural*

Close upon the rise of their party to power, Protestants everywhere considered the churches they had inherited and found them wanting. At first renovation satisfied the reformers. They stripped the medieval fabric of statues, screens, ornaments, and stained glass, leaving only a pulpit and simple altar table in place of the rich variety of Catholic church furniture. A handsome luminous interior resulted, but it was one in which the human figure had lost its scale. The new pulpits, the communion tables, the congregations themselves disappeared into vast reaches of brilliant space unbroken except by towering vertical Gothic piers. (Fig. 61.)

After 1600 the growth and divisions of continental Protestantism forced a boom of new church construction. In Holland a wide variety of church plans, octagonal, square, and rectangular, were designed to enable each member of the congregation to hear the preacher's word. Replacing the altar with the pulpit, these new designs met the needs of Protestant worship squarely. Oldest of these entirely new schemes, the brick octagon church at Willemstad must have seemed highly radical to the seventeenth-century Dutchmen. A perfect octagon 20 meters in diameter, the church became the center of a fortified town protected by eight bastions and two moats. Each of the church's eight walls was broken by a tall, nearly pointed window, and at each corner curious Doric columns masked the interior piers. A bell-like roof and cupola sat like a giant snuffer on the church walls. Until the invasion of the Netherlands in 1940 the fabric of the building remained almost untouched except for a large western tower which destroyed the original symmetry of the design. Within the church the pulpit stood against the northeast wall, and pews filled the whole body of the church.[2]

The internal prosperity of Dutch Protestantism contrasted sharply with the pitiful insecurity of the French Huguenots, but here too an original and influential form of church architecture emerged. In 1623 the world-famous Temple of Charenton introduced the use of galleries to enable the large Huguenot congregation to hear such pastors as the Parisian Pierre Dumoulin, favorite of Catherine of Bourbon.[3] (Fig. 62.) Built near the site of a small Protestant temple, fired by rioting Catholics in September of 1621, the second temple was designed by Salomon de Brosse and completed with royal per-

---

Historians (September, 1950). A very complete description of all Connecticut meetinghouses of the colonial period is given by John Frederick Kelly, *Early Meetinghouses of Connecticut* (New York, Columbia University Press, 1948).

2. Murk D. Ozinga, *De protestantsche Kerkenbouw in Nederland* (Amsterdam, H. J. Paris, 1929), pp. 12–19, Plates I–III. J. J. van der Meulen, *Nederland vanuit de Lucht* (Baarn, Bosch und Keuning, 1947), p. 133.

3. Pierre Dumoulin, born in 1568, was pastor of the Temple of Charenton from 1589 to 1619. In 1621, after the destruction of the Temple, he fled to Sedan, where he spent his remaining years.

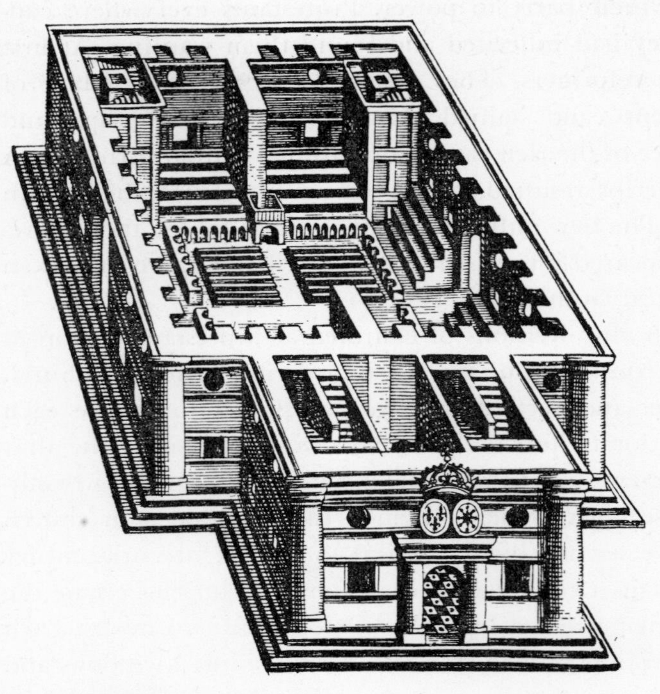

63. Jacques Perret's designs for a Protestant temple

mission.[4] From the time of its dedication the Temple of Charenton became a symbol of Protestantism, persecuted but militant. Though destroyed together with other Huguenot churches shortly after the revocation of the Edict of Nantes in 1685,[5] the building was widely imitated in both England and Holland and even today French Protestants regard it as the finest expression of their religious architecture.[6] Abroad it was copied closely. A Dutch engraving of 1630 shows workmen completing the Remonstrance Church in Amsterdam. In almost every detail the Dutch architect followed the plans of de Brosse. In each church two tiers of galleries were carried around all four walls of the church. In each the pulpit stood clear of one end wall so that the preacher was almost at the level of the first gallery and surrounded by his parish. Men and women sat apart and special seats were reserved for the elders.[7] All commentaries on the church point out its evident debt to Jacques

4. Jacques Pannier, *Salomon de Brosse* (Paris, Libraire Centrale d'Art et d'Architecture, 1911), pp. 86 ff.

5. A good reproduction of Sebastian Leclerc's engraving of the destruction is to be found in E. Lavisse, *Histoire de France* (Paris, Hachette et Cie, 1911), VII, Part 2, 78.

6. "Le Temple de Charenton, 1606–1685," *Bulletin de la Société de l'Histoire du Protestantisme Français,* V (Paris, 1857), 173–174, hereafter referred to as B.H.P. See also Jacques Pannier, *L'Église réformée de Paris sous Henri IV* (Paris, H. Champion, 1911). See also B.H.P., II, 247 ff.; III, 148, 418, 540; IV, 29; VI, 162.

7. The two are compared in nearly contemporary engravings. Ozinga, *De protestanche Kerkenbouw,* Plate XLIX. See also Pannier, *L'Église réformée de Paris sous Henri IV,* p.

Perret, who in his fascinating book of imaginative studies of fortress architecture interspersed plans of such widely separated projects as a skyscraper and a Protestant church. (Fig. 63.) Published in 1594, 1602, 1613, and 1620, *Des fortifications et artifices* could not fail to influence architects groping for a concrete expression of the Protestant ethic. Describing his own interior design Perret wrote, "au dedans tout à l'environ sont trois bancs l'un sur l'autre touchant la muraille en manière de théâtre. Puis les chaires pour les seigneurs et en après les bancs pour les femmes, ayant tousiours belles allées entre deux." [8]

The exterior of Charenton, while it did not suggest the theater, was not intended to awe or overwhelm. The tenuous political privilege which made the church possible was too uncertain to permit much ostentation. Situated near the slope of a low hill, the building had no true façade. On both the west and north sides central doors gave access to the services within. Three rows of windows surmounted by a hipped roof and atrophied bell tower reflected the simple internal arrangements and gave ample light to the interior. Although Doric columns supported the interior galleries, externally they were not used even for the main door in the fashion suggested by Perret. The structure's size, roughly 102 feet long and 60 feet wide, still impresses and exceeds that of most Protestant churches. The four sides of the steep roof met in a ridge some 60 feet high. Even if unfilled, a Protestant temple of this size must have caused no little misgiving when each Sunday as many as 4,000 Huguenots from neighboring Paris entered the plain north and west doors and, seating themselves without uncovering, sternly waited for divine service to begin.[9]

The extent to which English Protestants applied their religious convictions to architecture was governed chiefly by political considerations.[10] From Henry VIII's first suppression of the monasteries in 1535 to the restoration of the Stuarts in 1660, Englishmen of each shade of religious feeling hoped that their party might control the civil government and the extensive properties of the

---

454. Drawing by François Deublinger de Spire. It was also well known in England. George Wheler, *An Account of the Churches . . . of the Primitive Christians* (London, 1689), p. 117.

8. Jacques Perret, *Des fortifications et artifices* (Paris, 1594, 1620; Frankfurt, 1602), quoted in *B.H.P.*, XLIX, 521–522. In a similar work issued under the title *Architectura et perspectiva* (Frankfurt, 1602) Plate O shows the temple. Copies of latter at Yale and the British Museum (Oppenheim, 1613).

9. Many views of the temple have been published. One, a print by P. Mariette, shows the temple and village from the Park of Vincennes, which lay north of the church and is especially handsome. *B.H.P.*, XXXIV, 388. For an elevation and plan, see *B.H.P.*, V, 178, and for a cross section see Pannier, *Salomon de Brosse*, p. 87.

10. Parts of only two temples have been identified at Villeneuve and Montebeliard. *B.H.P.*, XLIV, 369–370.

Church of England. Indeed each party from Marian Catholics to the Puritan Cromwellians did, for a longer or shorter period, determine the official faith of England and during its incumbency remodeled the fabric of church buildings to suit its own needs.

The best example of this shifting policy of reconstruction was old St. Paul's Cathedral. Cleared of stained glass and statuary during the sixteenth century, the medieval fabric stood at the beginning of the Stuart period structurally unchanged. Under Charles I Inigo Jones contrived to mask the southern and western faces of the nave and transept with a screen of regular ashlar and classical details. Across the main façade a porch of ten giant Corinthian columns supported an entablature lauding "Charles by the grace of God King of Great Britain and France," whose somewhat bowlegged statue stood on the balustrade above the entrance. Elsewhere round arches were substituted for pointed classical doorways or Gothic vertical pilasters for flying buttresses, Dutch strapwork and classical pyramids for Gothic tracery and pinnacles. (Fig. 64.)

The effect from the ground of all this classical ornament designed as a screen was probably impressive. But it cowered meanly below the soaring transept tower, and the wall with classic balustrade could barely encircle the waist of the medieval chapter house. Hollar's masterful and bitter engravings make the classical work seem another of Inigo Jones' unreal stage sets and demonstrate that thin vertical walls of masonry and glass could no longer suit Protestant worshipers' taste and inclination.[11]

The Puritan reaction to such sham is easily imagined. No sooner had the Long Parliament convened than all moneys were withdrawn. The scaffolds for the new tower were pulled down, workmen tore out the stalls in the choir, ripped up the pavement, even used graves as saw pits, if William Dugdale is to be believed. The nave was occupied by cavalry troops. The choir was bricked off, and in 1649 "a Dr. Burgess gave a lecture and weekly sermons unto which divers citizens with some others do usually resort." [12] After the structure was nearly destroyed in the Great Fire, it remained only for Sir Christopher Wren to condemn any effort at repair and to insist on the construction of a new cathedral for London. Had his advices been followed a church more closely attuned to the "zentral-bau" churches of continental Protestantism would, after more than a century of turmoil, have replaced the medieval St. Paul's.[13]

Everywhere in England Protestants felt dissatisfied with the architecture

11. William Dugdale, *History of Saint Paul's Cathedral* (London, 1658), pp. 154, 163.

12. *Ibid.*, pp. 171 ff.

13. B. Pite, "The Design of St. Paul's Cathedral," *Sir Christopher Wren, A.D. 1632–1723; Bicentenary Memorial Volume* (London, Hodder & Stoughton, 1923), pp. 54 ff., 212.

65. St. John's Parish Church, Wapping

of their places of worship, but in general until after 1660 they contented themselves with alterations rather than with new construction. Externally the smaller churches were little changed except in the environs of London. There the alterations had extraordinary results. Maitland has left us prospects of many such churches, but perhaps St. John's at Wapping and St. Paul's at Shadwick best illustrate the complete lack of consistency or relation with the original structure which was characteristic of these early efforts to create a new church form.[14] (Fig. 65.) Ill-proportioned dormer windows were let into the roofs of tiny churches; Gothic tracery and towers disappeared under round arches and classic entablatures. Wherever possible eager workmen added ornamental spheres and pyramids, bell towers and flagstaffs, dials and clocks, and yet through all this sham or ornament the simple plan of the English parish church of tower, nave, and chancel still appeared.

Inside as outside, the problem of the chancel plagued the seventeenth-century English Protestant. About its humble walls theologians waged bitter controversy over the place of communion in Church of England liturgy, how it should be given and received, and the extent to which it could be regarded as a sacrament. During the reign of Edward VI stone altars were occasionally replaced by wooden tables.[15] Although this was not universally done at once, the wooden communion table in general had superseded the stone altar by the middle of the seventeenth century.[16] Supported on massive Jacobean legs and heavily carved, the earliest of these tables seem fit substitutes for stone altars.[17] No single custom was followed, however, as to the manner of their use at communion. Sometimes they stood against the east wall of the church as Archbishop Laud directed; sometimes the three walls of the chancel were lined with benches surrounding the table, which ran east and west so that the chancel became a kind of Lord's dining room. Often the sextons had to carry the heavy table into the nave of the church where communion was given to the elect either at the table or seated in their pews.[18] Such must have been the case at Bradwell-near-Coggeshall in Essex where a screen divided

14. William Maitland, *The History of London from Its Foundation to the Present Time* (London, 1775), III, n.p.

15. The complicated issue of the communion table (like many other aspects of the liturgy) is dealt with definitively by George W. O. Addleshaw and Frederick Etchells in *The Architectural Setting of Anglican Worship* (London, Faber & Faber, 1948), pp. 22–36.

16. Francis Bond, *Chancel of the English Church* (London, Oxford University Press, 1916), pp. 106–108.

17. *Ibid.*, p. 107. Handsome early and late Stuart tables were used at Earle Stoneham and Thorington. H. Munro Cautley, *Suffolk Churches and Their Treasures* (London, B. T. Batsford, Ltd., 1937), p. 183. For a New England example, see Luke V. Lockwood, *Colonial Furniture in America* (New York, C. Scribner's Sons, 1926), II, 169–170.

18. Bond, *Chancel of the English Church,* pp. 122–123.

64. West façade of old St. Paul's Cathedral

66. St. Paul's and the Piazza in Covent Garden, about 1640

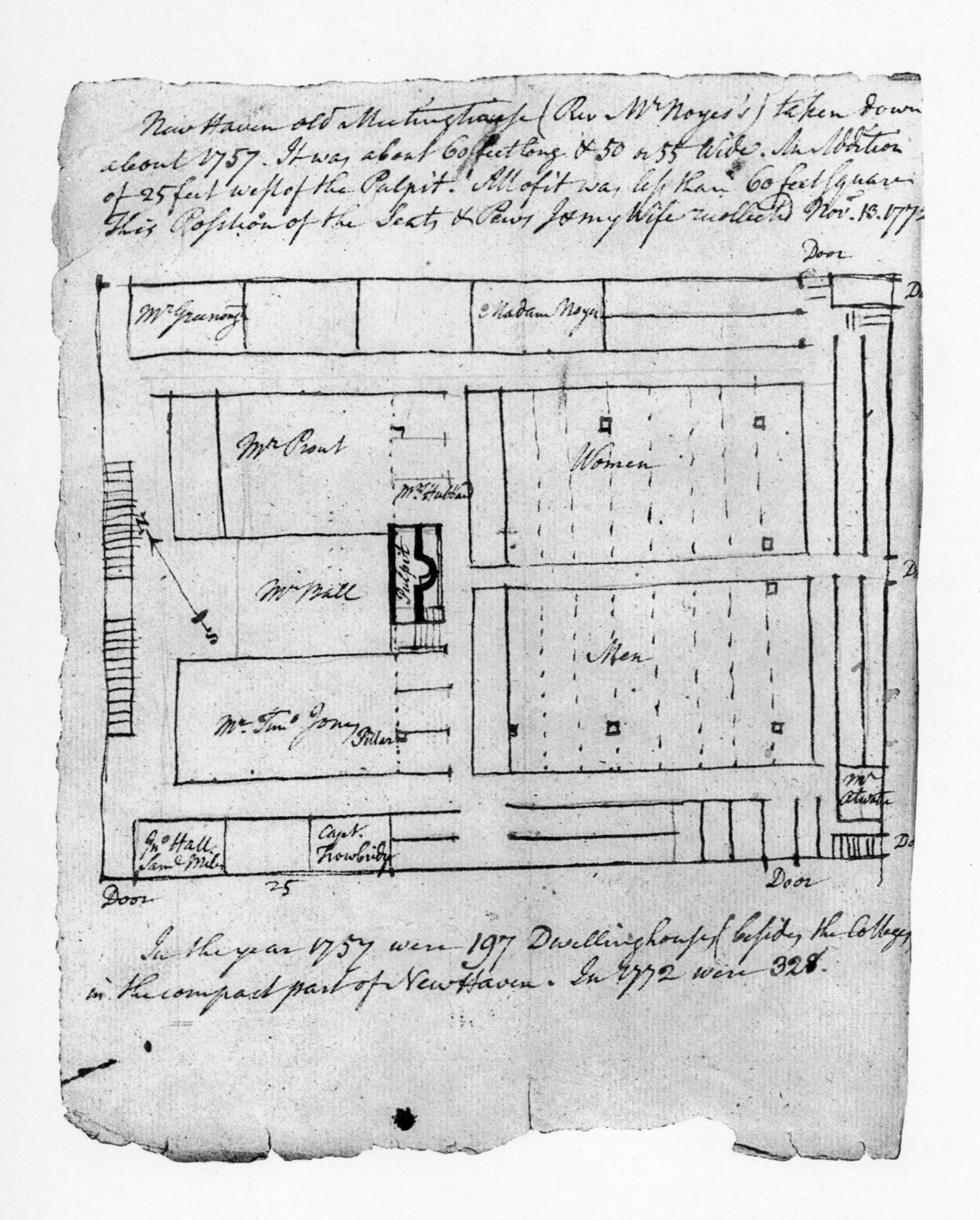

67. Ezra Stiles' plan of the New Haven Meetinghouse

the chancel from the body of the church and a fine Jacobean tomb of the local squire and his family filled the altar niche.[19]

Nor was the Lord's table the only new piece of church furniture the Protestants introduced into the nave of the English church. In the seventeenth century a growing population and the elaborate accommodations which were provided for a few elect families raised many seating problems in small country churches. Some solved their dilemma with galleries, first at the west end, then north and south, and occasionally across the east end of the nave.[20] Made from bench ends, the rood lofts which had been forbidden as idolatrous or originally designed and carved as galleries as at Pyddleton Dorset (1635) are themselves often very handsome, but their strong horizontal lines seem cramped and crowded by the low vaults of the average parish church.[21]

The liturgical emphasis all reforming Protestants laid upon the spoken word further affected church furniture. It is no coincidence that the earliest of the fine wood pulpits were handsomely carved with Jacobean ornaments. Such examples as Ashfield Magna (1619) or the triple-decker at Dennington (1628) with its place for reader, clerk, and preacher were raised high to overlook the steep sides of box pews that pressed them closely on every side. Their very richness, suggesting the court cupboards of the period, laid a duty upon the minister they served, as the 1635 joiner at Yaxley well knew when he carved on the steep sides and elaborate fretwork of his pulpit "Necissite is laid upon me yea woe is me if I preach not the gospel." [22]

19. Francis Bond, *Screens and Galleries in English Churches* (London, H. Frowde, 1908), p. 126. Roy. Com. Hist. Mon., *Essex,* III, 12–13, 34. Apparently the screen was reversed during the Reformation as its present east face is painted.

20. Bond, *Screens and Galleries,* p. 149. An especially fine gallery of bench ends was erected when box pews were substituted for benches at the western end of Churstanton Church. John C. Cox, *Bench-ends in English Churches* (London, Oxford University Press, 1916), pp. 43–46, 154.

21. A sixteenth-century gallery was preserved in the Berkeley Castle Chapel emblazoned with the arms of Henry VII and Henry VIII. Bond, *Screens and Galleries,* pp. 142–143. Bond listed seven other examples standing in 1908. Whitby illustrates the complete evolution of the gallery on all four walls. Edmund Vale, *Curiosities of Town and Countryside* (London, B. T. Batsford, Ltd., 1940), p. 121.

22. H. M. Cautley, *Suffolk Churches,* pp. 180–182. An excellent account of early pulpits is given by John C. Cox, *Pulpits, Lecterns, and Organs in English Churches* (London, Oxford University Press, 1915), pp. 98 ff. In rude country parishes they changed little. Witness Withersdale, seventeenth century; Thornably, early eighteenth century; Gislingham, late eighteenth century; and Shotwick, 1812. *Ibid.* Charles W. Budden, *Old English Churches, Their Architecture and Furniture* (Liverpool, Cathedral Bookstall, 1925), pp. 134–135. A perfect image of the interior of a church altered for Protestant worship is reproduced in a 1730 satirical engraving—triple-decker, box pews, reading congregation, and so forth. Gerald Cobb, *The Old Churches of London* (London, B. T. Batsford, Ltd., 1941–42), p. 18.

Eventually the former open nave of the parish church with its few stone benches for the old and infirm and rude backless benches for the rest of the congregation was completely changed by the reformers. Everywhere the box pew was introduced with high side walls and little doors securing its privacy. Families of prominence took the liberty of constructing high elaborate cubicles to protect themselves from drafts and malicious stares. The floor of the church and the base of its piers disappeared beneath a maze of boxes; its vaults were often hidden from view by a ceiling of horizontal timbers that kept the church warmer and at the same time suited the new furniture better than a pointed vault.

Even the dead rested under new stones. The engraved Tudor knight had stared stonily upward at the dim twilight of the roof timbers; not so his Jacobean or Stuart descendant. As in life, he limited his universe with architectural canopies and pyramids borrowed from Flanders. His own sculptured image was more realistic. No longer incised, he was carved in the round, lying fully clad beside his spouse; his head rested comfortably upon a pillow; his well-made armor sheathed his limbs of stone; with folded hands he dozed through the long afternoon, confidently ready to take up godlike affairs on the Day of Judgment. For the present he lay surrounded by carved stallions, children, hounds, and verses. In his own church he awaited the touch of his own God, a god inscrutable, perhaps, but certainly prosperous, successful, and intimate.[23]

Only one building built between 1600 and 1640 still remains which suggests the full effect of the new Protestant liturgy upon architecture. In 1631 the Earl of Bedford, a prosperous London land speculator, gave Inigo Jones the task of designing the residential square, Covent Garden. (Fig. 66.) Ironically the only structure that remains of his original design is St. Paul's Church consecrated in 1638 as a chapel of ease for the earl's tenants. Although Thomas Hardwick repaired the church in 1788 and rebuilt it after it burned in 1795, he is believed to have followed Jones' designs with care. A comparison, in fact, of Maitland's view (engraved in 1775) with Nightingale's illustration for *London and Middlesex* in 1815 shows Hardwick's fidelity and that the main façade was "a plain but noble portico of the Tuscan order; the columns . . . massy and intercolumniation large." [24] The broad, gently

23. The new fashion in tombs was perfectly illustrated at Ipsley on the north and south side of the chancel. On the south side John Husband and his wife Mary were buried in 1583 under a low rectangular engraved slab. Twenty years later his descendant was buried with his spouse under an elaborate, classical canopy. William Dugdale, *The Antiquities of Warwickshire* (London, 1730), p. 740.

24. Maitland, *History of London,* III, n.p. Joseph Nightingale, *London and Middlesex* (London, 1815), pp. 278–280. *Dictionary of National Biography,* "Thomas Hardwick."

sloping eaves of the roof were carried far out beyond the walls of the church, not only on the long sides but also over both the northeast and southwest walls where the roof made a crude pediment above the portals.[25]

The congregation might enter the church through identical high doors either under the portico facing the piazza or at the west end and then pass to their pews, which pressed closely around the pulpit. Along the two long walls were shallow galleries with three banks of seats. Since these galleries partially interrupted the flood of light from the tall windows that ringed the church, they are possibly a later addition.[26]

The windows themselves, which are indicated in every view of the church, are over 12 feet high and through their panes of clear glass brilliant light fills the interior of the little church. Box pews and a flat ceiling served to further enhance the lucid light of the Sabbath sermon. Space was closed, well lit, and rectangularly defined. No corner of God's house was hidden from the reasoning mind of the Covent Garden congregation. In all its elements—plan, use of the classic portico (although the choice of the Tuscan was peculiar to Jones), light within the church, galleries, box pews, and fenestration—the little church of St. Paul in Covent Garden anticipated the work of Sir Christopher Wren and James Gibbs and their American imitators. Not so skillful as Wren in his use of space, Inigo Jones, himself a Roman Catholic, completed in 1638 a too little recognized monument of Protestant architecture, the only building to fully interpret the Plain Style in England before the Great Fire of London.[27]

There is little question that the Protestant Plain Style was closely imitated in many Jewish synagogues in Holland and England at the end of the seventeenth century. The Sephardic Synagogue in Amsterdam and the London Great Synagogue closely followed Protestant models.[28] The larger question which still remains unanswered is the extent of Protestant knowledge respecting Jewish worship, liturgy, and architecture at the beginning of the seventeenth century. Certainly Calvinist emphasis on the Old Testament created curiosity as to the nature of Solomon's Temple and early Christian

25. *Ibid.* Colin Campbell, *Vitruvius Britannicus,* Vol. III.

26. Cross section and plan. K. E. O. Fritsch, *Der Kirchenbau des Protestantismus* (Berlin, 1893), p. 492.

27. It will be noticed that no mention of Puritan architecture in England was made. This is because the earliest of these structures date from after 1650, by which time the themes of Protestant architecture had already been interpreted for Englishmen by the Established Church. J. Betjeman, "Nonconformist Architecture," *Architectural Review,* LXXXVIII (December, 1940), 161–174.

28. Helen Rosenau, "The Synagogue and Protestant Church Architecture," Warburg and Courtauld Institutes, *Journal,* IV, 80–84. Article deals with some aspects of the problem, see Roy. Com. Hist. Mon., *London,* IV, 11.

worship.[29] The display of the Ten Commandments, the development of the pulpit, and even much of the new Protestant art of gravestone design all argue Jewish influence. Whether the use of an antiliturgical floor plan and of zentral-bau churches can also be attributed to Jewish influence is uncertain. The strong direction which Wren's London churches gave Jewish synagogues at the end of the seventeenth century suggests that the western European synagogue followed the Protestant counter-baroque rather than the reverse. The lack of detailed information, however, on places of worship of both faiths during the late sixteenth century precludes any definitive statement.[30]

When in 1630 the Great Migration to New England began, its ships carried not only Puritan settlers and Puritan theology but also a full-fledged Protestant aesthetic. The meetinghouses of New England were not haphazard or accidental responses to the demands of the American forest. The nonliturgical floor plan, the box pew, the movable communion table, the galleries, the two-story façade, the low ceiling, the elaborate pulpit, all were known to Protestant builders who by 1630 had striven for almost a century to create a Plain Style of church architecture. Carried not only to New England but to other American colonies, this aesthetic produced, because of the individuality of the colonies and their poor cultural intercommunication, a variety of church buildings; yet these churches in New England, the cosmopolitan middle colonies, or the plantation south obeyed the fundamental principles of the European Plain Style. In each, space was closely defined, linear, and well lighted; ornamentation was constrained and abstract, and the construction direct, simple, and apparent. Here was lucid, clear symbolism within which the rational, literate Protestant might reach his God.

Early church architecture in the colonies seems fumbling by comparison with Charenton or Covent Garden. As in Europe, each Protestant sect devised a plan suited to its own liturgy and reflecting at the same time an aversion to Popish tradition; unlike European builders, American workmen were busy farmers, merchants, or seamen and brought to their churches little of the skill which framed their homes. What in domestic architecture might pass for functional workmanship, in church or meetinghouse seemed only hasty and unconsidered.

As might be expected the Puritan settlers of Connecticut followed radical Protestant architectural practice in their meetinghouses. The walls of Ulster

29. An excellent example is George Wheler, *An Account of the Churches . . . of the Primitive Christians* (London, 1689).

30. Richard Krautheimer, *Mittelalterliche Synagogen* (Berlin, Frankfurter Verlagsanstalt, 1927), G. K. Lukomski, *Jewish Art in European Synagogues* (London, Hutchinson, 1947), and Alfred Grotte, *Deutsche, böhmische und polnische Synagogentypen* (Berlin, Der Zirkel, Architekturverlag, 1915) are the most useful works I have consulted.

and Virginia churches while clearly not Catholic still seemed to reflect a Papist twilight. The permanency of their brick and stone suited an established priesthood better than a Puritan minister subject to his congregation. Anglican floor plans, if not cruciform, still retained chancels, towers, and other Popish elements which ministers like Hooker and Davenport no doubt feared might be mistaken by unwary youth for symbols of inner light and saving grace.[31]

Deriving closely from the Huguenot, Dutch Reformed, and German churches, early New England meetinghouses resembled nothing built in England before 1650.[32] Their design scorned the squat sophistication of St. Paul's in Covent Garden; only after nearly a century would they return to the designs of Jones and the brilliant Wren. Instead, like the faith it served, the New England, and especially the Connecticut, meetinghouse pursued a course little affected by European taste until nearly 1740. These anachronistic buildings which had typified continental Protestant architecture in 1630 became almost inexplicable curiosities to the European traveler in eighteenth-century New England because the Protestant church in Europe had either been destroyed as in France or, as in Holland, waxed fat and inherited the temples of bishops. Only the rare Scotch-Presbyterian or English Nonconformist appreciated and understood the cold aesthetic of rude benches and drafty walls.

No Connecticut meetinghouse built before 1764 still stands, but the views, seating plans, and church accounts which have survived recall essentially an architecture of negation. The Cambridge and Saybrook platforms laid down no positive rules for divine service, and no other New England liturgy defined the form church building should take. In all matters of divine service the Puritans found the Westminster Confession satisfactory, but that assembly of divines, unable to foresee the demands of the New Albion, had only this to say of places of public worship: "As no place is capable of any holiness under Pretence of whatsoever Dedication or Consecration; so neither is it subject to such Pollution by any Superstition formerly used, and now laid aside, as may render it unlawful or inconvenient for Christians to meet together therein for the publick worship of God. And therefore we hold it requisite that the Places of publick Assembling for Worship among us should be continued and employed to that Use." [33]

31. Henry C. Forman, *Jamestown and Saint Mary's,* p. 160. *Phillips MSS,* pp. 12, 49, 133. Simpler rectangular churches suggest that the design of British churches in Ulster might provide a useful survey of English design. *Phillips MSS,* pp. 101, 113.

32. J. Betjeman, "Nonconformist Church Architecture," *Architectural Review,* LXXX-VIII (December, 1940), 162.

33. Assembly of Divines at Westminster, *The Directory for the Publick Worship of God* (1645), Appendix. *A Platform of Church Discipline . . . by . . . the Synod at Cambridge* (1649), Preface. *A Confession of Faith . . . Saybrook, 1708* (New London, 1710).

Such indifference scarcely suited New England conditions where no "Places of publick Assembling for Worship" existed. To build them the Puritan settler followed two principles. First, as the continental Protestant had done, he departed from Roman Catholic practice as far as he could and still shelter a congregation of worshipers. Second, he added nothing to the fabric or decoration of his church that was not explicit in the *Directory for the Publick Worship of God* drawn up at Westminster in 1645.[34]

Thus the New England meetinghouse was no longer oriented along an east-west axis; it was square or a shallow rectangle instead of cruciform; no statue, picture, or other symbol adorned it; Puritan practice approved its use for town gatherings as well as for Sunday worship. But despite these things the colonial meetinghouse and its post-Revolutionary successors have become the principal American religious symbol not only in New England but throughout the country.

Without any specific building instructions to be followed, the interiors of the early Connecticut meetinghouses became straightforward expressions in wood of the character of reformed religious worship. The long morning service emphasized the word of God, read and expounded from a tall pulpit, the only impressive piece of church furniture. The Westminster Confession provided for the reading of Holy Scripture by a teacher and, after a substantial prayer for guidance, the exposition of that or other appropriate passages by the minister in a sermon at once "painfull, plain, faithful, wise, grave, filled with loving affection and as taught by God." [35] In consequence the pulpit often had two levels or, more rarely, three; the highest for the minister, the next for the teacher, and, if three, the lowest for a clerk who took notes of the sermon.[36]

In Connecticut as at Charenton benches pressed closely about the pulpit, leaving narrow alleys that barely allowed the passage of the worshipers. The members of the congregation were assigned their seats, and each position in the meetinghouse signified its owner's rank and precedence by its distance from the preacher. Those responsible for church government, deacons and elders, sat almost under the shadow of the pulpit. Next came men of prominence and wealth. In the galleries or along wall benches sat the children and servants. (Fig. 67.)

34. This prescribed the order of divine service and specified the opening prayer, lesson, sermon, blessing, and occasional sacraments. It also substituted occasional days of Thanksgiving and fast for Catholic church feast days, which were all prohibited. *The Directory for the Public Worship of God, Westminster* (Philadelphia, 1745), pp. 10–30.

35. *Ibid.*, p. 20.

36. Kelly, *Early Meetinghouses of Connecticut*, p. 20. This outstanding work covers all sites which still have on them church edifices built before 1830. For pulpits, see *ibid.*, I, 49, 148, 270; II, 8, 157–159, 292, and Ezra Stiles, "Itinerary," MS, II, 414.

Although the decoration of pews in Connecticut never reached the elaborate extreme it had in English Stuart churches, at least by 1740 they had become private property and since the "Catholic or Universal church which is invisible consists of the whole number of the elect" and not of any public building, their elaboration did not signify sin or ostentation before God: the saints could not be saved or injured by the pews of a church.[37] Salvation was private, and election the principal source of grace; property was not the evidence of greed but of diligence.

For the elect one further privilege remained on designated Sundays. After the long sermon had been finished and a closing prayer repeated all except those accepted into the church as members rose and left. Then after an exhortation the minister sanctified the bread and wine at "a table decently covered and so conveniently placed the communicants may sit orderly about it." He next distributed the bread in "comely and convenient vessels . . . and the wine also in large cups." After which he blessed and sanctified the communion in the customary words.[38] Within the reserved, domestic-windowed walls of the meetinghouses the supreme ceremony of New England colonial life took place. There in the high Sunday noon God's anointed sat down at God's table to break bread with him. Only a faithless age ignorant of the joy of salvation can snicker at the dread severity of the Puritan plain way to God.

The often repeated truism that the meetinghouse was after all not a church and was habitually used as a civil meetingplace obscures the very real veneration in which the town held it. The deliberate effort to secularize all ecclesiastical symbols in less than two generations ended in a new architectural symbolism inherent in the New England scene.[39]

Probably the best documented of such symbols is the meetinghouse of the New Haven First Society. Although not a stick of its frame is left and its site is covered by later construction, it did impress many travelers of the eighteenth century, and their sketches, taken together with the existing church records, show it to have been a sufficient, if unpolished, pivot for the Puritan town.

The first meetinghouse, built hastily and probably of green oak in the English fashion, ripened into near collapse by 1657, less than twenty years after its erection. All efforts to repair this structure failed, and between 1668

37. Kelly, *Early Meetinghouses of Connecticut,* II, 34–36. Franklin B. Dexter, *Biographical Sketches of the Graduates of Yale College and Annals (*New York, 1885), II, 103. President Clap's pew was built in the meetinghouse.

38. *The Directory for the Public Worship of God, Westminster,* p. 26.

39. See Chapter III. Saybrook in the seventeenth century and later Voluntown, the Assembly towns of Litchfield, and a few towns in Windham County are almost the only Connecticut towns which were not planned around the meetinghouse.

and 1670 the second meetinghouse was erected, of frame construction, probably square. It had three entrances facing east, each leading to an alley running the length of the audience room. At least one tier of galleries was planned from the start, and casement windows were let into the wall to light them. The roof was hipped and, if Wadsworth is to be believed, had the lower slopes gambrel fashion, to provide light by means of dormer windows and more head room in the galleries, as well as to strengthen the frame. (Fig. 18.)

Within, the plan was simplicity itself. (Fig. 67.) At the western end a tall double-decker pulpit, fenced and flanked by steps, looked down upon eight rows of box pews, each divided by the central alley which penned the men to the south and the women to the north. Directly under the pulpit sat the ruling elder or teacher, and to his right small single-boxed seats were provided for three of the deacons.

Along the walls and in galleries slip pews or benches accommodated many more listeners. In 1698 crowded conditions necessitated a 20- or 25-foot addition west of the box pews on the ground level with stairs leading to galleries above; 1727 saw the last addition to the old fabric—a second gallery above the first, served by dormer windows. Division within the society over the fiery sermons of Whitefield, the introduction of Anglicanism into Connecticut, and the formation of nearby towns reduced attendance until about 1757, when a new brick building was first put into use.[40]

The further development of the meetinghouse style has been well known since the December evening when Noah Porter read his famous paper to the New England Society of Brooklyn. His thesis was that the simple square or rectangular meetinghouse gave way in Massachusetts by 1730, and in Connecticut by 1726, to the meetinghouse with attached bell tower, and that this type was in turn succeeded by the colonnade and integral tower near the close of the eighteenth and the beginning of the nineteenth centuries.[41]

Fortunately several of the towered meetinghouses of the mid-eighteenth century are preserved, though none without alterations. The Congregational Church at Brooklyn has the most characteristic exterior. On one long side the main entrance faces the pulpit window, which is set midway between the gallery and the first-floor windows. A bell tower with stair lights and a side door on the narrow west end balances a two-story stair porch at the east. A large rectangular meetinghouse has thus had two gallery stair towers added,

40. James Wadsworth, "Plan of the City of New Haven Taken in 1748," MS map. J. F. Kelly, *Early Meetinghouses of Connecticut,* II, 3–10. Ezra Stiles, "Itinerary," MS, II, 414.

41. Noah Porter, "The New England Meeting House," *New Englander* (May, 1883), p. 8. Guilford (1726); Old South Meetinghouse, Boston (1830); Trinity Church, Newport.

68. Second Nonconformist Meetinghouse, Brooklyn, Connecticut, 1772

69. Old Trinity Episcopal Church, Brooklyn, Connecticut

70. Interior of Old Trinity Church, 1771

one of which has a belfry, but the effect is handsome and functional.[42] (Fig. 68.)

Dissident church societies continued to build the simplest type of rectangular meetinghouse well into the nineteenth century. Their simplicity of design became a protest against the elaborate edifices of the established Congregational societies and a rural rejection of urban ostentation and wealth.

In the northeast corner of Connecticut Godfrey Malbone, a royalist and Anglican driven by misfortune from Newport in 1766, found himself about to be bound to pay some £200 toward a new meetinghouse for the Nonconformists of Brooklyn. In desperation and single-handed he planned, underwrote, and had built Trinity Church, which has stood almost untouched until the present day. The building is 46 x 30 feet, has a hewn oak frame with a hipped roof and arched two-story windows. All the exterior trim is precise and handsome Georgian work. (Fig. 69.)

In the interior most of Malbone's church furniture remains, although somewhat rearranged. (Fig. 70.) The box pews rise some 4 feet from the alley floor, and each has a paneled door on H iron hinges. The original reading desk and pulpit are still used though the altar has been replaced. The proportions of the clear glass windows and the galleries suggest the cool interior of St. Paul's, Covent Garden.[43]

Such civic architecture as the colony did develop grew in part from the same internal theological disputes which by Malbone's time had so enriched its religious architecture. In 1717 the colonists became agitated over the choice of a site for their college. Although the colony's only ministerial school might be presumed to bring some measure of prestige to the town in which it located I suspect that each town felt that orthodoxy in the younger generation of ministers would be best served if the undergraduates attended service with the preacher whom the townspeople knew and respected. In any event Hartford, Saybrook, Wethersfield, New London, and even Branford pressed their claims to the infant college.

That New Haven finally won was due to the quick action of one man, Gurdon Saltonstall, and the overwhelming persuasion of the great frame college building that Henry Caner of Boston built for him. The legislature would make the final decision—and both Assembly and Council were to convene in New Haven on October 10, 1717. Should the legislators be able to view a nearly finished building at that time, Saltonstall reasoned, they

42. See also Farmington (1772), Wethersfield in brick (1764), East Haven in stone (1774). Kelly, *Early Meetinghouses of Connecticut,* I, 39–43, 139; II, 290.

43. *Ibid.,* I, 16. For other examples of anachronistic architecture used by minority religious groups, see St. Andrews, Bloomfield; St. Matthews, East Plymouth; Tolland Methodist Church; Stratfield Baptist Church. *Ibid.,* I, 28, 145; II, 224, 229.

would more easily swallow their scruples and agree upon New Haven for the college. On October 8 Caner raised the mighty frame for the college. Saltonstall's surmise proved correct; the Assembly and the Council approved the new college after a few delays but in order to assuage the losers' pride voted funds for a state house at Hartford and a courthouse at New London.[44]

The building which Caner and Saltonstall began was not finished until 1718 and was razed in 1782, but fortunately its dimensions and plan can be accurately surmised from the "great timber" specifications which the college has preserved. These show it to have been substantially of "fair aspect in the market place of New Haven mounted in an eminent place thereof in length ten rods, in breadth twenty-one feet and near thirty feet upright." (The actual dimensions seem to have been 162 x 23 x 28 feet.) "A spacious hall and a spacious library all in a little time to be splendidly completed." It had three entries with stairs that ran through the building and a belfry with a bell. The dining hall was 31 x 21 feet and had a kitchen attached. Over the hall was the library, and the remainder of the building was devoted to twenty-two student rooms, each to house at first two and later three scholars.[45]

As may be well known this college stood upon Mrs. Hester Coster's 2-acre plot adjoining the Green. She had given her land, not to the college directly but to the church in New Haven, for the support of an educational lecture. The First Society had in its turn conveyed the property to the college and naturally assumed that the undergraduates would attend service at the meetinghouse on the Green, which for many years they did. The influence of the First Society was moreover reinforced by the presence of their minister, the Reverend Mr. Noyes, secretary of the Yale Corporation. (Fig. 18.)

When in 1750 President Clap planned the erection of Connecticut Hall to accommodate the growing student body, he also began to upset this cordial arrangement with the town and to isolate his college from its influence. His first step was to set the foundations of the new building well "back in the yard that there might be a large and handsome area before it and toward the north side of the yard with a view that when the old College should come down another college or chapel or both should be set on the south of the present house." Moreover, President Clap took care to see that the new building, named after the colony because the Assembly contributed hand-

44. Dexter, *Biographical Sketches and Annals,* I, 173. *P.R. Col. Conn.,* VI, 36. George D. Seymour, "Henry Caner, Master Carpenter," *Old-Time New England,* XV (January, 1925), 100.

45. Norman M. Isham, "The Original College House," *Yale Alumni Weekly,* XXVI (October 20, 1916), 115–120. The only modification to Isham's reconstructed frame is to turn the summer beams so they all run at right angles to the long walls and fit without further cutting. Thomas Clap, *Annals or History of Yale College* (New Haven, 1766), p. 24.

somely to its cost, had only student rooms, and so left the hall and library in the frame college as ruinous as ever. Clap spared no expense in the construction of Connecticut Hall and for many years it was probably the handsomest building in the colony. Built of brick under the direction of Francis Letort of Philadelphia and Thomas Bills of New York, it was "100 feet long 40 feet wide and three story high besides the garrots and a cellar under the whole, containing 32 chambers and 64 studies," had 124 windows, and 4 "great doors." [46] (Fig. 71.)

At first glance President Clap appeared to be only planning wisely for his growing institution, but his deeper purpose had long been clear. A violent Anti-New Light by instinct and officially since 1744, when he dismissed two students for attending an irregular religious meeting, he hoped to use the obvious unsuitability of the college hall room (31 x 22 feet) for Sunday service as an excuse to build a college chapel, install a college professor of divinity, and sever all of Yale's connections with the New Haven First Society and, to Clap, the suspect Mr. Noyes.[47]

That the old college had never been designed as a religious edifice or that the Assembly refused to vote funds to the college as long as Clap persisted in his arbitrary ways bothered the president not a whit. He pushed the construction with such funds as he could muster, appointed the Reverend Mr. Daggett as professor of divinity, brooked no compromise with the New Haven congregation though they offered many, and finally in the academic year 1762–63 he finished the chapel. The building had three stories of which the lower two were built as a chapel with galleries and devoted to religious meetings, debates, and so forth, while the upper housed the library. There was apparently an attached bell tower in the manner of meetinghouses of the period. The chapel survived as a nearly perfect colonial meetinghouse until the late nineteenth century when the college authorities tore it down and destroyed the last chance of the completion of President Clap's scheme to "the north and west for better accommodation." [48] (Figs. 71, 72.)

Clap's plan for Yale College, however cramped and primitive, seems to have been the only serious design of public architecture apart from meetinghouses in Connecticut until after the French and Indian War. Both New Haven and Hartford, as a result of the dispute over Yale College, built state houses, but they were plain structures. The Hartford state house had a

46. Clap, *Annals . . . Yale College,* p. 55. Thomas Clap, "Account of the Cost of the New College," MS in Yale University Library.

47. Dexter, *Biographical Sketches and Annals,* I, 772; II, 2, 71, 103, 227, 275, 320–322, 357–359.

48. Dexter, *Biographical Sketches and Annals,* II, 303, 320–322, 349, 440–444, 635, 682. Clap, *Annals . . . Yale College,* p. 72.

frame 72 x 30 feet with a door on each side and at each end. Two chambers, each 30 x 30 feet, with a 12-foot hall occupied the second floor while the first was left free of partitions for public meetings. That at New Haven, finished in 1720, stood on a corner of the Green and was even smaller. In fact, its description suggests a domestic design adapted to civil purposes. Only 45 x 22 feet, it was two stories high with a chimney at each end.[49]

Not until after 1763 did the growing importance of political life and the increased prosperity of the colony's ports lead to genuine civic architecture of importance. Only then did New Haven gain its imposing masonry court house, Hartford the state house, and New London its still extant sophisticated frame building. The erection of these three buildings and the refinement of the Connecticut meetinghouse according to London taste signaled the end of the period which had found the Plain Style a sufficient tradition with which to clothe the meetinghouses, framed to serve the needs of worship and local government. Civic and religious architecture in the European tradition may never again come so close in purpose and design as they did in colonial Connecticut.

49. *P.R. Col. Conn.*, VI, 36, 102, 157–158, 466.

A Front VIEW of YALE-COLLEGE, and the COLLEGE CHAPEL, NEW-HAVEN.

A compendious Hiſtory of Yale-College, and a general Account of the Courſe of Studies purſued by the Students.

YALE-COLLEGE was founded A. D. 1700; and ſubſiſted at Killingworth, in Connecticutt, until the death of Rector Pierſon, 1707; then at Say-Book, until 1716, when it was removed and fixed at NEW-HAVEN. Here the firſt College Edifice was erected 1717, being 170 feet in length and 22 feet in width, and three ſtories high, containing about 50 ſtudies in convenient chambers, beſides the Hall and Library. In 1714 Mr. Agent DUMMER procured a donation of 800 volumes in London for the Library; to which he afterwards obtained additions. Governor YALE contributed to this donation, and in 1717 added himſelf 300 volumes.—He was born at New-Haven 1648; became Governor of Fort St. George, in the Eaſt-Indies, where he lived about 20 years; and returning to London the beginning of this century became Governor of the London Eaſt-India Company. He made ſo reſpectable a benefaction to this academic inſtitution, that the appellation of YALE-COLLEGE was given to it, by the Governors of it, at the public commencement 1718. The preſent College Edifice, which is of brick, was built during the Preſidency of the Rev. THOMAS CLAP, 1750, being 100 feet long, and 40 feet wide, three ſtories high, containing 32 chambers and 64 ſtudies convenient for the reception of 100 ſtudents. The College-Chapel alſo built of brick, was erected 1761, being 50 feet and 40, with a ſteeple 125 feet high. In this building is the public Library conſiſting of about 2500 volumes. The firſt building of wood was taken down 1782, when a dining-hall and kitchen was built of brick 60 and 40 feet.

This literary inſtitution was incorporated by the General Aſſembly of Connecticutt. The firſt charter of incorporation was granted to eleven Miniſters 1701. The powers of the Truſtees were enlarged by the additional charter 1723; and by that of 1745 the Truſtees were incorporated by the name of the Preſident and Fellows of Yale-College, in New-Haven. The corporation are empowered to hold eſtates; continue their ſucceſſion; make academic laws, elect and conſtitute all officers of inſtruction and government uſual in Univerſities, and confer all the learned degrees. The ordinary inſtruction and executive government is in the hands of the Preſident, Profeſſors and Tutors. Beſides the four Tutors who give inſtruction in the learned languages and the whole circle of the ſciences, there have been three Profeſſorſhips, (although one is now vacant) viz. of *Mathematics & Natural Philoſophy*, *Eccleſiaſtical Hiſtory*, and *Divinity*. In 1732 the Rev. George Berkeley, D. D. then Dean of Derry, and afterward Biſhop of Cloyne in Ireland, made a generous donation of 880 volumes, and an eſtate in Rhode-Iſland, being an houſe and 96 acres of land: The annual rent of which being 100 ounces of ſilver, is divided into three ſcholarſhips of the houſe, and annually appropriated to the three beſt ſcholars in the Latin and Greek claſſics. This has proved a great incentive among the ſtudents, to excel in claſſical learning.

Major James Fitch made the firſt donation in land about 600 acres in 1701, before the firſt Charter. The honorable the General Aſſembly in 1732, made a donation of 1500 acres within this State. Dr. Daniel Lathrop added a donation of 500l. to the college funds, in 1781. Theſe are the principal benefactions.

The philoſophic apparatus is not compleat; it contains however a reflecting Teleſcope, an excellent microſcope, a compleat and elegant ſets of ſurveying inſtruments, the hydroſtatic balance, an excellent braſs aſtronomical quadrant fitted with a nonius and ſpirit level, a large planetarium and cometarium, a ſcioptic glaſs for perſpective views, an air-pump and receivers, with the other machines neceſſary for exhibiting the principal experiments in the whole courſe of experimental philoſophy and aſtronomy. The college-muſæum contains, though not a copious collection, yet ſome great natural curioſities, and is conſtantly increaſing. The number of matriculated ſtudents or undergraduates has been for ſome years from 150 to 250, and now is about 200, divided into four claſſes. The courſe of education in this Univerſity comprehends the whole circle of literature. The three learned languages are taught here, together with ſo much of the ſciences, as can be communicated in four years. It is expected that the youth at admiſſion be found able to tranſlate Virgil, Tully, and the Greek Teſtament. During their College reſidence they ſtudy, the firſt year the Languages, Decimal Arithmetic, the Proportions and Roots; they are alſo exercifed in public ſpeaking: The ſecond year, Engliſh Grammar, Rhetoric, Logic, Algebra, and Geometry, together with Engliſh Compoſition, Oratory, Geography and the Claſſics: The third is ſpent in Mathematics and natural Philoſophy and Aſtronomy. In Mathematics they are carried through the Conic Sections, the Menſuration of Superficies and Solids of all Figures, and Trigonometry with its Application to Navigation and Aſtronomy. In Aſtronomy they have not only a general ſyſtematical view of the Planets and Comets, but are taught the Law of Gravity, the ſeſquiplicate Ratio of revolving Bodies, and their deſcription of equal Areas in equal times, with the principia of the Aſtronomical Calculations, whether of the heliocentric and geocentric places of the Planets, the Eclipſes of their Satellites, or the Trajectories of Comets: In the fourth year they ſtudy Ethics and Metaphyſics or Moral Philoſophy, Criticiſm, Hiſtory, and the Belles Letters. During the whole academic life, the ſtudents are daily exerciſed in compoſitions, rehearſals, dialogues, and other oratorial performances, tending to give them a free elocution, and form them for public ſpeakers. Having finiſhed this courſe, the Degree of Bachelor of Arts is conferred upon them at the anniverſary Commencement in September: and three years after, they receive the Degree of Maſter of Arts. Thoſe who afterwards proceed to the higher Branches of Literature, and become eminent for Erudition, are admitted to the Doctorate in either or any of the Learned Profeſſions. About Nineteen Hundred have received a Liberal Education here, and have gone forth into the world with the honors of this Univerſity.

YALE-COLLEGE, June 26, 1786.

NEW-HAVEN: PRINTED BY DANIEL BOWEN, in CHAPEL-STREET; where every Kind of PRINTING is performed with Diſpatch, and in the neateſt Manner.

71. The first Chapel and Connecticut Hall, Yale College, 1786

72. The first Yale Chapel in 1869

Conclusion

The settlement and planning of the Connecticut colony were but one phase of the greater migration of Englishmen and English culture to America; yet the way in which the little New England colony was settled may have some significance for the larger movement as a whole.

For almost every aspect of the Connecticut townscape a precedent can be demonstrated in England with which many if not all the settlers were familiar. Practices as widely separated as the use of clapboard walls in construction and the division of land into larger rectangular lots for each proprietor had their origin in English practices, some as ancient as the use of the carpenter's saw pit and frows, some as recent as Bedford's Level and the draining of the Fens.

This work has been concerned chiefly with demonstration of the European precedents for the settler's customs, but clearly these alone do not explain the visual aspect of the Connecticut town as it developed. The straight rows of buildings fronting on the treeless common overlooked by a simple well-lit meetinghouse in the Protestant Plain Style, and, beyond the village, the alteration of commons, crisscrossed by the trails of domestic animals, with the long ladders of land allotments—all these were to be found in Stuart England. But in Connecticut as elsewhere in America environment determined the relative importance of each custom borrowed from England. Thus the West Indian barrel trade made shingles a practical substitute for thatch, the homogeneity and slow increase of Connecticut's population preserved and made honorific the English yeoman house, the high land-settler ratio led to the elaboration and perfection of the land division schemes of the Fens, the almost undisputed religious theocracy retained the seventeenth-century meetinghouse for nearly a century. Not all aspects of the Connecticut village remained static. The development of road and street plans soon far outpaced the sixteenth- and seventeenth-century English experiments in

Ulster and on the European continent. Security from natives and a wide base of property ownership combined to speed the exuberant exploitation of great areas of land, a practice that left in its wake houses widely separated and linked by road systems of very different capacities. Although few of these towns prospered, they and others like them added a new concept to the vocabulary of town-planning practice—the view that the town and its road system were not primarily instruments of communal life but the foundation of the rapid sale and exploitation of land.

If environment selected some of the transplanted customs which would flourish in the New World, other factors equally impersonal played a part in shaping the village physiognomy. At the outset the settler found most aspects of Indian culture quite useless for his purposes. The New England town had no native houses like those of the Irish in the English settlements in Ulster. No evidence of Indian decorative arts or Indian craftsmanship appeared on the interior of the settlers' homes. The levels of the two cultures were so disparate that the European found he could borrow only agricultural and hunting skills. In consequence towns did not reflect so much a merger of cultures as a transplantation of European civilization to American soil.

That the colonial town was never an exact counterpart of its namesake in Europe resulted from the accident of chronology quite as much as from the forces of change within English and colonial society. Thus after the first generation of settlement and construction the New England village was a homogeneous whole. Although its houses might differ from one another in size or in detail of design, they had all been built within a twenty-year period and by men of similar taste and inclination. The colonial meetinghouse could not be compared to older churches of more liturgical design since none existed; it remained until the eighteenth century the solitary Plain-Style house of worship for the theocratic colony.

This then was the architectural heritage of the second generation of colonists, a generation unaware of the wide possibilities of architectural design; these simple buildings, the only ones which as boys and young men the colonists had known, had to provide their models for new construction. Furthermore that second generation and to only a slightly less extent the third and fourth generation could not learn new techniques from the men who had helped rebuild London in brick or who had known Restoration architecture in their youth. Because Connecticut lay outside the main current of European migration after 1660, taste and architectural knowledge fixed upon the framework of the middle-class house of rural England before the Protectorate. To the colonist born in America the rich, varied architectural heritage of most English towns and villages would have seemed an alien panoply with few familiar parts. The Connecticut colonist had an architecture of great and small timbers, of drawknife and ax; the English fashion described in builder's manuals which was beyond the molding plane and chisel lay outside his imagination. The house frame and the severity of the meetinghouse remained throughout the colonial period visible links with the first generation of settlers and an outward symbol of that generation's influence upon the shape of New England tradition.

BIBLIOGRAPHICAL NOTE

Although curiosity about American colonial architecture and furniture has been a social fashion for more than a generation and is still commonplace, the tools of serious scholarship in the field remain to be forged. Despite the obvious utility of architectural bibliographies along historical lines only Henry Russell Hitchcock's list of books on architecture published in America before 1895 can lay any claim to authority.[1] Useful and suggestive bibliographical notes for each period can be found in *A History of American Life,* edited by Arthur M. Schlesinger and Dixon Ryan Fox (New York, Macmillan Company, 1927–44), 12 vols.

Houses and street plans which derive from the colonial period still exist in substantial numbers, although seventeenth-century remains have become very rare. The heavy industrialization of New Haven, Hartford, and New London counties has, until now, by-passed the northeastern and northwestern corners of the state where many later colonial towns remain relatively isolated. Any one of three official guides can lead the stranger and indeed the initiated student to most of the colonial sites.[2]

Photographic and other records of existing colonial buildings abound. Both private and public agencies have made state-wide surveys with different objectives and varying successes. Most comprehensive of these files is the Works Progress Administration, Federal Writers Project, which catalogued some 5,000 Connecticut buildings and prepared for each a photograph and data sheet. At least three complete copies of this material exist: at the Library

1. Henry Russell Hitchcock, *American Architectural Books before 1895* (Minneapolis, University of Minnesota Press, 1946).

2. Florence S. Crofut, *Guide to the History and the Historic Sites of Connecticut* (1937). A useful alphabetical compendium of town history and local lore. Edgar L. Heermance, *The Connecticut Guide* (Hartford, Emergency Relief Commission, 1935). Federal Writers Project, *Connecticut: A Guide to Its Roads, Lore and People* (Boston, Houghton Mifflin, 1938).

of Congress, the Connecticut State Library, and the Yale University Library.[3]

A richer depository of measured drawings, plans, elevations, and details of some Connecticut buildings is to be found among the more than 3,000 structures recorded by the Historical American Buildings Survey under the direction of the National Parks Service.[4] Unfortunately the records of early Connecticut insurance companies have either been destroyed or proved too fragmentary to be of much use in this study.

Private collections of data have been beset by the vagaries of the researchers, the collapse of funds, or neighborhood legend and have generally stopped far short of their ultimate goal. Out of many beginnings three such projects should prove of value to future researchers. Edwin Whitefield around the year 1882 traveled about New England sketching houses in danger of decay or destruction; his sketches are our only record of many houses that have since disappeared.[5]

The Historic Buildings Committee of the Connecticut Society of Colonial Dames of America supervised the collection of a still larger depository of architectural monographs on individual colonial houses. When edited, standardized, and opened to the public this file should provide excellent source material. At the time of my research (1942–46) I was unable to sift this collection properly and so used it only with caution. Bertha C. Trowbridge and Charles M. Andrews in their *Old Houses of Connecticut* (1923) leaned heavily on many of the best of these monographs.

Finally for the towns of the New Haven colony H. Rossiter Snyder made for the Yale University Library a modest collection of superlative photographs which can never be duplicated: he caught the Connecticut house just before the widespread introduction of paved roads, telephone wires, and automobiles.

All of these collections remain unpublished. Among published sources there are no well-illustrated volumes like the invaluable records of the Royal Commission on the Ancient and Historical Monuments, and Constructions of England or the *Survey of London* published by the London County Council, both of which gave me innumerable items of general and specific data which could be judged not only qualitatively but quantitatively.[6]

3. For each building an elaborate data sheet described the site, history of ownership, construction, fenestration, size, and plan, and in almost every instance had one or more photographs attached.

4. National Parks Service, *Historic American Buildings Survey Catalog* (Washington, Government Printing Office, 1941).

5. Edwin Whitefield, *The Homes of Our Forefathers* (1882).

6. Great Britain, Royal Commission on the Ancient and Historical Monuments and Constructions of England, *An Inventory of the Historical Monuments in Middlesex, Essex, London, Herefordshire,* etc. (London, 1910—); London County Council, *Survey of London* (1922—).

No similar archives of urbanism published or unpublished exist for Connecticut.[7] A competent atlas of colonial plans has appeared for only one town (New Haven), and even this atlas limits itself to the town's original nine squares.[8] For the remainder of the colony Edmund B. Thompson's *Maps of Connecticut before the Year 1800* (1940) furnishes a pioneer and useful (if incomplete) introduction to Connecticut cartography.[9]

Three official series of base maps and house locations adequately cover the whole state. Since each was drawn for a different purpose, all of them are informative. The United States Department of the Interior Geological Survey (date varies), scale $1/62{,}500$, and the United States Army Military Topographical Survey, scale $1/25{,}000$, are now very familiar. Less well known to the general researcher are the Connecticut State Highway Department's General Highway Maps of 1938, which give traffic flow, building sites, and functions of all structures adjacent to public roads.

Much attention has in recent years been focused upon the aerial photograph as a source of information about old roads, abandoned property lines, and the sites of destroyed buildings. Such materials proved of real value when I tried to apply the methods developed by Osbert G. S. Crawford in *The Strip Map of Littlington* (1937). Three agencies have made extensive aerial surveys of Connecticut. That flown by the Department of the Interior Geological Survey, was not available for my investigation. I did consult an incomplete copy of the United States Army, Corps of Engineers Survey, 1941–42. The body of my conclusions rests upon a survey flown by Fairchild Aerial Surveys, Inc., *Connecticut,* No. 8494, scale $1/24{,}000$, and *Fairfield,* No. 8437, scale $1/7{,}200$.

Contemporary town surveys had to be drawn from a wide variety of sources. That so many exist in reproduction suggests the rich store of such drawings still possibly remaining in Europe. John Speed's *Theatre of the Empire of Great Britain* (1611) leads any English list with its numerous plans of important towns and maritime ports. Jacob van Deventer gave a colorful view of defensive urbanism in the Lowlands.[10] Sir Thomas Phillips sketched the

7. Probably the only complete or nearly complete record of any American city is I. N. Phelps Stokes' *Iconography of Manhattan Island* (New York, 1915–28), 5 vols. The same author's *American Historical Prints* (New York, 1933) gives a summary review of most of the important prints and some views.

8. Dean B. Lyman, Jr., *An Atlas of Old New Haven* (New Haven, Chas. W. Scranton & Company, 1929).

9. Edmund B. Thompson, *Maps of Connecticut before the Year 1800* (Windham, 1940).

10. Jacob van Deventer, *Atlas des villes de la Belgique au XVIe siècle, cent plans . . .* (1884–1924). *Nederlandische Studen . . . Plattegronden von Jacob van Deventer* (1884–1924).

English colonization of Ulster in the early seventeenth century.[11] Wenceslaus Hollar's merciless pen caught the architectural detail of London before and after the Great Fire.[12] Numerous London livery companies and large owners of land surveyed their holdings; part of these terriers and plots have been published.[13]

Some writers who dealt with a particular English manor or town have employed the seventeenth-century survey as a guide to property and agricultural changes. Charles R. Straton, Edward Bateson, Hubert Hall, Charles S. Orwin, and others proved useful in this regard.[14]

Despite Connecticut's isolation and small population the colony proved relatively rich in manuscript survey material. The Connecticut State Archives, the Connecticut State Library, the Yale University Library, the Connecticut and New Haven Historical Societies all have cartographical collections pertinent to the study of the Connecticut townscape.

Edmund B. Thompson described a few of these manuscript sources but many maps for one reason or another fell outside his purview. I have listed the drawings upon which I leaned heavily; the more useful task remains—to gather and print a list of all the colonial land surveys of Connecticut.

The following maps and surveys are in the Connecticut State Archives

11. Sir Thomas Phillips, *Londonderry and the London Companies, 1609–1629* (1928). Ordnance Survey, *Memoir of the City and North Western Liberties of Londonderry* (1837).

12. Arthur M. Hind, *Wenceslaus Hollar and His Views of London and Windsor in the Seventeenth Century* (1922). William Dugdale, *History of Saint Paul's Cathedral* (1658).

13. London Topographical Society, Publications, especially Vols. LVIII, LXXII–LXXV. London Carpenters' Company, *Records of the Worshipful Company of Carpenters* (1913); London Salter's Company, *Short Particulars of the Manor of Sal* (1838); Henry L. Phillips, *Annals of the Worshipful Company of Joiners of the City of London* (1915); C. H. Ridge, *Records of the Worshipful Company of Shipwrights* (1939–46); Charles Welch, *History of the Cutlers' Company of London* (1923); John Nicholl, *Some Account of the Worshipful Company of Ironmongers* (1866); Arthur H. Johnson, *History of the Worshipful Company of Drapers* (1922).

14. William Pembroke, *Survey of the Lands of William, First Earl of Pembroke,* ed. by Charles R. Straton (1909); Edward Bateson, *History of Northumberland* (1893); Charles S. Orwin, *The Open Fields* (1938); Hubert Hall, *Society in the Elizabethan Age* (1887); William Dugdale, *The History of Imbanking and Drayning of Divers Fenns and Marshes* (1662); John Ogilby, *Itinerarium Angliae or a Book of Roads of England and Wales* (1675); Thomas S. Dorset, *The Buckhurst Terrier, 1597–1598,* Sussex Record Society, Publications, Vol. XXXIX; William P. Baildon, *Baildon and the Baildons* (1912–26); Charles R. Smith, *Antiquities of Richborough, Reculver and Lynne* (1850); George Dunston, *The Rivers of Axholme* (1909); C. F. Marmaduke Morris, *Nunburnholme; Its History and Antiquities* (1907); Pearl Finch, *History of Burley on the Hill* (1901); J. Shawcross, *A History of Dagenham* (1904); for Bermuda surveys see *The Journal of Richard Norwood,* ed. by W. F. Craven (1945), and Sir John H. Lefroy, *Memorials of Discovery and Early Settlement of the Bermudas or Somers Islands* (1877).

unless otherwise noted and in most instances the Yale University Library now has photostatic copies. The quality of these early surveys varies widely; but while I found many inadequate for this study these same maps may prove of use in other investigations. Mere boundary sketches have not been included.

Norfolk, 1760. Travel, II, 46, Green Woods road in Norfolk
——— Travel, II, 47, Lots in Norfolk affected by Green Woods Road
Bethlehem, 1724. Connecticut State Library
Barkhamstead Proprietor's Plan, 1733. Connecticut State Library
Harwinton Houses, 1740. Eccles., VII, 20
Simsbury, 1770. Travel, III, 353
Rocky Hill, 1721. College and Schools, I, 26
Durham, 1707. Town and Lands, II, 175
New Haven, 1724. Ezra Stiles' copy of Joseph Brown's map, Yale University Library
Tolland, 1754. Eccles., IX, 351
Plan of the Town of New Haven with the Buildings in 1748, James Wadsworth's map, Yale University Library
Coventry, 1715. Town and Lands, V, 22 (Bounds)
Coventry, 1715. Town and Lands, V, 45 (Lots)
Coventry, 1742. Town and Lands, VII, 162
Hebron, 1744. Eccles., VII, 352–353
Colchester, 1732. Town and Lands, VII, 170
New Salem, 1727. Eccles., III, 145, 148, 149
Preston, Groton, Norwich, and Stonington Meeting Houses, 1761. Eccles., X, 32
Parts of East Hampton, Westchester, and Middle Haddam, 1751. Eccles., IX, 53
Woodstock Town, 1759. Town and Lands, VIII, 237
Proprietor's Map of Voluntown, ca. 1705. Connecticut State Library
First Society in Lebanon, 1772. Yale University Library
Third Society in Goshen, 1770. Connecticut State Library
Eben North Survey of Colebrook, 1816. Connecticut State Library

Apart from the State Archives the Ezra Stiles manuscripts in the Yale University Library include the largest number of colonial maps available. No less than thirty sketches of Connecticut towns, property divisions, ferries, harbors, mill rivers, and meetinghouses are drawn upon the leaves of the six volumes of "Itineraries," which span the period 1755–94.

As for the tools and constructional methods used, English writers such as Blith, Markham, Best, and Moxon demonstrated the secrets and skills of each craft as well as the close connection which existed in the seventeenth century between surveying, standards of measurement, and architectural practice had created a wood and land technic.[15]

Authorities who deal with measurement in the seventeenth century are rare. Joseph Moxon, Stephen Primatt, and various Parliamentary committees give some consideration to local variations of the foot.[16] In the colonies no single work appeared to rival the detailed and explicit descriptions of Norden, Moxon, and their lesser successors. Their works provide the only large-scale printed account in English of tools and skills and, like Diderot's *Encyclopédie,* have become standards, however imperfect.[17]

Writers on civil and military architecture came during the seventeenth century to command a large and in part fashionable audience. Although they did extend the skills of the architect first to major and then to minor domestic building, their influence upon the colonies is, until after 1700, problematic. The works of Shute, Perret, Barret, Wotton, and Wheler represent architectural theory.[18] Dugdale, Salmon, Price, Maitland, and Gerbier probably come closer to the architectural practice of their predecessors.[19]

A number of collections of public documents throw more or less light upon architectural material. Chief among these are the colonial records of Con-

15. Gervase Markham, *Cheape and Good Husbandry* (1631), *Farewell to Husbandry* (1631), *The Inrichment of the Weald of Kent* (1660); Henry Best, *Rural Economy in Yorkshire in 1641* (1857); Walter Blith, *The English Improver Improved* (1652); Robert Reyce, *Suffolk in the Seventeenth Century* [MS title "The Breviary of Suffolk, . . . 1618"] (1902); David Loggan, *Oxonia Illustrata* (1675) and *Cantabrigia Illustrata* (1690) are the principal agricultural authors I consulted.

16. Joseph Moxon, *Mathematicks Made Easie: or, a Mathematical Dictionary* (1692); Stephen Primatt, *City and Country Purchaser and Builder* (1667); Hubert Hall and Frieda J. Nicholas, "Select Tracts and Table Books Relating to English Weights and Measures, 1100–1742," Camden Society, *Miscellany,* XV (1929); Great Britain, House of Commons, *Report from the Committee . . . to Enquire into Original Standards of Weights and Measures* (1759).

17. Joseph Moxon, *Mechanick Exercises* (1703); Richard Neve, *City and Country Purchaser's and Builder's Dictionary* (1736) were the most useful, together with John Norden, *The Surueyors Dialogue* (1607, 1618).

18. John Shute, *The First & Chief Groundes of Architecture* (1563); Jacques Perret, *Des fortifications et artifices* (Paris, 1594, 1620; Frankfurt, 1602); Robert Barret, *Theorike and Practike of Modern Warres* (1598); Henry Wotton, *Elements of Architecture* (1624); Sir George Wheler, *An Account of the Churches* (1689).

19. Sir Balthazar Gerbier, *Counsel and Advice to All Builders* (1684 and 1736); William Salmon, *Builder's Guide* (1736) and *The London and Country Builder's Vade Mecum* (1745); Francis Price, *The British Carpenter* (1735) and *British Carpentry* (1735); William Dugdale, *Antiquities of Warwickshire* (1730); Stephen Primatt, *City and Country Purchaser and Builder* (1667); Colin Campbell, *Vitruvius Britannicus* (1717).

necticut and the various compilations edited by both the census bureau and private persons.[20]

Recent studies of one or more aspects of colonial architecture are of course legion, but Fiske Kimball published what is still the best over-all account of colonial architecture. John Frederick Kelly examines existing monuments with architectural precision but hesitates to erect any new theoretical framework. Norman Isham in a far more limited scope presented the evolutionary hypothesis early in the twentieth century. Bertha C. Trowbridge collected and edited several competent monographs on individual houses.[21]

Accounts of European architecture generally ignore possible influences upon the colonies. Martin S. Briggs and Thomas J. Wertenbaker have actually examined minor English building from the American point of view. Charles F. Innocent's account of building techniques which is still standard deals in part with colonial methods. Reginald Blomfield, John A. Gotch, and Sidney O. Addy give detailed accounts of the development of the great and minor English houses. Following Francis Stevens in 1815 many sentimentalists and a few trained scholars have dealt with the English cottage.[22] Ronald P. Jones, Martin S. Briggs, and John Betjeman have done little more than call attention to the absence of records or accounts of Nonconformist architecture in England, but on the Continent far more extensive work has been done. Moreover, Addleshaw and Etchells have explored the liturgical aspects of the Anglican Church.[23]

20. *Public Records of the Colony of Connecticut* (1877); *Records of the Colony and Plantation of New Haven,* ed. by Charles J. Hoadly (1887); United States Bureau of the Census, *Heads of Families at the First Census of the United States Taken in the Year 1790* (1907–8) and *A Century of Population Growth* (1909); Evarts B. Greene and Virginia D. Harrington, *American Population before the Federal Census of 1790* (1932).

21. Sidney Fiske Kimball, *Domestic Architecture of the American Colonies and the Early Republic* (1922); John Frederick Kelly, *Early Domestic Architecture of Connecticut* (1924), *The Henry Whitfield House* (1939), *Early Meetinghouses of Connecticut* (1948); Norman M. Isham and Albert F. Brown, *Early Connecticut Houses* (1900); Bertha C. Trowbridge and Charles M. Andrews, *Old Houses of Connecticut* (1923).

22. Martin S. Briggs, *The Homes of the Pilgrim Fathers in England and America, 1620–1685* (1932), *A Short History of the Building Crafts* (1925), *The Architect in History* (1927); Charles F. Innocent, *The Development of English Building Construction* (1916); John A. Gotch, *Early Renaissance Architecture in England* (1914); Thomas J. Wertenbaker, *The Puritan Oligarchy* (1948); Francis Stevens, *Domestic Architecture; a Series of Views of Cottages and Farm-houses in England and Wales* (1815); Ralph Nevill, *Old Cottages and Domestic Architecture in South-West Surrey* (1889); W. Galsworthy Davie and W. Curtis Greene, *Old Cottages and Farm-houses in Surrey* (1908); Reginald Blomfield, *A History of Renaissance Architecture in England, 1500–1800* (1897); Sidney O. Addy, *Evolution of the English House* (1898); Louis C. Rosenberg, *Cottages, Farmhouses and Other Minor Buildings in England* (1923); Harry Batsford and Charles Fry, *The English Cottage* (1939); Hugh Braun, *The Story of the English House* (1940).

23. Ronald P. Jones, *Nonconformist Church Architecture* (London, 1914); Martin S. Briggs, *Puritan Architecture* (London, 1946); John Betjeman, "Nonconformist Architec-

Local historians, although often biased and narrow, provide a wide variety of topographical and biographical detail which no other authorities supply. Florence Crofut has compiled a two-volume summary of historical information on Connecticut towns, while Hans Kurath has shown how this material might be applied to the study of dialectical variations.[24] Trumbull's and Barber's accounts now have great value, since they demonstrate local history at the beginning of the nineteenth century.[25] Among the most reliable town and county historians for the general researcher are Francis M. Caulkins, Edward E. Atwater, Isabel MacB. Calder, Elizabeth Schenck, Henry R. Stiles, and Ellen D. Larned.[26]

Despite the recognition that land formed the chief economic base of colonial society a definitive account of land ownership and town planning still remains to be written. At present many of the specific practices discovered by detailed monographs are at variance with the generalizations drawn by writers with a wider perspective. Pierre Lavedan, the principal continental writer, seems confused by this divergence and tends to minimize American town planning. Roy H. Akagi, Amelia C. Ford, Leonard W. Labaree, Charles M. Andrews, Melville Egleston, Herbert L. Osgood, and Anne B. Maclear represent the principal authorities. It is hoped that Glenn T. Trewartha will soon publish a larger survey based upon his provocative articles.[27]

---

ture." *Architectural Review,* LXXXVIII (December, 1940), 529; A. L. Drummond, *Church Architecture of Protestantism* (Edinburgh, 1934); George W. O. Addleshaw and Frederick Etchells, *The Architectural Setting of Anglican Worship* (1948); K. E. O. Fritsch, *Der Kirchenbau des Protestantismus* (1893); Jacques Pannier, *Salomon de Brosse* (1911); *L'Église réformée de Paris sous Henri IV* (1911).

24. Florence S. Crofut, *Guide to the History and the Historic Sites of Connecticut* (1937); Hans Kurath, *Handbook of the Linguistic Geography of New England* (1939).

25. John W. Barber, *Connecticut Historical Collections* (1936); Benjamin Trumbull, *A Complete History of Connecticut* (1818).

26. Francis M. Caulkins, *History of New London, Connecticut* (1852), *History of Norwich, Connecticut* (1866); Edward E. Atwater, *History of the Colony of New Haven* (Meriden, 1902); Isabel MacB. Calder, *The New Haven Colony* (1934); Elizabeth H. Schenck, *The History of Fairfield* (1889); Henry R. Stiles, *History of Ancient Windsor* (1859); Ellen D. Larned, *History of Windham County* (1874–80).

27. Roy H. Akagi, *The Town Proprietors of the New England Colonies* (1924); Amelia C. Ford, *Colonial Precedents of Our National Land System as It Existed in 1800* (1910); Leonard W. Labaree, *Milford, Connecticut: The Early Development of a Town as Shown in Its Land Records* (1933); Charles M. Andrews, *The River Towns of Connecticut* (1889); Melville Egleston, *The Land System of the New England Colonies* (1886); Glenn T. Trewartha, "Types of Rural Settlement in Colonial America," *Geographical Review,* XXXVI (1946).

Index